W9-CFJ-068

# FLORIDA
## FOR FAMILIES

# FLORIDA
## FOR FAMILIES

### LARRY LAIN

Interlink Books

An imprint of Interlink Publishing Group, Inc.
Northampton, Massachusetts

First published in 2008 by

**INTERLINK BOOKS**
An imprint of
Interlink Publishing Group, Inc.
46 Crosby Street
Northampton, Massachusetts 01060
**www.interlinkbooks.com**

**Library of Congress Cataloging-
in-Publication Data**
Lain, Larry, 1947–
Florida for families/by Larry Lain.
    p. cm.
 Includes bibliographical
references and index.
 ISBN-13: 978-1-56656-695-7
(pbk.)
1. Florida—Guidebooks. 2.
Family recreation—Florida—
Guidebooks. 3.
Children—Travel—Florida—
Guidebooks.
I. Title.
 F309.3.L27 2008
 917.5904'63—dc22

2007031874

Printed and bound in China

*© Varina and Jay Patel/
Dreamstime.com*

# CONTENTS

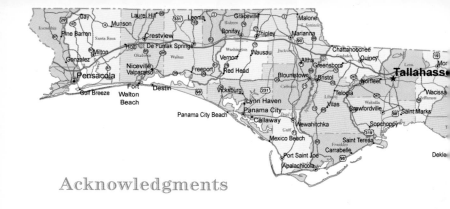

# Acknowledgments

I appreciate the help and advice of the many friends and acquaintances who have steered me toward things I didn't know about in Florida, and away from things that would waste my time. (But which, to be honest, I often checked out personally myself. My friends were always right.)

Some of the friendliest and most helpful guides, museum directors, and public relations people I have ever met, I've met in Florida. They include Lynn Hobeck Bates, Ringling Estate; Ed Boon, Sarasota Classic Car Museum; David Christensen, the Titanic Experience; Michelle Curtis, Clearwater Marine Aquarium; Molly Ebersold, St. Augustine Alligator Farm; Dave Herbst, Walt Disney World; Phyllis Klym; Carol & Mike McGlaughlin, Pelican Apartments, Indian Rocks Beach; Jim Moore, Gamble Plantation; Jessica Neikirk, Ripley's Odditorium St. Augustine; Michelle Reyna, Fountain of Youth Archaeological Park; Lisa Sbuttoni, Edison & Ford Winter Estates; Stacy Seff, Wannado City; Jann Snellings, Manatee Observation Center; David Talley, DaytonaUSA; Dana Zucker, Clearwater Marine Aquarium.

What's a family travel book without family? My son, friend, and illustrator Mike accompanied me on one of my research trips to Florida, and my wife Barb, my collaborator in everything that's worthwhile in my life, came on another one. And, of course, our other sons Rik and Doug were part of the original Lain Family travel contingent to Florida, and I've used their experiences here, too. My mother Betty Lain gave me ideas from the many trips she and my father took there over the years, and my brother Dave and sister-in-law Jeffrin had lots of advice based on trips with their daughters. To all of these, and everyone else who has provided help, advice, and support, I offer the deepest thanks.

# Introduction

If you've read previous books in the *Family Travel Series*, you'll find this one a bit different. Each of the other books focuses on a single city, usually with some suggested excursions to nearby cities or attractions. Not so this book. Here I'm going to take your family to an entire state, lead you across 500 miles (800km) of spectacular scenery, unforgettable attractions, and memorable experiences.

Unless you have more time (not to mention money!) than we've ever been able to set aside, you're probably not going to tackle the whole state at once. If you visit everywhere in this book on one family trip, I'd like to hear from you. In fact, I'd like to shake your hand, and will when I visit you in whatever asylum you've been committed to.

Florida is a place you can go back to many times and always find new things to see and do that are every bit as fabulous as anything else you've ever done here. Florida may exhaust you—but you will never, ever exhaust its possibilities. People from around the world vacation in the state every year, and even after decades of trips, there's always something wonderful that's new to do.

I'm going to take your family to Florida in the next seventeen chapters, show you the scope of what's here, and give you enough exciting things to do to keep you busy for years' worth of holidays. If this is your first family trip to Florida, you'll get everything you need in this book, not just the usual list of attractions, but practical, family-tested suggestions on how to find reasonably priced places to stay, how to avoid the worst of the crowds and the weather, and how to plan your time so you all still like each other at the end of the trip! If you've been here before, you'll find enough new ideas and approaches in this book to make it feel like your first visit.

I'll take you not only to the famous theme parks and beaches that everybody visits, but to some places that you might not have thought of, places that will make your family's vacation special and unlike the cookie-cutter holidays of your friends. Florida is unique: beautiful and kitschy, crowded and isolated, surprising and predictable, the most varied place in the country—and always memorable! We're going to have a great time here. Let's go!

*Key Largo sunset; photo by Juliana Spear*

Sanibel sunset image by Juliana Spear

# PART ONE

## The Basics of Family Travel

So you're thinking about going to Florida? Nice move! Whether you've already made the decision to go, or are just beginning to explore the possibilities, you'll get a lot of ideas in *Florida for Families*. It's a real challenge to take an entire family on a trip of hundreds or thousands of miles, to try to ensure that everybody has a good time and are still friends when the trip is over, and to find ways to do all this without running up a debt that will last for generations. That's why I began the *Family Travel Series*.

In Part I we'll talk about the logistics of taking a major family holiday—how to travel, where to stay, how to plan something that seems about as easy as getting a herd of elephants across the Alps. The focus throughout this section will be on making sure that things go as smoothly as possible, but on doing things economically without sacrificing the great family times that are the reason you're taking the trip in the first place. Now, if you're ready, let's talk about how to plan a trip that will be even better than you ever dreamed it could be.

# 1
# America's Back Yard

I WAS A LUCKY KID, BECAUSE WE LIVED IN A SMALL TOWN AND I always had a big back yard to play in, complete with swing set, sandbox, a blow-up wading pool, and room to throw a ball around or to play games from baseball to badminton. My friends and I could spend endless summer days in the yard without getting bored, never running out of things to do as we went from one activity to another, or just relaxed in the shade of one of our big old trees.

It was idyllic.

Alas, I grew up. The older I got, the more chores I was expected to do, and my days of living in a perpetual resort faded away. I was expected to mow the grass I had lolled in, paint the garage that stored all the sports equipment I played with, even give up my life of leisure and earn my own spending money by delivering newspapers. Oh! The cruelty! The injustice!

And it's been that way for decades now. I mow, I paint, I earn a paycheck, and I seldom have a chance to recreate the endless, irresponsible summers of my youth: That's what being a grownup is all about.

Those days don't have to be gone forever, though. This is a book about Florida, one of the country's most popular tourist destinations, and as far as I'm concerned, it's the biggest, coolest back yard in the United States. Think about it:

*The Swing Set:* Hoo, boy, does Florida ever have some great swing sets! Try Walt Disney World. Did your swing set at home have a couple of swings, maybe a glider and a slide? Well, the playgrounds at Disney, at Universal, and at other amusement parks large and small are the greatest swing sets imaginable, with countless rides that cover the full range from tame to terrifying.

*The Sand Box:* Florida has more than 660 miles (1070 km) of beaches where you can soak up the sun and get sand between your toes. There's plenty of room for quiet walks, noisy games, picnics, sand castles, shell hunting, and burying Dad up to his neck.

*The Wading Pool:* The state is surrounded on three sides by water, a coastline almost 1200 miles (1940 km) long. The little wading pool to the east is the dramatic Atlantic Ocean. To the west, you've got the warmth of the Gulf of Mexico. Sure beats anything in *my* back yard! What's more, you can splash to your heart's content at any of the innumerable water parks in the state.

*The Tree House:* I didn't have one of these, but Florida has lots of their grownup equivalent, the Resort. The tree houses of my acquaintance were pretty Spartan, but not so these! You can be catered to and pampered to your heart's content all over the state, and get perks like special admission to the best local attractions.

See why I have always thought of Florida as the best back yard in the world? This is a metaphor I could probably torture forever, to your certain dismay, but I'll allow myself just a couple more.

*The Vacant Lot Next Door:* We had lots of fun hiding behind bushes and watching for animals in the overgrown lot nearby. In Florida, visit the animal habitats at Disney's Animal Kingdom, Busch Gardens, Monkey Jungle, or Lion Country Safari. Or explore the Everglades—but don't feed the gators!

*The Island in the Pond:* Bowman's Pond, with its little island with the dug-out fort in the middle, was only a block away. It took just a couple of minutes by raft from shore to the island, the most exotic place in the neighborhood. It will take you longer than that to reach Florida's exotic islands, The Keys, and you're honestly better off getting there in a car or ferry than on a raft, but the trip is more than worth it to this tropical paradise, where the clocks seem to run so much slower than on the mainland.

So how do you tackle a truly overwhelming neighborhood like this? You've already taken the first step: You've picked up this book.

*Florida for Families* will help you make sense of this diverse state and create a memorable family trip that pleases everybody. When you first think about a holiday like this, each member of your family might have a different vision. The youngest child thinks of nothing but Walt Disney World. The oldest wants to spend the whole trip seeing how movie special effects are done at Universal Studios. Mom wants nothing more than endless days of reading on the beach, with somebody else doing the cooking. And Dad can't get the vision out of his head of life on a fishing boat, far from the sight of the shore, ending with landing a marlin bigger than he is.

You can't do them all.

But I'm here to help you sift through the endless possibilities. I'm pretty good at some things, really bad at many others, but what I am probably best at is *planning*. That's the key to a successful vacation, and that's the focus of the first section of the book. Florida is too big, too varied, too packed with possibilities to not plan your trip carefully, and I'll show you everything you need to know to do it.

And yet, oddly enough, I'll talk about the wonderful virtues of spontaneity. Some of the grandest moments of every trip I've ever taken have been things I *hadn't* planned ahead of time. So this book will help you plan every detail of your trip to Florida, but also have you ready to take advantage of the unanticipated spur-of-the-moment opportunities that will certainly come your way.

Florida is a great destination for five days or five weeks, and this book will help you decide on just what sort of vacation you want. Your trip will probably be a mix of famous big attractions and fascinating little-known ones. Of noisy places and quiet times. Of surf and shore. *Florida for Families* will lay out the possibilities, help you to put together your itinerary, and show you how to budget both your time and your money (probably saving more of each than you would have thought possible). Attractions large and small, finances, logistics—they're all here.

Everybody in the United States probably knows at least 50 people who have been to Florida in the past two years. Are you from outside the U.S.? You probably know at least five. I'll bet you don't want your trip to be exactly like everybody else's. Your family is certainly different from your neighbor's or your brother-in-law's. Your vacation should be, too! It should be tailored specifically for your own group. That's what we'll be doing in the next couple hundred pages—tailoring that trip the same way we'd tailor a suit: measuring for size, texture, and color, until it fits your family perfectly.

The journey begins.

## *Recommendations*

‰ We're about to begin planning a trip. Savor this process! It's fun, and it's important.

‰ Remember: This is *your* trip. What was right for somebody else's family might not be right for yours. Listen to everybody's advice, but it's your own family you have to keep in mind. Even—perish the thought— some of the ideas in this book might not be best for your particular situation.

# 2
# A Blueprint for Blue Sky and Blue Water

I'D HATE TO BE AN ARCHITECT. IF I HAD A COMMISSION FOR A building and were faced with a drafting table, a pencil, and a blank sheet of paper, I'd just freeze. Where would I begin? As soon as I draw one line, I eliminate an infinity of other possible lines. But if that building is ever going to get built, draw that blueprint I must.

But on reflection, I suppose every job is like that. All of us, in one way or another, make something out of nothing practically every day of our lives.

Are you laying a brick wall? It doesn't exist until you mix the mortar to what you decide is the right consistency and place the bricks in what you feel are exactly the right positions.

Are you cooking a meal? There will be no food for the family until you decide what to fix and settle on exactly how much of each ingredient to include, what sort of pan to use, how long to cook it, and so on.

For that matter, if you're writing a travel book, you're faced with a blank page as soon as you turn on the computer, and each time you select one word, you've eliminated several million other possible words.

Our lives are a never-ending process of drawing blueprints. But this one is going to be more fun than most.

In this chapter, you will begin to make some decisions about what sort of vacation you're going to take: where and when you'll go, how you'll get there, how long you'll stay, where you'll live, how you'll eat, how much money you'll spend, and so on.

If that sounds like a pretty tall order for a 3,000-word chapter, don't worry: This is just to get us started, a sort of a rough sketch before the final drawing. We'll fill in the details as we go along.

# Where To Go

"Going to Florida" isn't much of a plan, really. Florida's a big place—more than 65,000 square miles (168,000 sq. km). That might be more territory than you want to cover. Let's narrow it down a bit, keeping in mind that Part II of this book might give you some new ideas. Here are four basic choices:

· a theme park vacation
· a beach escape
· an urban getaway
· the hodgepodge holiday

## *Theme Park Vacations*

This is the first thing most families think of nowadays, and often the planning process stops right here. You can't beat Florida's theme parks—no one will argue that: the Disney World parks, the Universal Studios parks, Busch Gardens, SeaWorld, even the oldies like Cypress Gardens and Weeki Wachee Springs. Florida was a big travel destination even before the first architect began designing the first theme park, though. There is nothing in the world wrong with a theme park vacation if everybody's heart is set on it; millions of people spend significant parts of their time and money there. But before you buy each person in the family a set of mouse ears, be sure to talk about the rest of what the state offers.

## Beach Escapes

If the idea of sun, sand, surf, and sea appeal to you, Florida is the place to go. Endless miles of beaches, cool breezes off the water dispelling the heat on even the most broiling days, glorious sunrises and sunsets over the water, the sound of waves on the sand lulling you to sleep each night, millions of sea shells laying about waiting to be discovered, family picnics along the shore—Ah! Makes me want to set down my laptop and phone my travel agent. If there is anything not to like about this that can't be taken care of with a good sunscreen, I don't know what it is.

## Urban Getaways

If you're familiar with the rest of the titles in my *Family Travel Series*, you will notice that they are different from the one you're reading now. The other books all cover a single city, while I take on an entire state in this one. I enjoy big-city vacations, filled with bustle and densely packed attractions unlike anything I can contrive at home. If that's what you want, Florida's got it. The Miami-Fort Lauderdale metro area consists of 5 million people. The Tampa-St. Petersburg area is well over 2 million. Both areas include the sorts of museums, cityscapes, culture, pro-sports, and ethnic diversity that make big-city vacations exciting.

### Hodgepodge Holidays

Can't decide? Things aren't far away in Florida. Use the Gulf Coast beaches around Largo as home base, but enjoy the amenities of nearby Tampa, with a day or two at Busch Gardens for good measure. Or do the Orlando theme-park thing, but on your way home, spend a day at Cape Canaveral and another at Daytona Beach. If you vacation by exploring Miami's urban delights and Atlantic beaches, add on a trip to the Keys or an excursion to the Everglades. A completely different Florida is always just a few miles from wherever you happen to be.

## When To Go

Decades ago, Florida was mostly a winter getaway for northerners who found two feet of snow dismaying and had enough money to flee from it. "Snowbirds," the native Floridians called them, seasonal flocks migrating down to the sunshine when the temperatures dropped below freezing up north, and staying until the blossoms were on the trees again back home.

That's not the case any more. Every season in Florida has its plusses and minuses. Often you just travel whenever you have the chance and take the positives and negatives as they come. But if you have the flexibility to choose your timing, here's what you need to know.

### Summer

This used to be the slow season in Florida, but that was long ago. Now it's probably the most popular time of year for families. School is out!

Everything will be open maximum hours, the days are long and warm, the swimming is great. The long school break makes this an easy and attractive time of year for families.

The weather will be hot and humid, though. That usually doesn't deter kids, but you need to be prepared for it with cool clothes, plenty of sunscreen, and bottles of water. The heat is less of a problem if you plan to spend most of your trip on the beach or at water parks. Cities and theme parks are less comfortable in the summer heat. Temperatures of more than 90 degrees (32°C) are the norm, perhaps a bit less in the Panhandle.

Summer is the wettest time of year, as well, with June through September getting significantly more rainfall than most other months—except, oddly, in Miami, where July gets 30 percent less rain than either June or August. But rain doesn't have to be a problem. Our first family trip to Florida was a June trip to the beaches of the Gulf Coast, and we had a lot of rain. But it always came in the form of a thunder-storm about 5:30 in the afternoon. We just learned to schedule dinner for that time. By 7 o'clock the rain had passed, the sky was blue again, and we were playing in the sand.

### Autumn

This is a wonderful time of year. The temperatures are beginning to moderate, there is less rain, the waters of both the Atlantic and the Gulf are still comfortably warm, and the crowds have diminished as the kids head back to school. If you're able to travel at that time of year, the weather can be great.

But what about hurricanes? Everyone is more conscious of these violent tempests after the terrible storm season of 2005.

The hurricane season runs officially from June through November, with most storms occurring between August and October, and susceptibility increasing as you move south, although the Panhandle carries some risk as well. But despite all the problems of 2005, you shouldn't worry about this very much. Hurricanes are uncommon, and unlike tornadoes in the Midwest or earthquakes in California, you can see them brewing days or even weeks ahead. The chances of being in Florida when a storm like that threatens are very small and the chances of being unable to leave if one strikes are nil.

Don't let this worry ruin a great vacation. If you refuse to go anywhere in the Midwest in the summer because of the threat of tornadoes ... or anywhere in the Northeast between November and March because of the threat of blizzards ... or anywhere in California ever because of the threat of earthquakes—then maybe you don't want Florida in the fall. But the rest of us might be there.

### Winter

If you want to get away from the cold and ice, this is a great time to visit Florida. Winter is when seasonal residents move to Florida, but visiting families with kids are fewer, except at the holidays. The snowbirds have already seen most of the attractions, and their children are usually grown, so you may find the theme parks and tourist sites less frenzied than at some other times of the year.

It's more difficult to travel if your kids are in school, but this is when the weather is at its best. Many schools now have midwinter breaks, and you might find the places you want to visit a little less crowded then, especially between late November and Christmas, or in January, late February, or early March.

Temperatures are much cooler in the winter. Those 90 degree days we talked about in the summer are more like 72°F (22°C) in the winter. And the winter months are much drier as well, averaging just 2 inches (3 cm) per month.

### Spring

This is the Florida travel season that is second only to summer. Nearly all U.S. schools have spring breaks, and by March or April, northerners are eager to get away from the snow-covered ground and the cloud-covered skies for a week. Spring breaks used to be clustered on the week before or after Easter, but they're a bit more evenly distributed through the early spring nowadays, so not everyone is converging on the state all at once.

If there's a drawback to a spring trip, it's the fact that large numbers of spring-break revelers are university students, whose activities are sometimes more rowdy than many families might be comfortable with. No letters, please—I am completely aware that you can't lump all the college vacationers together. Some spend all their time relaxing on the beach getting caught up with their textbooks, and go to church on Sunday. Others, uh, do not. I've made my living teaching those students for a long time, so I know the variety of flavors they come in.

Student antics, when they occur, are usually beach-oriented, with places like Ft. Lauderdale, Daytona, and Panama City perennial favorites. Personally, I try to avoid the popular beaches in the early spring, because even the large majority of well-behaved college students create larger crowds and louder music than I like. You shouldn't avoid Florida in the spring if that's the most convenient time to go, but you might want to pass on the beaches that are the most popular college hangouts.

## How Long To Stay

State tourist bureaus collect information about everything imaginable, and Florida, trying to keep track of 80 million visitors a year, does it better than most. That's an amazing number of tourists. There are only fourteen countries in the world that even have that many people full time! That's like every single person in Great Britain and Australia deciding to visit in the same year...or everyone in Turkey and Sweden ... or in Canada and Argentina...or every American west of the Rockies!

Because of Florida's relentless record keeping, we know that the average length of stay for Americans who visit the state is five days, and that overseas visitors average twelve days. But the average might not be right for everyone. How do you decide how long to stay?

I usually recommend a formula of one day for every two to three hours of travel time. If you drive to Orlando from Chicago or New York City, a distance of about 1100 miles (1750 km), you'll spend at least twenty hours on the road—one-way! Less than a week at your destination will leave everybody feeling crabby and hurried. But an hour's drive to O'Hare or LaGuardia airport, a couple of hours waiting for a flight, two hours in the air, and an hour to pick up a rental car and drive to your accommodation amounts to just six hours of travel each way. You can get away with a 3- or 4-day weekend trip, if that's all the time you have.

If you're coming from London or Buenos Aires, you'll face a flight of eight hours to Miami. Add getting to the airport, waiting around once you're there, going through immigration on arrival, and getting to your accommodations, and you're looking at another day-long journey. You'll need a minimum of a week to get much out of the holiday. A trip from Australia needs to be longer still. It's 9700 miles (16,000km) from Melbourne to Miami, fourteen time zones, 24 hours in the air, one or two changes of plane, an arduous two-day experience. If you don't stay for two weeks, you'll return home needing a vacation!

These are averages, of course. Families who are used to doing a lot of long-distance traveling adjust more quickly. Pace makes a big difference. But if in doubt, err on the side of taking an extra day or two. When we talk about building an itinerary, you'll see how we put those days to good use.

## So—What Will It Cost Us?

Oh, man! I knew you were going to ask that. And I can't really answer it without knowing a lot more. It's like saying, "Larry, I want to buy a car. How much will it cost?"

And I'll answer, "Oh, in the $200 to $50,000 range."

The answer is in the details. So: What do you want?

I'm really into saving money without giving up the fun of travel. If we hadn't found a way to do that, our family travel would have been limited to walks around the block. I'm still committed to saving money, because I think travel is a lot more fun if you don't live like a maharaja when you visit someplace, but live a life very much like the people of the place you're visiting. My travel philosophy has always been, "Live Like a Local."

But back to your question about how much this escapade is going to cost.

Part of the answer is in your travel arrangements. This is a big item if you're flying from Melbourne, and not a very big one at all if you're driving from Georgia. In Chapter 4 we'll look at the possibilities—driving, flying, even taking the train—and show you how to do it most efficiently *and* most economically. There are tricks to getting good airline fares, and I'll show you how it's done.

Accommodations are another potential budget breaker. Some theme parks really push hard to get you to stay at their resorts. Those can be fine facilities with vast numbers of amenities—many, many of which you will never use, yet pay for every day. A cheap motel nearby might be a better alternative … or might not be if it has too few money-saving amenities, or if you plan to visit nothing but the theme park. Chapter 5 will give you a rundown of possible places to stay, some of which you might never have considered.

Food can be another budget-buster. Restaurants charge five to ten times or more what it costs you to fix the same meal yourself. We *had* to learn some strategies for coping with meal costs, because at one point we were traveling with three teenage boys, a thought that can still produce nightmares. In chapter 5 I'll give you some great ways to save serious money on food.

The cost of attractions can vary wildly. A week on the beach costs almost nothing. A day at a big theme park, including resort, meals, admission, and souvenirs, can cost a family more than the gross national product of a small country. But even in Chapters 8 through 14, where I talk about the state's attractions in detail, you'll find dozens of money-saving tips, ways to cut lots of dollars—but not a bit of fun.

The last chapter of this book provides a place to put it all together. Chapter 17 consists of easy-to-use worksheets to help fliers get the best deal on airfare, to help everyone get the best accommodations at the best prices, and to estimate just how much the total trip will cost. These are exactly the approaches the Lains have always used in planning family travel, and thousands of readers of the *Family Travel Series* now do too.

Some surprises on a big family vacation are a good thing—discovering a special secluded beach, an unexpected view, a great shop, a hidden restaurant. But not all surprises are so much fun. You *never* want your money to run out before your vacation does. The chapters that follow will save you money, but without sacrificing the very best Florida has to offer, and showing you what marvelous fun the planning can be.

# Recommendations

∽ The best family vacations are the ones where everybody helps with the planning. Start talking about the trip far enough in advance for everyone to become excited and to think about what they want to do.

∽ Don't plan on seeing all of Florida. It's too big and complex for that. Stick to one or two themes for the trip.

∽ Don't rule anything out from the beginning. The more something costs, the more ways there usually are to save money doing it.

# 3
# Cooking Up the Perfect Family Trip

I LIKE TO COOK, AND I HATE TO FOLLOW RECIPES. COOKING TO ME is art, not science, and I'm always asking myself, "I wonder what it would taste like if I'd add *this* and substitute *that*."

Mostly my concoctions are pretty tasty, I think, but you'd have to ask Barb, who might have a more realistic view of what they're like. Cooking something by just making it up as you go along can produce some fabulous meals ... or a disaster worthy of two full minutes on the late-night news.

One thing I would never, ever do, however, is tackle a family vacation the way I'd tackle Tuesday's dinner.

In fact, as a guy who writes about family travel, I'm asked one question more than any other: *How can I be sure everything will go as smoothly as possible?*

And my response is always, "Let me share my recipe with you."

This chapter is that recipe. When you invest a lot of time, money, and excitement on a fancy dinner party or on a major family trip, you want to make sure everything goes perfectly, and I'll share all the ingredients with you here. Be assured, though, that there will be plenty of opportunities to season this holiday to your family's individual taste. You might not like all the cooking that comes from my kitchen, but you're sure to get a lot out of the tasty morsels that fill this chapter.

## The Main Course

If you're planning an elegant dinner party, you don't begin by charging into the kitchen and flinging pots and spices around. You sit down and plan. That's every bit as true when you cook up a big family trip. Barb and I can enjoy trips now where we're almost completely spontaneous, but we wouldn't have dared to risk our money and our sanity by doing it that way with three kids.

I'm convinced that our planning is the biggest reason why every single holiday we took, whether it was two days or two weeks, was a success. Well, except for the time we all went tent camping in a monsoon. That could have worked out better.

Monsoons aside, here are the ingredients you need to put together your big Florida adventure.

### Everybody Helps with the Planning

Once kids are old enough to understand you're going on a big trip, they're old enough to help plan it. I'm not suggesting that you put your 6-year-old in charge of finding a motel in Tennessee on the drive down, of course, but with the help of a good guidebook (like *this* one, for instance), talk about all the possible things there are to do. Otherwise, the kids—especially the youngest ones—will just focus on the same trip their friends' families took, or on whatever they've most recently seen advertised on television. There's so much more to do!

If kids help plan the trip, they don't feel like it's just Mom and Dad's ideas: They're being listened to and taken seriously. They have a real stake in the success of the vacation.

Older kids can read guidebooks for themselves, of course, but younger family members will need to have most things explained, and that's a great way to get everybody involved. Chapter 15, *Top Attractions*, provides a comprehensive list of all the attractions I'll talk about in the rest of this book. The idea is for everybody in the family to think about all the many things to see and do in Florida.

One thing the Lains used to do is to make a big list of all the possibilities, and have people decide what they think about each. I've made the list for you in Chapter 15. Each member of the family can mark each attraction with numbers or letters, or smiley and frowny faces, or anything that translates into

> **Tip:**
>
> If you're one of those lucky families that still has a chance to get everybody around the table together at dinnertime, that's a perfect time for these discussions. If kids' activities or parents' work schedules make that more difficult, a half hour before bedtime or on Sunday afternoon will work, too. But it's best if you can have everybody together.

"Yes, I'd like to do this," or "I don't care," or "I'd rather go to the dentist." It doesn't have to be a formal voting system—just something that starts to limit possibilities.

Once that's done, you'll have a good idea about what sort of vacation your family wants. Remember, in the last chapter we talked about a theme park vacation, a beach escape, an urban getaway, and the hodgepodge holiday.

This is the time to decide. Once that's done, you can begin to talk about the specifics of the trip.

*Make a List*

When you've narrowed the field from the whole state of Florida to focus on just the Daytona or Tampa area, or on the theme parks of Orlando, or some other more manageable approach, you've got a home base and can begin to do some specific planning.

For example, when the Lains went to Florida for the first time, we wanted to spend most of our time along the Gulf Coast. We're from the landlocked part of the country and everybody wanted to be on the water most of the time.

Besides, I had a grandfather who lived there and we wanted to be able to visit him and have our kids get to know him, because he was a neat guy who had led an interesting life. So we found a beachfront apartment at Indian Rocks Beach, just a short drive from his home in Largo, and spent most of our holiday on the beach.

But Florida has so much to offer that wherever you base yourself, there are going to be plenty of attractions nearby that will give variety to your days. There's nothing wrong with spending two solid weeks baking on the beach, but there's nothing wrong, either, with taking an afternoon or a day now and then to explore the other nearby wonders.

For us, that meant not only letting the kids spend time with Great-Grandpa Smitham, but trying some other things, too. More than half of our time in Florida was spent on the beach, but one of the kids especially wanted to see the Circus Museum at the John Ringling estate in nearby Sarasota, and that made a great afternoon trip.

Tampa offered museums and loads of possibilities at Busch Gardens. We spent an entire morning watching the fishermen compete for their catch with pelicans on a nearby pier. And if we'd been so inclined, the theme parks of Orlando were little more than an hour away.

We even planned our trip so when we drove home, we'd take a different route, driving to the east side of the state and up the Atlantic coast, stopping at the Kennedy Space Center, something that was right at the top of another son's wish list.

Once you begin to talk about all the possibilities for your Florida "home base," it won't take much time to come up with a list of lots of things to see and do nearby.

### Make Sure Everybody Gets Their First Choice

This is one of the most important ingredients in our vacation mix. You're taking a family trip; you want everybody in the family to enjoy it. You've spent weeks, perhaps, talking about it and thinking about the possibilities, and everybody is excited.

But not everybody is excited about exactly the same things. When you've talked about all the things there are to see and do, each member of the family will have a slightly different idea about what's most important. That's how you set your itinerary. Make sure each person gets his or her first choice.

No insurance company will sell you a policy guaranteeing a great holiday or your money back. But the principle of making sure that everyone gets to do the one thing that is most important to them is the best kind of insurance you can have.

This is very closely related to our first ingredient—having everybody help with the planning. Kids who know that everyone will make sure they get what's most important to them are *much* less likely to complain about what other members of the family want. Everyone in the family has something really special to look forward to, and understands that it comes with a fair price: *"Nobody will complain about doing what I want in exchange for me not whining about what's important to other people."* Every kid (and grownup!) will understand a bargain like this.

As much as possible, schedule each person's "special" activities early in the trip, especially if it's something that is a one-time opportunity, could be rained out, or become unavailable in some other way. It would be a shame for one of the kids to be the only one to miss something like a special fishing trip out on the ocean because you'd saved it for the last day of the trip, and you wound up with a day full of lightning storms.

## *Maintain Regular Meal and Sleep Schedules*

This is especially important if you have small kids ... or grumpy dads like me! I've known too many people who think the only way to justify spending a lot of money on vacation is to start having a good time as early as possible every morning and work at it relentlessly all day and far into each night, grudgingly stopping only occasionally to take on food.

That's not a vacation, it's a forced march!

If a child's normal bedtime is 9 o'clock, he or she ought to be tucked away each night pretty close to that, except for an occasional special evening activity. And unless you need to get up before the birds for a special outing, let people sleep until they wake up naturally. Vacations are tiring!

(That last suggestion about sleeping late might not apply to many of the teenagers I've known, however. At 16, I could have easily slept past lunchtime most days. Ah, memories.)

Kids (and parents) who are tired or hungry get cranky. You don't want cranky people on vacation. Travel is naturally stressful and hard on the body. The time zone might be different, the food different, the air different, even the

*Sanibel Island Sunrise at Lighthouse Beach on Sanibel Island, Fort Meyers.* © *David Davis/Dreamstime.com*

sunlight coming at you from an unfamiliar angle. The body adapts, but might become fatigued more easily, especially at first. Keeping a regular schedule, so it knows when it will be fed and when it will be able to rest, will make your body like you more.

## Plan Free Time

This is unquestionably one of the hardest pieces of advice to follow and people always look at me like I'm a lunatic (which is perfectly possible) when I suggest it: *"You want me to travel thousands of miles at a cost of thousands of dollars and spend time just reading a book or watching television?"*

Yep.

While I won't apply this too sternly to a holiday spent entirely on the beach, I will to just about every other sort of trip. In a nutshell, I'm suggesting that you occasionally take a vacation from your vacation.

As I said a moment ago, travel is stressful, tiring, and demanding. Having fun can be a lot of work. Kids—and parents, too—need a break if they've spent three solid days experiencing the thrills of Disney World, or tramping from museum to museum, or spent a day in St. Augustine followed by a drive for a day in Daytona · followed by a drive for a day at Cape Canaveral.

Once in awhile, you have to stop and let your mind catch up and your sore muscles relax. Schedule an afternoon when you do nothing but splash in the motel pool. Spend a day at a beach. No sightseeing allowed, just relaxation. Trips became more fun once we'd figured this one out.

I know you're investing a lot of time and resources on a Florida trip. Downtime is a good investment, though. No matter how much time and money you spend on a trip, it will be wasted if this great family experience is spent grumbling and arguing. Fatigue makes people grouchy—and I'm an expert on grouchy. Trust me.

## Be Spontaneous

Poet Walt Whitman wrote: "Do I contradict myself? Very well. I contradict myself." I quite agree. I've harped on and on about the importance of good planning, and will several more times in the pages that follow. But there are times when the only right thing to do is to just forget the planning and go with the flow.

I don't believe I've ever taken a trip where one of the highlights wasn't something I did on the spur of the moment, and often hadn't even known about ahead of time: a festival, a secluded beach, a building with an important historical connection. If I'd have stuck too firmly to my travel plans, I'd have missed two of the most phenomenal buildings I've ever seen. One was a treasure in Washington, DC, that nobody knows about, and the other was, improbably enough, an abandoned hotel in southern Indiana.

If I hadn't poked my nose into a university building in London one afternoon I'd have missed an exhibit odder than anything in any museum in the city. If I hadn't followed a nondescript sign south of San Francisco once, I wouldn't have seen some of the most remarkable animals I've ever encountered.

Of course it has happened in Florida, too. I followed a highway sign once and found the home of a strange utopian cult that thought we were all living inside the earth, rather than on its surface. Near a museum I had intended to visit, I discovered a wonderful primeval garden that left me with a feeling of having just missed a dinosaur walking past. I found an odd, surprisingly engaging museum to a second- (or perhaps third-) tier actor.

Planning is essential, but don't be afraid to turn aside from your itinerary if something catches somebody's interest, or if you stumble across something you didn't know was there. And, frankly, the kids are usually the quickest to spot those opportunities. I was too often the person with one eye on my wristwatch and the other on the odometer. I'm better now, but still have to fight the tendency to be too relentless. Relax! This is supposed to be fun, and few things are more fun than a nice surprise.

> *Tip:*
>
> Related to this is the Two Hour Rule, which applies to most indoor activities like museums. Two hours is enough in one place: After that people start to get bored and restless. Obviously that doesn't apply to places like big theme parks, which offer a wide variety of activities, or to days on the beach, where the whole purpose is to bake yourself medium-well. But everybody gets a little stir-crazy from too long indoors.

## Seasonings

Here are a few ideas to help you spice up your vacation. Like oregano or garlic, they're not suitable for every occasion, but when appropriate, they will really make your vacation something to savor.

### *Vary Your Activities*

When I write about urban holidays, I encourage travelers to not do things that are too much the same on the same day— don't visit two great cathedrals or two art museums back-to-back, for example. Each will diminish the special-ness of the other.

The same is true of this sort of trip. I wouldn't go to two or three different beaches on the same day. You won't appreciate the unique qualities of any of them as much. If you only want a half day on a beach, spend the other half exploring on old settlement, visiting an alligator farm, or taking a boat ride.

Of course if the whole point of your trip is to soak up as much winter sun as possible, you'll stick with beaches most of the time. But when you're looking for a variety of activities, separate similar ones by a day or two.

### Split Up Sometimes

Cancel this one if you're traveling with three kids under the age of 8. But even on a *family* vacation, it's perfectly possible for some members to go their separate ways occasionally. At Universal, the 9-year-old will have a very different agenda from the 16-year-old much of the time. Once everyone has a lay of the land, splitting up might be a way to satisfy everybody, with an agreed meeting time and place. Or Mom might take some kids in one direction and Dad and the others go another way for awhile.

Even on a day at the beach, older kids might want to spend the afternoon walking down the shore on their own, enjoying the solitude or meeting new friends (and, honestly, checking out the opposite sex). If you're someplace where you feel comfortable doing that, it's okay, and the kids appreciate it.

You don't even have to do the same sort of thing. If you're in Miami and father and son want to go to a Florida Marlins baseball game while mother and daughter want to shop Bayside Marketplace, everybody's happy. And that's the point of the trip, after all.

## Side Dishes

So much for the main ingredients. Let's talk about a few other things you'll want to consider in planning your menu of activities, some things it will help to know about or that will make the trip more memorable.

### Daily Life

If you're basing yourself in a single spot, pick up a copy of the local newspaper each morning. Not only will you be able to keep up with what's going on in the world that way (although

# Let's Talk About Money

Long, long ago, when dinosaurs roamed the earth, I used cash for all my expenses, even when I traveled. I was lucky, and never suffered a lost or stolen wallet. I'm smarter now, and have many more options.

I never carry more cash in my wallet than I expect to spend that day. I have extra tucked away in the money belt I talked about on page 27, and an extra credit card, too. Now a lost wallet will merely mean inconvenience, not disaster.

Travelers cheques used to be the best choice for families on the move, and they can still be a good one. Most places will let you spend them like cash, although clerks sometimes have to fetch the store or restaurant manager to authorize them. And some places won't take them. They're safe, though, since you can replace them if they're lost or stolen. Be certain to keep a record of their serial numbers in a safe place away from the cheques. Most people can get them from their bank for a fee of about 1 percent of the value, although auto clubs and many credit unions offer them at no fee to members.

I don't use them very often any more, though. Bank machines are now everywhere you look in Florida, making it easy to get cash whenever you need it. Money is withdrawn directly from your account, so you have to make sure there's plenty available. Bank cards may also be used as debit cards, taking the money from your account right at the point of purchase.

Credit cards are the fourth option. The biggest danger here is overextending yourself, and winding up with more debt than you really want, and facing exorbitant interest rates as you pay it off. It's a good idea to let your credit card company know you're going to be traveling. Once or twice I've been away from home and made three or four major purchases in the space of a few hours, and the credit card company has put a hold on my card, fearing it stolen. Then I've had to get on the phone and prove my identity by reciting my mother's maiden name, recalling the name of my childhood pet dog, singing my college fight song, and doing the other things a pickpocket probably can't do.

If you're visiting from abroad, be aware that *nobody* will take cash or travelers cheques in foreign currency. You'll have to change it at a bank: bureaux de change are rare, except at airports, where the commission is very unfavorable. In many countries, money can even be exchanged at post offices, but not here.

Bank machines in the U.S. almost always have 4-digit PIN codes, but most foreign bank cards will work just fine in American machines. U.S. banknotes are all the same size, and come in denominations of 1, 2, 5, 10, 20, 50, and 100, although the $2 bill is rare. Coins come in denominations of 1 cent, 5 cents, 10 cents, 25 cents, 50 cents, and $1, although the latter two are also rare.

it's not necessarily a bad thing to get away from the bad news that too often fills our world), you'll get a local weather forecast and information about interesting local events and places you might otherwise miss—festivals, parades, restaurants, and all kinds of unique local attractions.

For example, we were driving through our first New England visit some years ago and when evening drew on, we stopped in a small town in Vermont for the night. That's no big deal: *All* towns in Vermont are small. But when we looked at the local paper we got from the lobby of the motel, we discovered the town was the headquarters of Ben & Jerry's Ice Cream. *That* got our full attention.

So instead of setting out first thing the next morning for the Maine coast as we'd planned, we lingered long enough to take a tour of the plant, accept the free samples that came with it … and buy a little extra for the road.

We've also gleaned other sorts of useful information from local papers, like road closures due to fires, and highway construction updates, that saved us considerable travel time.

*Clothes and Laundry:* I usually travel light, though I have a friend who easily outstrips me, cramming enough clothing for a month abroad into a carry-on about the size of my briefcase. I'm not that good. I'm better, though, than some of the college students I've taken to conventions in New York City: One girl a few years ago took two large suitcases and a large carry-on for a three-day conference. I have no idea what was in them. Her boyfriend, maybe.

Florida is a very casual place, and you're not likely to go anywhere on a family vacation where you'll be expected to dress up. The most common wardrobe in the state consists of shorts, sandals, and t-shirt. More than that is verging on fancy. Still, depending on your plans and comfort level you'll probably want to take along slacks and a decent shirt or top for going to church, to a nice restaurant, or something like that. But leave your neckties and cocktail dresses at home.

If you're staying for more than a week, don't try to pack enough clothes for the entire trip, even if you're driving. Take a couple of hours and stop at a self-service laundry. You'll find them in every neighborhood.

If you're renting an apartment or condo, laundry facilities might be on the premises, and even some motels have washers and dryers that are available to guests. One roll of quarters (that's $10, for overseas visitors) should take care of a week's worth of wash.

And you can always wash out a few things by hand. In Florida's perpetually warm weather they'll dry overnight.

*Security:* Wherever you go in Florida, you're likely to be just as safe as wherever you're coming from. But just about every area in Florida is a high-traffic area, and it's possible for your possessions to become somebody else's possessions if you're careless. Don't leave your wallet or camera on your beach blanket while everybody runs into the water. It might be there when you come back ... but it might be a half-mile down the beach in somebody else's picnic cooler.

Big cities in Florida aren't a lot different from big cities anywhere else. Almost everywhere you go will be perfectly safe. But it's always best to stay away from deserted areas at night, to avoid flashing your cash, and to put valuables in the trunk of your car instead of leaving them visible through the windows.

Wherever you travel, it's *always* best to carry no more cash in your wallet than you expect to need that day. Some of the best money you'll ever spend is on a money belt or pouch, where you can keep your cash reserve, an extra credit card or two, and even your passport if you're traveling from abroad.

They usually come in three styles. My wife Barb wears one that fastens around her waist, under her clothes. I wear one that loops onto my belt and tucks inside my trousers next to my side pocket. A colleague I often travel with prefers a neck pouch that goes under his shirt. All are so comfortable you cease to notice them after ten minutes, but they're better than an insurance policy.

None will do much good if you go swimming, of course; they're not waterproof. You'll want to leave valuables in the trunk of your car, or people can take turns staying on shore to watch them. That's a very small price to pay for a day at the beach.

In an emergency, dial 911 from any telephone to get immediate police, fire, or medical help. If you're calling from a cell phone, you might need to give details of your location, since many cell phone systems can't pinpoint you fast enough.

**Tip:**

If you're flying with film, buy a lead-lined bag at the camera store and put it in your carry-on bag, never in your checked luggage, where the much stronger scanners will ruin the film. Security at U.S. airports will hand inspect your film, usually grudgingly, if asked, but that's often not true in other countries. Digital cameras, memory cards, and video tapes are not harmed by x-rays. Film and undeveloped slides are, no matter what the security guards tell you.

*¿Usted Habla Español? (Do you speak Spanish?):* If you do, you'll feel very much at home in most of south Florida and in any of its big cities. Spanish is virtually a second language—and in many parts of Miami is the primary language. It's not uncommon to walk down the street and see hand-lettered signs reading "English Spoken Here" in shop windows. You'll find Spanish language newspapers and television stations, and Spanish radio stations abound.

Miami is the most frequent port of entry for travelers and immigrants from Central and South America, and the area was flooded with Cuban refugees in the 1950s, many of whom have made it a home away from home and have preserved their culture, even, now, into a third generation.

*Daypacks:* When you're traipsing around, it's often helpful for everybody to carry a daypack, with snacks in case lunch is delayed, a water bottle, a map if you're wandering around a city, a camera and spare film and batteries, a book or personal electronics gear, and whatever else each person might need. They're also great for carrying small purchases or souvenirs you pick up during the day. I've got a small cloth briefcase with a shoulder strap I often use, but a small backpack or a tote bag that will zip or snap shut will do the trick. Each member of the family can carry his or her own, if they're old enough, or can share one and take turns carrying it.

If you're at the beach, though, you shouldn't put seashells in your daypacks. They're wet and sandy and might make a mess of whatever else you've got in there, and sometimes the shell's owner is still living inside. Dead shellfish toasting inside a bag all day will lend an unforgettable aroma to your belongings. A plastic shopping bag is better for the shells. When you get back to where you're staying, you can wash them and set them out to dry thoroughly.

You now have all the makings of a real gourmet vacation. Good planning and a realistic view of what your family wants to do—and can do in the time you have available—will produce a holiday all of you can relish, and with no need for salty language!

## Recommendations

↝ Get everyone involved in the planning from the beginning.

↝ Make sure each person in the family gets his or her first choice. Knowing that people will do what *they* want almost always makes kids more tolerant of the things others want.

↝ As important as preparation is, don't try to plan every minute. Leave room to be surprised by unexpected opportunities.

↝ Have lunch *before* you sit down to write a chapter like this.

# 4
# On the Move

FLORIDA MIGHT BE TUCKED AWAY IN THE LOWER RIGHT-HAND CORNER of the country, but it's probably the easiest place to get to in the entire Unites States, way easier than someplace you'd think would be accessible, like Kansas, which is smack-dab in the middle.

You can drive, you can fly, you can take the train, you can arrive by sea, you can probably even pedal your unicycle into the state if you have the balance and stamina for it. I have neither, so I'll restrict myself to more conventional modes of transportation.

We really have two separate issues to discuss when it comes to transportation: getting to Florida, and getting around once you're there. The first, getting there, is ridiculously easy; the second, getting around, depends partly on how you got there to begin with, where you are, and what your plans are. Let's take the easy one first.

## Getting to Florida

Visitors from the eastern and central United States and Canada have several choices for getting to Florida. Travelers from further west, or from abroad, are pretty much limited to flying. Before you decide for sure, though, let's look at all the possibilities. Or all except unicycles, at least.

### Flying to Florida

Few other places on the planet are as well served by airlines as Florida. No matter where you want to go, it won't be much more than an hour's drive from a major airport: Florida is served by 14 international airports and three other municipal and regional airports with commercial flights.

Because Florida is a major tourist destination, all the airlines want a piece of the Florida tourist pie, so there is a lot of competition, and prices are usually low. Few destinations are available in the United States at more consistently low fares than here. That's the upside.

The drawback to flying is that once you get to Florida, you will almost certainly need a car unless you're staying at an all-inclusive resort where you never leave the premises, or staying somewhere that has shuttle service to wherever you want to go. Public ground transportation is not very good in the United States except in some large cities, and covering much ground without an automobile in a large state like Florida is nearly impossible.

Fortunately, there is as much competition among rental car companies as there is among airlines, and weekly rentals at lower-than-usual rates are common. I've always paid less for a rental car in Florida than I've expected to. Chapter 17 includes a sidebar, *Don't Get Taken for a Ride*, that gives some good tips for finding a rental car at a good price.

## Taking the Train

Not even I am old enough to remember when you could travel the country by train. Unless you live along the Atlantic Coast, train travel to Florida is all but impossible. If you do live along that route, though, trains are a neat way to go, one the kids are sure to enjoy.

Train travel usually costs a little less than flying and takes a little longer than driving, but it is relaxing in a way that neither of those can be. The seats are roomy, meals and snacks are available, the scenery can be fabulous, passengers can get up and walk around whenever they feel like it—I love train travel, but seldom get the chance to do it in the United States because rail service has been largely abandoned for decades except in a few narrow corridors.

What I said above about needing a car when you fly into Florida also applies to train travelers, of course. In some cases, train stations are convenient to the center city, but often they lay some miles from where you want to be, so a rental car is in your future this time, too.

## Cruising

Passenger liners dock in Jacksonville, Fort Lauderdale, Miami, Tampa, and Port Canaveral. Most of these are cruise ships rather than point-to-point service, but the voyage is more the attraction in a case like this, rather than the destination. There are direct services, however, and all I can say is that if I lived in England and wanted to go to Florida, I couldn't think of a better way to go than an 8-night voyage to Fort Lauderdale on the Queen Mary 2.

Maybe in my next life....

## Driving to Florida

Major highways throughout the East and Midwest do a good job of funneling drivers right into the heart of the state. Interstate and federal highways can get you anywhere from the Panhandle to the Keys, and more scenic roads often hug the coastline. Florida is more than 400 miles (650 km) long, but mostly quite narrow, less than 100 miles (160km) wide in some places below the Panhandle. So it's easy to make one place your home base and cover an entire region of the state on your visit.

But Florida roads can be crowded, especially during the winter when "snowbirds" from the frozen north swell the population, and in the middle of the summer, when kids are out of school and family vacations abound. So while the speed limit on a Florida highway might be 70 mph (112 kph), heavy traffic will mostly leave that speed in the realm of the theoretical.

Actually, the worst part of driving to Florida is getting there. Because Florida *is* tucked into the corner of the country, it can be a very, very long way away from wherever you're starting from. From where we lived, one family trip to the state required almost exactly 24 hours of actually driving, with three boys (aged 10, 9, and 6 at the time) shoehorned into the back seat and a trunk full of what seemed like all our worldly possessions.

But for many families, it's that way—or no way. Even with the cost of gasoline and two nights in a motel each way, our trip was affordable. At that time in our lives, airfare for five people and a rental car once we got there would have been out of our price range. So we drove.

It wasn't all concrete tedium, though, but a good experience for all of us, especially the kids, who got a taste of just how big and diverse their country is. We watched the relentlessly flat cornfields of the Midwest gradually give way to the foothills, then the lushly rolling summits of the Smokey Mountains, then down through the red clay country of Georgia, to the tall palm trees of Florida. None of us had ever seen anything like that.

So if you must, or prefer to, drive, make that part of the attraction of your holiday. Look at it as an opportunity to experience the wonderful variety that's part of the United States. Stop frequently to snack, walk around, and talk with

*Bridge over Boca Ciega Bay. Madeira Beach Florida*
© *Jeff Kinsey/Dreamstime.com*

# Florida Airports

Daytona Beach International Airport (DAB)
Fort Lauderdale International Airport (FLL)
Fort Myers-Southwest International Airport (RSW)
Jacksonville International Airport (JAX)
Key West International Airport (EYW)
Melbourne International Airport (MLB)
Miami International Airport (MIA)
Naples Municipal Airport (APF)
Orlando International Airport (MCO)
Orlando Sanford International Airport (SFB)
Palm Beach International Airport (PBI)
Panama City-Bay County International Airport (PFN)
Pensacola Regional Airport (PNS)
St. Petersburg-Clearwater International Airport (PIE)
Sarasota-Bradenton International Airport (SRQ)
Tallahassee Regional Airport (TLH)
Tampa International Airport (TPA)

# Florida Train Stations

Amtrak stops at eighteen stations in Florida. From north to
south they are:

Jacksonville
Palatka (near St. Augustine)
DeLand (near Daytona Beach)
Sanford (near Orlando, auto train only)
Winter Park (near Orlando)
Orlando
Kissimmee
Winter Haven
Lakeland
Tampa
Sebring
Okeechobee
West Palm Beach
Delray Beach
Deerfield Beach
Fort Lauderdale
Hollywood
Miami

other travelers. End your drive each day early enough to play in a motel swimming pool and have dinner in small local restaurants instead of at the ubiquitous highway chains that are the same everywhere. It'll be lots more fun than you think.

And when you head home, take a different route, if you can, extending the vacation by seeing even more new things.

## Getting Around in Florida

Most of my books are about big-city vacations in places that have good public transportation. That's fine for a city, but what about an entire state?

Well, as I said a few pages ago, a car is pretty much a necessity.

You can do without one if you're going to an all-inclusive resort where everything is on premises. That means it's tough to break away even if you want to, but at someplace like Disney you might not care that the Orlando area has endless other attractions.

If your focus is surf and sand, many of the attractions are walkable in someplace like Daytona Beach, with others accessible by city bus or beach trolley. You'll find large city bus systems in Daytona Beach, Fort Lauderdale, Fort Myers, Gainesville, Jacksonville, Miami, Orlando, Tallahassee, Tampa-St. Pete, and West Palm Beach. In fact the transit systems of West Palm Beach, Fort Lauderdale, and Miami are nicely interconnected.

Miami also offers Metrorail, a 22-mile-long elevated rail service with stations about every mile. Visitors have little use for it, however, because it doesn't get very close to many attractions. The same can be said for Tri-Rail, the railway line that runs from West Palm to Miami: commuters find it useful, but tourists really don't.

Many beachfront areas like Daytona, Fort Lauderdale, and Clearwater have inexpensive trolleys that can take you for miles up and down the beach in search of a more secluded spot, an arcade, good restaurants, or shopping. If you're staying close to one of those beaches, lack of your own car might be only a small hardship.

If you need a car and don't bring your own, though, shop around among several companies. When there's a lot of competition, there can be a difference of $50 a week or more among companies.

Caution is a must when driving in Florida. Few places have

## No Buss for the Bus

Americans seldom travel by bus. A staple in most of the rest of the world, long-distance bus travel to most Americans is as unthinkable as a ride on the Space Shuttle. There are some good reasons for that—and some bad ones.

The United States is a country of automobilists: almost everybody owns a car and drives wherever they go, except for big-city dwellers who have access to cheap and reliable public transportation. And even they often rent cars for out-of-town trips. Most Americans perceive interstate bus travel as the domain of the rowdy young, the poor, and those on the margins of society. That's not entirely accurate, and I suspect, unfortunately, that at least some would-be riders steer clear of buses because they see more minority faces than they're used to.

It's often true that many bus riders are those who can't afford cars or more expensive modes of travel. Those people are no more unsafe to be around than your elderly Aunt Agnes. But I'm not entirely comfortable with encouraging unaccompanied female friends or family members to use them for lengthy, multiday trips. Anyway, bus travel, aside from its lower cost, doesn't leave its passengers in much better shape that air or train travel does: They arrive someplace, but are stuck there unless they rent a car to get around.

more visitors, and many of them aren't as sure how to get where they're going as they would like to be. Many visitors are from other countries, who are less familiar with American highway signs and driving practices than the natives are—especially tourists who come from countries like Great Britain, Australia, and Japan, where drivers drive on the left-hand side of the road. I've seen more sudden turns and unexpected lane changes on Florida roads than I have almost anywhere else, even in places like New York City and Boston that have well-earned reputations for fearsome drivers.

Remember, too, that the proportion of Florida residents older than age 65 is higher than any other state in the country—and that only two states have a higher percentage of residents over age 85. Statistically, older people are among the safest drivers, but the physical tools all of us put to use behind the wheel—sight, hearing, reflexes—do fade, and you might encounter more drivers in Florida than you do at home whose most skillful days behind the wheel were some years in the past.

## The Key to the Keys

If you're going to the end of the line—Key West, Florida's Caribbean—you've got a couple of other pretty neat choices.

Bus travel is not as big in the United States as it is in most of the rest of the world. And unless you're in Miami, the major national bus line, Greyhound, makes it difficult. For example, from some places even in South Florida, the trip to Key West is an interminable twelve hours, arriving in the middle of the night. But for a little more money, TransFloridian Shuttle runs comfortable luxury services from numerous Florida cities. Service is best along the Atlantic Coast, but on-demand services operate from other cities.

### A Disillusioned Arrival

It's only fair for me to tell you about the disenchantment that came in our first ten minutes in Florida. We had spent two days driving from Ohio with three rambunctious boys, aged 10, 9, and 6 squeezed into the back seat, and we were all excited about finally being there and seeing palm trees for the first time.

The morning of our third day on the road, endless miles of I-75 concrete behind us, we could see it at last—the state line, the Welcome Center, and a handful of the most anemic looking palm trees on the planet. We could have grown better looking palms in a pot.

But we gave them a pass on that. We knew that in truth, we were still too far north and too far from the warmth of the sea for palm trees to really flourish. They probably had to replant new ones twice a year. But tourists expected palms, and palms they would get.

What happened next was the real disillusionment. We went into the Welcome Center for our free glass of orange juice. Mmm, our mouths were watering at the prospect of delicious fresh Florida orange juice. We stepped up to the counter, asked for five cold glasses, and the attendant said, "I just ran out. Wait just a minute while I make some more."

Did he grab a big bag of plump oranges, a knife, and a juicer? He did not. He pulled out a can of frozen concentrate—the same brand we bought at home—emptied it into the dispenser, added tap water, mixed it with a big metal spoon, and handed us, smiling, five glasses of exactly what we drank in Ohio.

Even more fun might be to take a ferry from Fort Myers. The three-and-a-half hour trip on the Key West Express takes no more time that driving, and is much more fun. Mom and Dad can even play the slot machines while the kids watch movies on the 48-inch (1.2m) television screens. What a great way to go!

## *Recommendations*

∾ Most people will need a car. If you don't drive to Florida, you will find rental prices very competitive in most places.

∾ Look for inexpensive shuttles and trolleys in beach areas.

∾ Driving to the Keys is fun, but consider a bus or ferry so even the usual driver can enjoy the spectacular scenery.

*Road to Key West © Mauricio Thomsen/Dreamstime.com*

# 5
# At Home in Florida

YOU CAN SPEND AS MUCH MONEY AS YOU WANT ON SOMEPLACE TO stay in Florida. No matter how rich you are, you can find plenty of places that will really batter your budget.

But I don't suppose that's the sort of information you're looking for, is it? Unless you are very different from most people I know, you're hoping for some advice on *saving* a little money, not on shoveling hard-earned dollars at some multinational resort chain that has more money than some continents do.

Good. I know a lot about traveling cheap but haven't had much experience in spending money like it didn't matter. And while it's true that you can spend sanity-shattering sums on someplace to stay in Florida, the state has a wider variety of good-value accommodations than almost anywhere else I've ever been. Moreover, Florida offers a variety of different *types* of places to stay as well. You're sure to find someplace that is perfect for your family's needs, at a price you can afford.

You might also want to eat while you're visiting the state. I can give you some ideas there, too. The Lains have seldom been caught missing a meal, and I've got some ideas on how you can feed a hungry family for less than you expect. So let's talk now about how to make Florida your home away from home.

## Affordable Accommodations

You're not a reckless college kid anymore and have a family to think about, so maybe your days of sleeping on a blanket on the beach are best left to memory. You still have an array of accommodation choices that range from posh resorts that will send in a maid to brush your teeth every night to basic but clean motel rooms that cost less than the gasoline you put in your car. In this chapter we'll talk about those almost endless possibilities.

## Hotels and Resorts

Countless places call themselves resorts in Florida, but for the most part, we're talking about fancy hotels with recreational facilities. All-inclusive places like Club Med and similar mostly-Caribbean destinations are scarce in Florida; there are just too many things in this state to lure people away from resort facilities.

And if you do stay in a place like that, you don't really need this book. All your activities will be part of the resort package. Your valet will handle all the arrangements.

You can find hotels and "resort" hotels aplenty, though. There's not necessarily a big difference. I've seen business-district Holiday Inns with indoor pools and video arcades call themselves resorts at $79 a night, and elegant beach-front lodgings with extensive recreational facilities, a broad range of activities for kids, teens, and couples, luxurious rooms and dining, private butler service, and prices starting at $500 a night that are content with the simple designation of hotel.

A resort can also be a series of beachfront cottages on a private island. Or apartments on a marina that offer guests the use of watercraft, a private pier, and guided excursions to nearby attractions. Or a lakefront guesthouse with home-cooked meals, lots of personal service, and no activities at all. Or anything else somebody wants to call a resort.

It pays to know what you want and to investigate carefully. If all you're looking for is a base of operations and plan to spend your days on forays to surrounding attractions, you might not want to pay for a lot of amenities you'll never use. On the other hand, if you plan to spend most of your time using your hotel's own waterfront facilities, children's programs, and excursions, that's a different matter altogether.

Especially if the latter is the case, I really did mean it when I said to investigate carefully. Check places out on the Web, but remember that a talented photographer and clever copywriter can make a garden shed look like an elegant property. A phone call to the manager (not the reservation clerk) can confirm that all the services trumpeted on the website are available and operational, and also give you your best opportunity to negotiate a good rate.

You can also get a lot of information from internet travel advice sites like *tripadvisor.com* or *travel.yahoo.com*, or from travel discussion boards and Usenet forums like *rec.travel*. Remember, though, that most posted reviews will be negative.

One inexpensive dining option available throughout Florida is the buffet. If you eat early, before 6 p.m. or so, these all-you-can-eat establishments can even fill up a hungry teenager for very little money. Florida is home to large numbers of retirees on limited budgets who like to eat early and stretch their pensions as far as possible, and there's no reason why you can't benefit from places like this that cater to them.

Satisfied customers are much less likely to add to forums than unsatisfied ones are. But you can get some good information from such sites.

Travel agents have had a hard time in the internet age, but they are still a great source of information; because when they work with customers, they hear about both good and bad experiences. The best agents have taken familiarization tours of the places they're sending you and have seen hotels and attractions first hand. It's hard to duplicate that personal touch on a website.

I seldom recommend specific places to stay in my books, but like to talk about strategies for finding suitable places at a good price. The sidebar *How Low Can You Go* gives you a step-by-step guide for doing just that.

I have to mention the Disney and other theme park resorts here because they're a different sort of creature from most other places that call themselves resorts. If all you plan to do is to go to Walt Disney World, there are real advantages to staying on the property, which might include early and late admission to some of the parks each day, ease of transportation, priority for certain activities, discounts on others—Disney, especially, has numerous packages, and several different levels of luxury. You'll find more detail on that in Chapters 10 and 11.

## Motels

Less fancy, less packed with amenities … and less expensive … motels can be a good choice if you're only spending a night or two in one place before moving on, or if you're happy with basic, no-frills accommodations.

The difference between a hotel and a motel might not be obvious. I guess it depends on whether the letter "M" or the letter "H" was on sale the week the owner bought the sign. I think of a motel as a place where the rooms open directly to the outside and a hotel as a place with interior corridors.

But I've stayed at some of each where the opposite was true.

Of course motels come in many different flavors. We've stayed at well-priced motels right on the beach in Florida in May for no more money than I'd spend for one on the Interstate in Ohio in February. We've found motels with kitchenettes, motels with adjoining rooms for just a little more than one room, motels with large free breakfast buffets—motels of all imaginable descriptions, for half of what I'd have been willing to pay for the amenities. I've also seen places that would have been overpriced at a dollar a night.

We've found a lot of advantages to motels with kitchenettes (see the sidebar *Now You're Cookin'* in this chapter) and saving money on meals might make it possible for you to get two adjoining rooms where everyone can spread out and the kids can have their own space, instead of packing everybody into one room.

It's perfectly okay to ask to see your hotel or motel room before you actually register. Europeans do this all the time, but Americans seldom do. Check to make sure the room is

clean, that the air conditioning works, and that everything is as it's supposed to be. We were offered a 50 percent discount on a room once because the television didn't work. We took it happily; it was late, we were tired and ready for bed, and wouldn't have used the TV anyway. But because it *was* late, that room probably would have gone vacant if we hadn't taken it. Both the Lains and the motel profited from the deal.

If the room is not acceptable, you have a right to one that is. Except occasionally for peak season, you won't have any trouble finding another place to stay right down the road. We've turned down rooms with serious problems many times, in Florida and elsewhere, and sometimes accepted rooms with minor problems—but at a discount! Except at the very height of the season, there are nearly always plenty of rooms available nearby, and motel owners know it. Even without making reservations (which we seldom do unless

*Motel in Islamorada; photo by Juliana Spear*

we plan to stay in one place for several days) you can be picky about location, amenities, and price.

## Apartments and Condos

Motels with kitchenettes (or, at least, a microwave and refrigerator) may be your best low-budget option. We often travel like this when we're visiting multiple cities on one trip and staying just a night or two at a time.

Resort hotels with endless amenities where your beds are turned down for you every night, where a mint is left on your pillow, and where the concierge will come to tuck you in are the high-end option. I never travel this way myself unless I can get somebody else to pay the bill.

The approach that offers the best combination of value and economy, especially for a stay of a week or more, is to rent an apartment or condominium. For less money than most medium- to high-end hotels charge, you get a home away from home with separate bedrooms, living room, full kitchen, and much else. This much space in a hotel could cost you $1,000 per night. You can find condos where the same money gets you a full week, and sometimes much more.

And that apartment or condo might be right next door to the luxury hotel, sharing the same beach, the same view, the same local attractions—but *not* the same price!

The appeal of a place like this is that you can live as comfortably as you do in your own home, but in a much more exotic location, unless you're already used to watching the sun rise (or set) over the ocean each day ... in which case, why are you here? You save money by fixing many of your own meals, and it's no trick to find a place where the beach is just steps from your door.

Besides that, many vacation rentals are part of resort developments, so you just might have the same sort of pool, hot tub, fitness center, and tennis courts that you would have at the luxury hotel next door.

Nowhere else in the country has as many places like this to stay as Florida does. Ask friends, co-workers, or your travel agent for recommendations and you'll get more than you have time to check out. There are also some excellent websites in the appendix that provide extensive information on apartments and condos in all price ranges.

While many places you'll hear about are big blocks of condos run by corporations, we like to look for independent places run by live-in owners. One St. Petersburg-area

## Getting the Best Hotel Deal

1. Decide what sort of place you're looking for—resort hotel, motel, condo, or campsite.

2. Gather as much information as you can from the web, brochures, travel agents, and so on. Look for rates not only for the place you want to stay, but for comparable places nearby. Hotels will usually at least match the competition.

3. There is one overarching rule: Never pay rack rate. That is a hotel's "official" listed rate. Every experienced traveler knows you can always do better, usually a lot better.

4. Telephone the manager directly. If you book by phone, reservations agents are limited in what discounts they can offer. The manager is the boss: he or she can do things no one else can. Don't book through the web, either, especially through third-party sites like Expedia or Travelocity. Tell the manager what price you found online and he or she can probably beat it. Tell managers right away that you're trying to get the lowest possible rate so you can afford to take this special family vacation. Get them on your side: They are probably parents themselves. Telephoning works just as well if you're calling from another country, maybe better, because people know you're serious about working with them.

5. Flexibility is important. If you are not tied to specific dates but can come when hotel or apartment bookings are slow, you'll always be rewarded with a lower rate. Ask if you can provide your own bed linens for a rollaway, or bring a sleeping bag so one of the kids can camp out on the floor instead of using an extra bed. You might not be charged for an extra person. In some places if you offer to forego maid service and clean sheets and towels every day, you can lower the price a bit more.

6. After you've made your best deal, ask about other packages and incentives that might be in effect for the dates you want, or for nearby dates.

A room that's sold at half price still makes a lot more profit for a hotel than a room that sits empty, so if you can take your Florida trip during slow periods when hotels are much less likely to be full, you've got an edge. I've never met a manager who wasn't willing to beat the "best" price the reservations agent was able to give me. A savings of $20 a night for a 10-day vacation gives you $200 to spend on things that are a lot more fun than listening to Dad snore.

# Now You're Cookin'

This might be the best money-saving tip in the book: Find accommodations where you can do your own cooking.

I know this is meant to be a vacation, and I emphatically do not want anybody slaving away in a kitchen every night. But if you stay in a motel with a kitchenette, or in a condo or apartment with a kitchen, you can save big bucks.

After transportation and accommodations, food might be your biggest overall holiday expense, unless you plan to eat all your meals at Burger Bash. But with your own cooking facilities—even a microwave oven in the room—you can prepare simple, inexpensive meals and tuck away the savings.

Here's a simple example. Take your family of four to Olive Garden and you'll probably average at least $10 each for your main course. Add at least $1.50 per person for drinks, $4.50 for dessert, add tax and tip of at least $12, and you won't get out of there for less than $76. And that's with no appetizers, no coffee afterwards, and sticking to the low side of the menu.

Or you could stop at a Winn-Dixie grocery store and get a box of spaghetti for $1, a large jar of spaghetti sauce for $3.49, a loaf of crusty bread for $1.99, some salad greens for $1.49, milk or soda for $2.50, and a half-gallon of ice cream for $3.69. No tax, no tip. Your total is $14.16, less than the price of one person's meal in the restaurant.

Even without a full kitchen, you can prepare meals in the motel's microwave in the lobby, keep sandwich meat and milk in a cooler in your room (motel ice machines are almost always free), and have plenty of fresh fruit around.

We've done this many, many times and, in fact, when our family was young and we weren't making much money, it was this strategy that made it possible for us to travel at all.

You don't have to live like paupers; part of the fun of traveling is going out to eat sometimes. But to really make a trip affordable, you look for ways to save money and this is a dandy. If you pack a lunch of sandwich, fruit, and cookies for every member of the family each day instead of eating exorbitantly priced park or museum food, you can save $30 a day or more. Use that money to have dinner at nicer places, to extend your stay, or to sock away toward next year's vacation.

woman, who has run such a place for decades, naturally agrees. "If you can call and talk to the owner himself who lives right there, your odds are good of getting a place that's clean and well taken care of," she advises.

We began vacationing like this when our kids were small and we needed to save money, and have used this approach not just in Florida, but in London, Paris, Washington, New York, and elsewhere. We feel like we're putting down roots in a place, even if it's only for a little while. With a home of our own in Florida, even just a temporary one, we feel less like visitors and more like a part of the place we're staying. If I can't have a patio or balcony overlooking the ocean all the time, at least having a place of my own like that for a little while is just the sort of vacation I need to feed my retirement fantasies.

## Camping and RVing

I'll admit, the Lains have never been very good campers. We've tried tent camping and it wasn't the lack of heat or air conditioning, the absence of bathrooms, or the nightly attacks by mosquitoes the size of pigeons that deterred us. It was the fact that monsoons followed us. Drought-stricken farmers begged us to camp on their parched land, knowing a downpour would follow just about the time we decided to go to bed.

And since our family car for years was an old Oldsmobile about the size of a 747, we never thought about getting an RV. We could have held a medium-sized wedding reception in the back seat as it was. So we, at least, have never camped in Florida.

But we know lots of people who camp, and Florida is a favorite destination. There are hundreds of places to choose from, and it's a great way to see some of the state's most beautiful areas.

If you've got a camper or an RV, campsites and hookups will be only one-third to half the cost of a motel room, or less. Lots of opportunities for tent camping exist, too. Florida has a great system of state parks, and you'll find plenty of independent campgrounds and RV parks near every city. You can even fly to Florida and rent a camper or RV. You'll find links to some dealers in the appendix.

Perhaps the best source of information about where to stay is the Florida Association of RV Parks and Campgrounds. Their 64-page guidebook is free and their website, which is listed in the appendix, lists hundreds of facilities around the state.

From a tent to an estate, you'll have no trouble finding accommodations in Florida that fit your family's taste and budget. I'm always surprised at how inexpensively I can stay here, compared to other popular destinations, but competition keeps prices down. Take advantage of it.

## *Recommendations*

✐ Always inspect your motel room before you present your credit card.

✐ Save money by looking for motel rooms with kitchenettes, and prepare some of your own meals.

✐ For comfort and economy for stays of more than a few days, rent an apartment or condo. Good units are everywhere, and present more privacy, space, and value than any hotel.

✐ Prices on hotel and motel accommodations, and often apartments, are always negotiable, especially if you talk directly to the owner or manager.

# 6
# Under the Florida Sky

WRITING THIS CHAPTER TODAY IS PROBABLY A BAD IDEA. I'M SITTING in front of a large window at home, looking out on a frigid February morning with snow as far as I can see and a wind that's making a thick old oak tree next door creak and shiver. The squirrels are wearing hats and mittens.

And I'm going to give you a completely objective assessment of Florida? Don't count on it.

I'm scheduled to leave for a few days in Florida a month from tomorrow, and ten minutes after I arrive, my feet will finally be warm again. Until then, all I can do is think about it—and chat about it with you. So while dozens of specific places to go in Florida fill Part II of the book, let's talk about the great variety of mostly outdoor activities you can do almost everywhere in the state. From Pensacola to Key West, and everyplace in between, these are the activities that fill the free time of residents and visitors alike. Without them, Florida would just be, well, Ohio.

Let's spend a little time looking at Surf and Turf in Florida. And no, I'm not back to that food thing from Chapter 3—the description just seemed to fit.

## Surf

You've already guessed it: *Surf* is a collection of Florida activities on or near the water. This has always been my own favorite dimension of Florida, and never more so than now. I can go to baseball games or play golf in the U.S. Midwest but oceans are scarce here. Florida has endless numbers of non-water-related attractions, it's true, and the next part of the book is filled with dozens of the best of those. But the first thing I want to do when I get to Florida is to head for the shore. I'm not alone in that. Just look at the possibilities!

*Near the Water*
I don't know anybody who doesn't love a day on the beach.

It's perfect for lounging about, napping, reading, and just letting all those tense muscles go slack.

You won't have a bit of a problem finding a beach here, of course. I said in Chapter 1 that Florida has 660 miles (1070km) of beaches, so you're never far from one. Even if you're staying as far from the ocean or gulf as you can possibly get, you're no more than about 70 miles from the water—not much more than an hour's drive.

And don't assume that all those beaches are going to be jammed. It's true that you'll never be lonely on Daytona Beach or Miami's South Beach. But if all you're looking for is a quiet stretch of sand and water, and don't need a video arcade, snack bar, and deck chair rental, you'll find public access points up and down each coast. There are areas where you can drive for ten miles of nothing but Private Property and No Trespassing signs cutting you off from the shore. But you'll soon come across a public path or a county park that gets you right to the water.

Parking isn't always free, especially in cities, where parking meters or attended lots might cost a dollar an hour. I'm a cheapskate, though, and have seldom failed to find free parking within a few minutes' walk.

Lifeguards patrol the most-frequented beaches, but at other places you're on your own. If there are frequent rip tides or dangerous currents, that might be posted—or it might not be. Be careful everywhere, but especially on unattended beaches.

There's lots to do in a day at the beach. Swimming is obvious, of course. It's also great fun to dig a big hole and bury Dad up to his neck—but not too near the water if the tide is coming in, please, and don't forget to dig him out again before you go home. Kites are great fun because there's almost always a breeze at the shore and there are no buildings or trees for them to fly into.

If there's no snack bar (or even if there is—it's a lot cheaper), bring a lunch and plenty to drink. You'll go through a lot of water and soft drinks on a day in the sun.

*Children strolling on a Florida beach © Jennifer Boyd/Dreamstime.com*

Alcoholic beverages are almost never permitted on public beaches, just as well, since they're dehydrating anyway.

And don't get me started on shells. They're everywhere. Best time to find the prettiest ones is after the tide goes out, or after a heavy downpour. Most of the ones you find will be broken, of course, but every day you'll find something lovely worth saving. My father stubbed his toe on something in the sand one day, dug it up, and discovered a large, beautiful piece of coral that my brother mounted for him. The sidebar in this chapter tells you how to clean your favorite specimens.

My own favorite thing to do on the beach sounds boring to most kids, although they really will enjoy doing it at least once—watching the sunrise or sunset. These are the most magical times of day for me.

You have to remember where you are, though. After I grew up and left home, my parents and brother took a Florida trip with my aunt and uncle and their 10-year-old daughter, staying at their usual apartment right on the Gulf Coast.

Early one morning my mother went out just after first light to look for shells and found my cousin already sitting on the beach. Mom asked, "Denise, what are you doing up so early?"

"Oh, Aunt Betty," she replied, "I've always wanted to watch the sun rise over the ocean!"

If the sun had risen over the Gulf that morning, everybody would have had *way* more trouble than they could have handled that day.

### In the Water

I think the only reason I passed my required swimming class in college was because the instructor was convinced that if I had to retake it, I'd drown for sure the second time. I did, however, have the good sense to marry a girl whose summer job was being a lifeguard. But even given my very limited aquatic skills, I love splashing in the ocean.

There's something wonderful about standing in waist-high water and letting a big wave wash over you and knock you on your face. The saltiness of the water you come up sputtering is a real surprise if you've grown up in landlocked areas with only freshwater lakes to paddle around in. The first time we swam in the ocean, everyone in our family was surprised at how salty the water really is, and how its saltiness helps you stay afloat.

Even if your *real* life is headquartered at your beach cottage on the coast of Maine or your Mediterranean villa in the south of France, you'll love frolicking in Florida's waters. Don't forget to rinse yourself off thoroughly in fresh water afterwards, or you'll itch like crazy.

There's more to do than swimming, however. Some areas are just made for snorkeling, and the color of the tropical fish in Florida's waters are unforgettable.

## On the Water

There's no reason to limit yourself to the shore, however.

Boat rentals are everywhere and you can find anything from a rowboat to a yacht. Unless you're renting a rowboat, rentals are usually by the half day, full day, or longer term. Obviously you're not going to do this (except for the rowboat) unless you're an experienced sailor. I don't want to read about you being the guest of honor at a Coast Guard rescue. You can also rent water skis, jet skis, and any other sort of watercraft you can think of.

Even if you're not a sailor yourself, you can't leave Florida without taking some sort of cruise. Every coastal town has a marina where

> *Tip:*
>
> If you don't snorkel and don't want to learn, you can get a peek at what's below on one of the numerous glass bottom boat trips that are advertised everywhere.

you can book anything from a one-hour sightseeing trip along the coast to a daylong voyage far from the sight of land. Choose from whale cruises, dolphin cruises, manatee cruises, marine ecology cruises, jazz brunch cruises, dinner cruises, moonlight cruises, pirate cruises, and every kind of cruise you can imagine except Tom.

Expect to pay $25 to $50 per adult for a two-hour cruise, depending on the amenities. Kids will usually pay half to two-thirds of that. Passengers seldom have problems with seasickness on short cruises close to shore, but motion-sickness aids like Dramamine are available over the counter at any pharmacy, and Scopolamine patches, available by prescription, are highly effective for even very susceptible travelers.

If you like fishing, you'll have a field day here, if we can say that of an activity that can't actually be done in anything like a field. Fishing piers abound. Walk down the city piers at Daytona, Clearwater, or scores of other places and watch the competition—both for fishing space on the pier among the anglers, and with the pelicans that try to snare the things they catch.

You don't even have to bring your own equipment. Either near the pier, or halfway down it, you'll find a bait shop where you can rent gear as simple or as complicated as you like. A small fee gets you everything you need from a pole or rod and reel, to bait, to a temporary license. It's a cheap and relaxing morning's entertainment.

If fishing from a pier is too tame, deep sea charters abound everywhere along the coast. It can cost $500 or more for a half-day deep sea charter, but if you can join a charter group that's sharing the cost, it's affordable, and you might bring back a trophy of the sort you'd never get off the pier.

There's one more exciting on-the-water option. But perhaps I should list it as *above* the water. Try parasailing.

I'll admit, it's not the sort of thing I'm into myself. And parasail operators would take one look at my size, my age, and my general state of cowardliness, and start looking for other customers to help. Friends and family members who have done it, though, say it's a phenomenal experience, even my sister-in-law, who would rather be locked in a closet for a week than get within a hundred yards of an airplane.

Parasailers are strapped into a harness with a parachute and pulled behind a speedboat. In no time, they're soaring hundreds of feet above the ocean or Gulf, looking down on spectacular scenery no one else can see. What a high—literally! The sport is safe because the crew gets you up and down gradually, and you don't even have to get wet on the landing unless you want to. Most operators have harnesses that will take two or three people up at a time. Some vendors charge a flat fee, others according to how high you want to go, but you might find yourself more than 1,500 feet (457m) above the waves for a sight you'll never forget.

## Beach and Water Safety

Unless you're from a similar climate, you don't realize just how hot the Florida sun is, and how quickly you can get a sunburn that will ruin the rest of your vacation. Not only is Florida warm all year round, the rays of the sun are more direct, because it's closer to the equator, so fair-skinned people will tan—and burn—more quickly than they will at home.

The most important thing you can do is use a good, high SPF sunblock—at least SPF 15, and ideally more. Don't forget your ears, nose, backs of your neck and knees, and

Dad's bald spot. Reapply the sunblock frequently. Seawater and perspiration will dilute even so-called "waterproof" products. And remember that it's perfectly possible to get a sunburn on a cloudy day; clouds won't block the rays that are most harmful to the skin, even if you can't see them.

Avoid being on the beach or in a boat during the time when the rays of the sun are most direct, between 11 a.m. and 3 p.m. most of the year. Or make sure you have shade. It's worth renting that big beach umbrella on shore or rigging a tarp on the boat for shade, unless you *want* to look like a slab of charred prime rib.

Wear sunglasses and hats, and always have your water bottle handy.

Pay attention to the warning flags posted on beaches that indicate the presence of strong currents or dangerous creatures. Here's a rundown of what they mean:

> *Green: calm water and safe conditions. Swim, but be careful.*
> *Blue: dangerous marine life, like sharks or jellyfish. Stay out of the water.*
> *Yellow: moderate surf or currents. Exercise extreme caution.*
> *Red: high surf or strong currents. Being in the water can be dangerous.*
> *Two Red Flags: The water is closed because of dangerous surf, currents, or marine life.*

Rip currents (sometimes called rip tides or undertow, although there are technical differences) are very dangerous currents that can pull even strong swimmers away from shore. Children should always be closely supervised in the water, and it's best to stay away from piers, large rocks, or jetties, places where rip currents often form.

In small boats, everyone, but especially children, should wear life jackets; cruise boats will make a safety drill the very first order of business when you embark. Pay attention.

Few things are more fun than a day ... or a week ... on or near the water. Following just a few safety tips will make it all the more fun for everyone.

## Turf

We are often told that the human body is 98 percent water. It seems like Florida is, too. Except for the northern extremity which connects it to the rest of the continent, Florida is surrounded by the stuff. And even the dry land

## Cleaning Shells

Everybody brings back shells from Florida, dozens of shells, hundreds of shells. My mother's home is filled with shells from the numerous Florida trips she and Dad took, and I discover shells in odd and unexpected places in our own house. I'll bet you a dollar—a sand dollar—that somebody … or everybody … in your family brings back a bunch.

If you want them to look good, and not smell bad, here's what you want to do with most shells. First, make sure nobody is still living in the shell. If it's occupied, throw it back in the ocean and get it on your next trip.

Next, soak the shells overnight in a mixture of half water and half bleach, and brush off any barnacles that are still clinging to the shells. If they're stubborn, you might need to use a toothpick or the tip of a small nail or screwdriver to pry them off. Finally, wipe the shells with a soft cloth dipped in baby oil to bring out the colors and shine.

Sand dollars should be soaked in clean water first, changing it several times as it discolors, then for no more than 10 minutes in a 50-50 bleach-and-water solution. Rinse them in clear water again, then let them sit out in the sun to whiten.

isn't all that dry. The Everglades is an enormous swamp—fascinating in countless ways, ecologically significant, biologically mesmerizing, but still a vast swamp.

In fact, most of Florida is, technically, classed as wetlands. Well drillers in the state work with spoons rather than augers. Try to put a basement in your house and what you end up with is an indoor swimming pool.

But while water activities might be what Florida's best known for, there's more than enough to keep even confirmed landlubbers content. The chapters in Part II will lead you to dozens of my favorite places, but here I want to talk about land-based activities you'll find in every corner of the state.

### Participant Sports

Name your favorite sport. Unless it's alpine skiing, you can do it in Florida. For that matter, there are active ski clubs in Florida, but they sponsor trips out of state. Florida even has more than a dozen ice rinks.

Let's be honest, though. Nobody goes to Florida for winter sports; anything else, however, and you're in business. Outdoor sports of every sort are available here in unimaginable quantity and quality. I gave you a glimmer of the breadth of water sports a moment ago. But what can you do on dry (okay—dryish) land?

*Golf:* To say that golf a big deal in Florida is sort of like saying that oxygen is kind of important to the body. I'm not sure anybody knows how many golf courses there are in the state. One "comprehensive" guidebook to Florida golf lists 700 courses. I've managed to count 1,286. The Florida tourism marketing organization claims 1,370. Suffice to say that the World Golf Hall of Fame is here and the PGA plays several major tournaments here.

You can almost always rent clubs if you don't bring your own, and greens fees can be moderate, especially if you're not here in the winter. Courses often have spectacular oceanside scenery. You may encounter some of golf's more unusual situations, like the rule that entitles you to a free drop if your ball lands too close to an alligator.

*Bicycling, rollerblading, and skateboarding:* You can rent bikes in almost every city and pedal yourself across the state. I've seldom seen anywhere with more wide, accessible bike paths, often well separated from roadways. If you don't like coasting along the shore with the ocean breeze in your face, I can't imagine what you're looking for in a ride.

These are great places to stretch your legs on skates, too, and there are dozens of skateboard parks located throughout the state.

*Competitive Sports:* Tennis courts, baseball fields, basketball hoops, shuffleboard courts—they're all here in abundance. If you enjoy playing it at home, you'll find it here. (And don't forget those indoor ice rinks.)

Be sensible about playing in the heat of the day, take the advice I gave to beach-goers a few pages ago, and take along lots of water to drink.

## Spectator Sports

The pro sport I probably least associate with Florida is ice hockey. They've got it. There are NHL teams in Miami and Tampa and East Coast League teams in Pensacola and near Fort Myers. If Florida's got *that*, it's got everything! I'll admit, though, that the Big Four are baseball, football, basketball, and auto racing.

*Baseball:* Aside from the fact that there are major-league teams who play the regular season in Miami and Tampa Bay, about 18 big-league teams comprise the "Grapefruit League" for spring training every February and March. This is a great time to get inexpensive tickets in small ballparks that get you close to the stars of the game.

There are no teams in the Panhandle, but from Orlando south, you're seldom far from some team's training facilities. The largest concentration of teams is in the Tampa Bay area, but the Atlantic side has Grapefruit league teams about an hour's drive apart all the way down the coast. Besides major leaguers, you'll find more than two dozen minor league teams in the state during the summer, playing in every corner of the state. If you like baseball, this is the place to come.

*Football:* If anything can rival golf in this sports-mad state, it's football. Competition is intense from Pee Wees to pros, it's a statewide fixation from August to January.

The NFL has teams in Jacksonville, Miami, and Tampa Bay, and the Super Bowl is played in the state about half the time—not that you stand a chance in the world of getting tickets to that one!

For a truly electric atmosphere, though, try college football. Three of the country's traditional powerhouses are in Florida: the University of Miami Hurricanes, who play in Miami, naturally; the University of Florida Gators in Gainesville; and the Florida State University Seminoles in Tallahassee. But there are many other colleges and universities in the state where excitement runs just as high.

*Basketball:* The Miami Heat and Orlando Magic play in front of packed houses all winter long, and offer visitors an opportunity to see some of the best (and tallest) athletes in the world. Pro basketball in person is nothing like the game on television. The action is so intense that I've come away from pro games where I was only a spectator feeling like I had bruises all over my body.

*Auto Racing:* The Indianapolis 500 has claimed to be "The Greatest Spectacle in Racing" for decades, but the Daytona 500 is at least its equal. I don't know which one is better; it's like choosing between steak and lobster. (And now we're back to that Surf-and-Turf business again.)

I'll take you around the big track at Daytona in Chapter 8 and the sports car track at Sebring in Chapter 14, but if you can't make it to one of those, look for smaller tracks throughout the state, the kinds of dirt and asphalt tracks where today's NASCAR drivers got their start. Saturday night at the local small-town speedway is a lot of fun. There are more than a dozen fairly large tracks around the state and innumerable local ones.

### I Bet You'll Like These

As long as we're on the subject of racing, what about horses? Florida has several race tracks, and they provide inexpensive family fun. Admission to most tracks is no more than about $5 per person, and kids are often free, or pay no more than a dollar or two.

How can they do it so cheaply? They count on wagering. You don't have to bet, though. Just going to the track for an afternoon of color and pageantry, and the chance to see the sheer power of the only athletes in the state more fine-tuned than NBA players is enough for me.

The top tracks are Gulfstream in Hallandale, just north of Miami; Calder, also in Miami; and Tampa Bay Downs, north-west of Tampa. There's also harness racing at Pompano Park near Miami.

There are also about fifteen tracks that feature greyhound racing. Kids are welcome here, too, as long as they stay out of casino and betting areas. Mom and Dad can place bets, of course, and even a $2 wager makes a race seem more exciting.

That's Florida—more to do than you can imagine, and if you can imagine it, you can do it here. Except alpine skiing.

## Recommendations

∽ You haven't really been to Florida if you've spent your trip in theme parks and arcades. Get out on, in, or over the water.

∽ If you're a golfer, a round on a waterside course is a must.

∽ Sports venues of all types are every-where and can be an inexpensive afternoon or evening of fun.

# 7
# Your Vacation Strategy

I HOPE YOU'RE CONVINCED THAT YOU JUST HAVE TO TAKE A FAMILY holiday in Florida, and that it will be easier than you thought. The next step will be to decide what to do once you get here, and now the real fun begins. I love the excitement of planning a trip like this!

And I really, really hate it.

The good part is seeing all the possibilities, all the fabulous things I never knew existed at our new destination, the dozens—hundreds!—of things I'd love to do: museums to visit, walks to take, scenery to admire, famous places to experience. The list is endless.

That's why I hate this part, too, because I know I'm going to have to leave out most of what I'd really like to do. There's always just too much! I won't have time to do everything unless I become compulsive and unpleasant, and besides, I can't think of just myself, but of the people I'm traveling with, too. If this is a family trip, it's not going to be very much fun if we only do what Dad wants. We're all in this together!

The problem is compounded when you make the decision to go to Florida, because the first question will be ...*Where?* You can't cover the whole state unless you're even more compulsive than I am at my worst. You have to narrow it down: Panhandle? Gulf Coast? Atlantic Coast? Orlando? The Keys?

Even that's not enough. If you choose the Atlantic Coast, for example, exactly where along the 350-mile (560km) stretch from Jacksonville to Miami are you going to base yourself? Each time you make a choice, you're eliminating dozens of other wonderful options from your trip.

But cheer up! There are really no bad choices. It's like deciding between ice cream and cake—it's all good!

Here's what matters about making the choice: It should be a family decision. If your kids are old enough to be able to make their own choices about other things, they can help decide how the family should spend the holiday. Little ones won't be able to see beyond Orlando theme-park vacations.

They don't know enough.

But if any of your kids are more than age 10 or so, they're old enough to take a broader view of things and can contribute serious ideas. Maybe you'll end up in Orlando anyway—but once kids realize just how much more there is to Florida than coming home with a pair of mouse ears, they'll get excited about the possibilities, too.

*Tip:*

Chapter 15 provides an easy form for discussing all the places and attractions in Part II, and is just what you need for having all the possibilities in a handy, easy-to-use format for making the final decisions.

These discussions are the best insurance you can get for planning a vacation that everyone will enjoy. Kids who help plan trips like this, whose ideas have been listened to, who have helped prepare the itinerary, have a personal stake in the success of the trip. If the trip isn't just something Mom and Dad cooked up one night after they were in bed, kids will almost always have more fun, complain less, and be more tolerant of the things other family members want to do. And I guarantee they'll come up with ideas you'd have never thought of—fun things that might be a real highlight of the trip.

The actual planning is a pretty straightforward four-step process.

### 1. Survey the entire Florida landscape

Everybody in the family should read Part II of the book or, if they're too small to read it for themselves, Mom and Dad can summarize the things in each chapter for them.

Chapters deal with large geographic chunks of the state. That's a practical approach because unless you're planning some sort of traveling road show, you're going to base yourself in one place and focus on the attractions there. If you choose Daytona, for example, it means you're going to miss the neat things around Fort Myers and that's too bad. But you do want to be sane and financially solvent when you get home, so you can save Fort Myers for next time. It will still be there.

The key here is just to get everybody familiar with what each part of the state has to offer. Then you can start to narrow it down.

## 2. Make decisions on the sort of vacation you want

After everybody is familiar in a general way with the endless opportunities Florida offers, your next task is to try to resolve how people want to approach the holiday. Remember the choices I gave you in Chapter 2?
· a theme park vacation
· a beach escape
· an urban getaway
· the hodgepodge holiday

Now is the time to get that part sorted out. But even if no one is interested now in doing anything other than lying in the sun and splashing in the surf, you're bound to want a change of some kind over a period of a week or two—or at least have alternatives in case a day or two of your beach escape turn cool or rainy. That's the next step.

## 3. Narrow the possibilities to something manageable

Now you know what kind of vacation you're going to focus on, and what fun things are available in every corner of the state. So—where will you make your home base? Maybe that choice will be easy because you want to stay near family in Clearwater, or because you can borrow a neighbor's condo in Fort Lauderdale. Otherwise, though, your biggest choice comes right here:
· You want to be in or near the excitement of a big city, so will it be Miami or the Bay Area?
· You want to bake on the beach and just wander around a bit, so do you choose Daytona or Panama City?
· Your life will be a ruin if you can't go to a big theme park, so pick Tampa or Orlando.
· You want variety, something different every day with cities, shopping, beaches, museums, parks, everything within an hour or two away, so you decide between—oh, I don't know … pretty much everywhere!

That's why these chapters are so valuable: They fill you in on the coolest family spots in each area.

## 4. Pin down the key things you want to do

Once you've made the hard choice of what area to base yourself in, you can begin to plan an itinerary. Chapters 15 and 16 will be especially helpful with that. Take note of all the great things to do in the part of Florida you've selected, and have every member of the family list the things they want to do—and to identify the one thing on the list that each *most* wants to do.

This is one of the great secrets to a successful family vacation. Everybody gets his or her first choice. If a child knows that what she most wants to do on a vacation will be a family priority, she's bound to be more tolerant of everybody else's choices, even if she's not crazy about them. Once you've finished this step, you're ready to book accommodations: You know where you'll be going and what the main things are you plan to do when you get there. Chapter 16 will show you how to put together reasonable itineraries for your visit.

## How the Chapters Are Organized

Each chapter in Part II begins with an overview of the region, how to get there, and the best ways to get around. There's not much in the way of intercity public transportation in Florida, and city-based bus and rail services in Florida cities are much more useful to local commuters than to visitors, except trolleys along the beach in some areas. I'll point out the exceptions where they exist, however.

Next I'll focus on the key cities in each region, places that offer families a good base of operations with choices of accommodations, restaurants in a variety of price ranges, and lots of activities that should appeal to members of almost every family.

In these chapters, however, I will *not* try to give you a list of every single attraction in the state. The hallmark of books in the *Family Travel Series* has always been to show you places other than "the same old stuff." If your kids want to go to a water park, that's fine. There's one within a couple of miles of wherever you're staying. There's not *that* much difference in approach between Adventure Landing and Buccaneer Bay. (Tomorrow morning I will get 23 e-mails from water park directors heatedly explaining in painful detail exactly why theirs is very different from, and so much better than, all the rest. *Sigh.*)

There is a nice zoo in every major city and quite a few minor ones. In Florida, you can't throw a stone without breaking a fish bowl in an aquarium. If you want those things (and they have always been fun for our family, as they have been for yours), go to the nearest one. For that matter, you probably have a nice one (water park, zoo, aquarium—whatever) within an easy drive of home.

I'd rather spend the pages talking about the less usual attractions. I might mention a zoo or two in passing, but for animals, I'd be inclined to try *Lion Country Safari*, where the animals roam free and the people are caged up. Aquariums abound in Florida, and while some are better than others, you get a similar experience in each. But not in the *Clearwater Marine Aquarium*, a very special place that does more than exhibit sea creatures—it saves their lives.

And don't get me started on Florida beaches. You will find an assortment of wonderful ones wherever you go, unless you spend your entire vacation in Sebring. I couldn't possible list them all—and don't feel I need to.

I have no quarrel with guidebooks that try to be comprehensive; I borrow a forklift and load two or three thick volumes into the trunk of my car before planning every trip. But this book will focus for the most part on longer reviews of places that seem more special to me for members of families trying to make sure that their own particular holiday isn't just a copy of the one that Aunt Molly and Uncle Charlie took in 1996. When I travel, I look for special, memorable places. I think you do, too.

I do try to provide a guide to the days attractions are open, although I seldom list specific admission prices or opening times, since those often change seasonally or, sometimes, weekly. The appendix at the end of the book contains websites for every attraction that has one. That's where to go for the most up-to-date information on those things.

One more point. I know I've said it before, and you shouldn't be surprised if it comes up another time or two. But don't *over*-plan. You don't want to get to the Florida state line and just start to wander about aimlessly with your family—kids are not patient creatures. But don't try to map out every move, every visit, every attraction. That's obsessive and I know a psychologist or two who would be happy to work with you on that problem. Leave room to be surprised.

If I'd been unremittingly compulsive on various Florida trips, I'd have missed the very odd Castle Otttis. (yes—spelled with three T's). I'd have missed the kitschy Burt Reynolds Museum. I'd have missed the headquarters of the fascinating Koreshan group of Utopians. You have to leave room on a trip, as in life, to be surprised. And Florida is full of surprises.

## Recommendations

&#10097; Get every member of your family involved in the planning. It's the best insurance you can have for a successful trip, because everybody has a stake in making it work.

&#10097; Start with the broader questions of what sort of vacation you want, and gradually narrow the focus to specific attractions.

&#10097; Leave room for surprise.

# PART TWO

## The Very Best of Florida

Now that we've dealt with the logistics of the trip, let's talk specifics. What will you actually do once you're there?

You are absolutely spoiled for choice. I can't possibly list every attraction in the state unless you want a book you'll have to take home in a wheelbarrow. I assume you're coming to Florida because it offers things you can't find at home. Those are the things I'll focus on in Part II of the book. I won't go into a lot of detail on every zoo or art museum, as much as I like them: You've got some good ones near where you live and don't have to go to Florida to see them.

Instead, I'll spend this part of the book introducing you to the special places that make a trip to Florida unlike a vacation anywhere else in the country. Florida is a lot more than just big theme parks, and while I'll talk about those, there is so very much more. Turn the page and you'll start to see just what I mean.

# 8
# The East Coast

WHEN PEOPLE TELL ME ABOUT THEIR FLORIDA VACATIONS, THIS IS the part of the state they seem least likely to mention. I've heard so many tales of the wonders of Orlando, the vibrancy of Miami, the warm waters of the Gulf Coast, the seclusion of the Panhandle—but, aside from college students describing their spring-break trips to Daytona, I hear very little about the northeastern corner of the state.

To be perfectly honest (as I always am with you), the first Lain venture into this part of Florida was something of an afterthought, too. We had spent our holiday in the Tampa area and wanted to visit Kennedy Space Center on the way home. We cut across the state and saw Kennedy, then hightailed it for the border. We had to take an extra day because I got sick in St. Augustine and saw nothing of the city but the inside of our motel room, and I couldn't wait to leave once I started to feel well.

I should have taken more time; now I know better.

You'll find more than enough for a memorable vacation along Florida's Atlantic Coast, and you'll have less problem here than most other places in the state finding accessible, uncrowded beaches, parks where you don't have to wait in line for hours, and attractions that are like nothing else in Florida—or anywhere else. I've never been able to decide if I have a favorite part of Florida. The state has so many different sorts of experiences to offer. But if I did have a favorite, this might be it. Unless it were somewhere else.

## Getting Around

This could be said of almost everywhere in Florida, but the only easier way to get to East Florida would be to have been born here.

If you're flying, you can choose from three international airports (Jacksonville, Daytona Beach, and Melbourne). Amtrak trains stop in Jacksonville, Palatka (close to St.

Augustine), DeLand (just west of Daytona), and Orlando (a short drive from the Space Coast). And if you've rented a car or have driven your own, going north and south in Florida is the easiest thing in the world, especially along the Atlantic Ocean side of the state.

Your map will show three main north-south highways, and the choices are clear-cut.

The really boring option is I-95. This interstate highway runs all the way from the Canadian border in Maine to the south side of Miami, about 1,900 miles (almost 3,100km). You don't want to drive through Florida that way unless you're in a real hurry. I-95 looks just like every other interstate highway and motorway in the world, except with palm trees. It's crowded, but efficient. High-speed traffic is usually one of the things people are trying to get away from on a holiday.

A slightly better choice is U.S. Highway 1. It, too, runs the length of the country. In fact, it starts further north in Maine and runs clear to the end of the Florida Keys. But at least it goes through towns along the way. You can pull off at a roadside restaurant if you're hungry instead of waiting for the next exit, which might be 30 miles away. You see people in their front yards, kids on bikes—normal life!—instead of endless miles of sterile highway.

It's slower. There are stoplights and congested areas. And, honestly, most of it is not very picturesque, just utilitarian. But there's a third way, my favorite.

Route A1A might not even show up on some small maps, and occasionally the highway disappears altogether, joining up for several miles with U.S. 1. But this is the one you want. A1A hugs the coastline. While there are dull stretches, for much of the trip you'll be within sight of the ocean on one side of the car or the Intracoastal Waterway on the other ... and sometimes both at once!

On A1A you'll pass countless quiet public beaches, amazingly luxurious homes (and, it must be said, some downright silly architecture, too), lush golf courses, yachts with more bedrooms than your rich uncle's house, and tourist attractions galore.

In fact, that last part is one of the best features of A1A. Many of the things you've come to Florida's East Coast to see are on or within minutes of this highway. It, too, can be busy during the height of tourist season, but you're more likely to cruise along without a car in sight, as we've done, listening to radio reports of lengthy delays on I-95 a few miles to the west.

From Jacksonville to Melbourne is less than 200 miles (300km), but there's more to do than you possibly have time for. Each of the principal cities along this route offers a terrific array of possibilities…and not just the cities, but the coastline between them.

In fact, you should get used to people referring to the coast as much as to the nearest important city. There's the Palm Coast, the First Coast, the Space Coast, the Treasure Coast and more. Some of the names have been around for years, others are more recent marketing inventions. Some overlap, some are meaningless to people just a few miles away, and some are known to everybody. Figuring out the names is a real roller-coaster.

## DESTINATION
## Jacksonville

This is Florida's largest city, with more than three-quarters of a million people, more than double the size of Miami, the next contender. Like all big cities, Jacksonville is host to the usual array of museums, zoos, and parks. In fact, if you're driving in on I-95 from the airport north of the city, you might have to stop Dad from turning off at the very first tourist attraction you come to, the Anheuser-Busch Brewery tour. A little further, though, will get you to a more family-oriented attraction, the **Jacksonville Zoo** *[370 Zoo Parkway, east of I-95 Exit 360. Open daily. Adm.]*.

If you're staying in the city, you'll probably end up sooner or later at **Jacksonville Landing** *[Water & Laura Sts. downtown at riverfront. Open until 8 p.m. M-Th, 9 p.m. F-Sa, 5:30 p.m. Sun.]* an attractive riverfront shopping, eating, and entertainment complex.

Within a five-minute drive are several museums. The closest, the **Jacksonville Museum of Modern Art** *[333 N. Laura St. closed M. Adm.]* is a quick walk away. Kids will probably like the owl perched above the street looking down at traffic from atop a stack of books, the stark white interior, and the unusual approaches to art. A few minutes west, the **Cummer Museum of Art and Gardens** *[829 Riverside Ave. Closed M. Adm.]* is a more conventional art gallery. Across the bridge is the improbably named MOSH—the **Museum of Science & History** *[1025 Museum Circle. Adm.]* with a nice variety of exhibits and hands-on activities that focus on Florida animal life and local history.

*Florida coastline © Scott Pehrson/Dreamstime.com*

I think the best bits of Jacksonville aren't really in Jacksonville at all, however (unless you can get tickets to an NFL football game at Alltel Stadium downtown). Jacksonville is actually about 15 miles inland, and I'm heading for one of the best beachfronts in a state famous for its beaches. The best way to get there is straight east on Beach Boulevard. Along the way you'll pass **Adventure Landing & Shipwreck Island Water Park** *[1944 Beach Blvd. Open daily. Adm.]*, one of dozens of water parks of varying quality in the state and one of two in the area owned by this company alone. (Be alert. It's not well marked and you can zip past it if you're not watching. Turn south at 20th Street.) This is a pretty good one, as these things go. The best water ride is the Hydro Halfpipe, where people braver than I am sit in a big yellow inner tube and shoot down a water-covered 35-foot-high ramp like skateboarders and travel almost as far up the other side of the pipe, back and forth until their momentum runs out. The park also has an arcade, kiddy rides, and dry-land activities, too, including one of the best go-kart tracks I've seen.

But if you're after the *real* water, make tracks for the ocean. There are miles of big, broad beaches here, with plenty of close-by parking. The beach is well guarded, offers nearby restrooms and food, a great fishing pier, and always seems to have a delicious charcoal smell from somebody's barbecue in Oceanfront Park on South Fifth Avenue. They've even got street signs on the beach to keep you oriented so you can find where you came in. We've seen dolphins playing in the water here just beyond the swimmers, so keep your eyes open.

When you leave the beach—which is so hard to do— head south on Third Street. This is the Route A1A I talked about earlier. It will lead us to just about everywhere we want to go in this part of the state.

It's a pleasant drive. Keep your eyes open for unusual mailboxes. Along this road, we've seen dolphins, sea turtles, sea horses, conchs, pelicans, and manatees. I've never seen mailboxes like any of those in Ohio! You might also watch for interesting street names. If you were sharp-eyed on your way along Beach Boulevard heading for Jacksonville Beach, you probably wondered about *Parental Home Road*. There's got to be a story in that. On this part of the drive, you might spot *Mosquito Control Road* as you go through Ponte Vedra. I don't think I want to know about that one. And the elegant homes will make you wonder "Does everybody here have twenty children? Who needs houses this big?"

But coastline houses (many in a faux Spanish style) are always interesting, mailboxes and extravagance aside. Many are set on stilts, which is as good a way as I can think of to add to the view, catch the ocean breeze, and keep the basement dry during unusually high tides. And many are capped with crow's nests—rooftop observation decks for watching the waves.

The drive from Jacksonville Beach to St. Augustine is about 30 miles (50km). Once you reach Vilano Beach, on the northern outskirts of St. Augustine, watch the west side of A1A for one of Florida's most unusual sites—*Castle Otttis*. Yes, with three T's. Built by three local men between 1984 and 1991 to look like a thousand-year-old Irish castle, it offers non-denominational worship services every Sunday from 11 a.m. until noon, and allows sightseers for an hour after that. It is also a popular place for weddings, but is a startling addition to the local landscape. The castle is on Third Street, about 2.6 miles (4km) north of where A1A turns sharply west to cross the Intracoastal Waterway and goes into St. Augustine.

# DESTINATION
## St. Augustine

The next stop is America's oldest city, and old is something I can really relate to.

Juan Ponce de Leon landed here in 1513 in search of the legendary Fountain of Youth, and in the process gave Florida its name because of the abundance of flowers he found here: *florida* means "flowery" in Spanish. He was the first European to discover this place, but he didn't find eternal youth here and didn't establish a settlement. That happened in 1565, two generations before the first English settlement in Jamestown, VA. This history is St. Augustine's stock-in-trade, and there's enough to see and do here to provide plenty of variety in even a lengthy beach vacation.

## *Touring Old St. Augustine*
Whether you find eternal youth here or not, you're just an infant compared to most of what you'll see in St. Augustine. Even if you're committed to a vacation spending as much time as possible on the beach, a half-day walk through St. Augustine's Historic District will provide an interesting change of pace, and hard-core history junkies like some of the Lains might clamor for a full day.

But park your car. Streets are old and narrow, and some prohibit vehicles altogether. Best bet is leave your car near the *Visitor Center* (across San Marco Avenue from Ripley's Believe It Or Not) at the north end of the Historic District. You can pick up maps and brochures at the center, but it's very easy to find your way around. The area is very compact, everything is well marked, most places are accessible for visitors with mobility problems, and just wandering around looking at the two- and three-hundred- year-old landmarks is free.

If you want to tour any of the buildings, admission prices are low. You'll find plenty of places to shop or eat and public toilets are easily available, so this is an area where everyone will find a lot to enjoy.

Enter the old *City Gates* near the Visitor Center, walk down St. George Street, and you're already spoiled for choice. The country's *Oldest Wooden Schoolhouse* will be on your right and the old grist mill on your left. When you reach Cuna Street you can visit the *Colonial Spanish Quarter*, where you can sample life in 1740s St. Augustine.

As you stroll down the street, you can enjoy the buildings, many built in the 1700s and 1800s. When you reach Cathedral Place, you can turn left and visit the *Basilica Cathedral*, the oldest Roman Catholic parish in the country. Although the present church dates only from the 1790s, parish records go back to 1594.

If you want to walk up another block to King Street, a left turn will take you to the *Spanish Military Hospital* (the building is a reproduction, not authentically old) or you can turn right and walk to the *Plaza and Government House*, which contains a museum of local artifacts. The statue of Ponce de Leon in the plaza makes him out to be just 4-foot-11 (1.5m) in height, forcing us to wonder if his search for the

*St. Augustine © Chad Van lue/Dreamstime.com*

fountain of youth wasn't as much for an eternal puberty where he could continue to grow as it was for an indefinite lifespan.

Three blocks more along St. George and you can turn left on St. Francis Street, and a block to the left is the *González-Alvarez House*, the oldest house in the United States, built about 1702. Exhibits show more of life in the old city, and it's easy to picture household members at work in the separate kitchen building. There's a small museum in a modern building with archeological finds from the site, and the adjacent *Tovar House* has an exhibit of military uniforms that have guarded St. Augustine for 400 years.

If you're not sated by history yet, retrace your steps back along St. Francis and go one more block to Cordova Street. Turn right here. At Bridge Street you can visit *Old St. Augustine Village*, a city block of 100- to 250-year-old buil-dings, gardens, and public spaces with guides to demonstrate how people lived long ago.

As you make your way back north on Cordova Street toward the parking lot, you'll also pass the *Lightner Museum*, *Flagler College* with its dazzling collection of Tiffany glass, the *Oldest Drug Store*, and much more. This is a great area to turn aside from your walk whenever you see something you think might be interesting—because it almost certainly *will* be.

### The St. Augustine Alligator Farm

From downtown St. Augustine, cross the Lion Bridge on A1A to Anastasia Island. Just beyond the lighthouse (see page 79) you will come to Florida's oldest (1893) continuously operating attraction, the **St. Augustine Alligator Farm** *[999 Anastasia Blvd. Open daily. Adm.]*, perhaps the best of the several gator farms in the state. That's not my opinion alone. Here's a direct quote, overheard in the crocodile exhibit, from a boy who appeared to be about 6 years old: *"Mom, I want to stay here for the rest of my life."*

Can there be a better endorsement?

Even if you're not a 6-year-old boy, you're going to be fascinated by this place. From the dwarf caimans you'll meet just inside the entrance (mean-enough looking to make you not want to meet a big one in an alley on a dark night) to the enormous croc Maximo—more than 15 feet long and 1,250 pounds (4.7m, 570kg)—to the rare albino

alligators that supposedly bring good luck to those who look on them, you'll see creatures you've never seen before around every bend in the path.

This is the only place in the world where you can see all 23 of the earth's varieties of crocodilians. From a safe distance above them, you can throw food to the gators and watch them snap and scramble for a bite, a sight that will probably make you hold just a little more tightly to the guard rail over their ponds. And the birds! Ah, the bird exhibits are phenomenal, from the brilliantly colored parrots, toucans, macaws, and cockatoos to the huge natural rookery filled with herons, egrets, ibises, storks, and spoonbills.

Everything is completely wheelchair accessible, and places with solid walls even have viewing windows cut into them for the benefit of small children and visitors in wheelchairs. Near the back of the Land of Crocodiles, is a small play and picnic area called Kids Zone—but with *no* petting zoo!

## Other St. Augustine Attractions

I'm not a person who takes many organized city tours, but in St. Augustine we took the *Red Train Sightseeing Tour* and got a good look at the highlights in less than 90 minutes that made it easy to know where we wanted to return to later. You can even get on and off as much as you like for three days. *Old Town Trolley* operates a similar tour, and both also run shuttles to other attractions like the Alligator Farm, the beach, and San Sebastian Winery. Our guide said all drivers have to score at least 145 on a 150-question test about the city and its history.

We tried the water at the **Fountain of Youth Archaeological Park** *[11 Magnolia Ave. Open daily. Adm.]* but I've had more gray hairs sprout since my visit, so I don't think it helped me. Evidence that this was Ponce de Leon's headquarters is less than conclusive, but there is an hour or so of historical artifacts to see, kids will enjoy the stories, and the grounds are beautiful. Look for the gorgeous snow-white peacock. He likes to pose for the camera. Of course you'll check out the spring reputed to be the Fountain itself, and might be tempted to buy a bottle of its water. Is it the real deal? Well, Ponce de Leon died at age 61. You decide.

More authentic history is available at **Castillo de San Marcos** *[1 S. Castillo Dr. Open daily. Adm.]*, the sort of old fort you usually see only in Europe. Begun in 1672, this was an active military outpost for Spain, England, Spain again, the

United States, the Confederacy, and United States again for 200 years. It was handed over peacefully as control of St. Augustine changed over the years, and survived lengthy bombardments and sieges, but was never taken in battle. Now you can walk through the fort and see the guardroom, barracks, chapel, and prison. Kids and nimble adults can crawl into the powder magazine, and everyone will want to climb to the bastions, look out over the landscape from the sentry boxes, and see the old cannons that still line the walls. Small children need supervision up here, since the walls are low. This is one of the coolest places in the city.

The oddest place in town might be the **Ripley's Believe It or Not! Museum** *[18 San Marco Ave. Open daily until 8 p.m. (7 p.m. Su-Th in winter) Adm.]*. This is the sort of kitschy place we usually run from, but it's actually a lot of fun to see a suit of clothes from the world's tallest man, an enormous erector-set Ferris wheel, assorted instruments of torture, and a variety of some of the oddest oddities you'll encounter. There are other branches of Ripley's in Orlando and Key West, too, but this is the original home of unbelievability.

No matter what you're interested in, you'll find some satisfaction in St. Augustine. Golfers might visit the **World Golf Hall of Fame** *[1 World Golf Place. open daily until 6 p.m. Adm.]* eight miles north of the city at Exit 323 on I-95. Determined museum-goers will like the **Lightner Museum** *[75 King St. Open daily. Adm.]* for its collections of clothing, musical instruments, and period furniture. And if your family liked the Castillo de San Marcos, check out the **Fort Matanzas National Monument** *[8635 Highway A1A S. Open daily. Free.]*, a watchtower built by the Spanish in the 1740s to guard the southern approaches to the city. It is about 18 miles south of downtown.

I can't think of a single bad thing to say about this wonderful city. Okay, maybe one: The horse-drawn carriage rides produce a byproduct that is remarkable for its pungency. At the intersection of Avenida Manendez and Cathedral Place, at the entrance to the Bridge of Lions, is what locals claim is Florida's longest traffic light. The lengthy light forces the horses to wait too long in one place, allowing the, uh, byproduct to accumulate, which creates an unmistakable aroma, especially in the summer heat. There's a very friendly restaurant nearby, the A1A Ale Works, with balcony seating that overlooks the intersection. When the temperature rises and the horses are busy, indoor seating is far, far better.

(And here's an odd side note on this restaurant: The french fries were crisp—and hollow! I used one as a straw to slurp up their homemade root beer. It was a revelation even to our waitress. My son just shook his head wearily. Nothing I do embarrasses my kids any more.)

As you head south from St. Augustine, you might want to stop at the **St. Augustine Lighthouse and Museum** *[81 Lighthouse Ave. Open daily. Adm.]* It's just off A1A on Anastasia Island. You can climb the 219 steps to the top for some great views, or to burn off the kids' energy, and see the remains of old shipwrecks in the museum.

A little further south is *Marineland*, which was the world's first oceanarium. If its remodeling is complete, you won't have to walk a couple of hundred yards across a landscape that resembles the surface of the moon to get in, as visitors have had to do lately, and once there, you can probably see dolphins swimming in tanks—but you might not be told when you buy your tickets, as we weren't, that the last dolphin performance of the day has concluded, a disappointment to everyone. If you're willing to pay fees of about $65 to almost $300 you can get close to or into the water and spend some time meeting a dolphin in person. These aren't the only people who offer this. Everyone in Florida with a big bathtub seems to offer dolphin swims. I probably won't bother stopping here again on my next pass through the area.

The 50-mile (80km) drive to Daytona down A1A is another eye-opener if you like expensive real estate, cozy public beaches, and wonderful views. You'll find private beaches all along the route, but public ones, too, mostly without lifeguards or toilet facilities. But if you've ever wanted to drive on the beach, you'll find more and more access points, with better facilities, as you get closer to Daytona.

You'll also pass, both along this route and elsewhere in the state, several abandoned go-kart race tracks. I suppose they failed because of the sheer abundance of them in this NASCAR-crazy state.

Once you reach Ormond-by-the-Sea, you'll have your pick of places to stay. There are staggeringly expensive places, of course, but lots of budget options because of the competition. I like Ormond because it's less crowded and hectic that Daytona, but you can't make a bad choice.

# DESTINATION
## Daytona Beach

Time stands still here. This is the city of the perpetual spring break, regardless of your budget, your age, or the time of year. Inexpensive motels and cottages sit beside exclusive resorts; burger chains stand across parking lots from white-tablecloth restaurants. Shoppers can wander from thrift stores to nearby boutiques. Soda, beer, and champagne are all available to the thirsty.

The city claims a population of 65,000, but there are probably twice that many or more here at any given time. The big attractions are at opposite ends of town, however, so there's plenty of room for everybody. Let's talk first about the two big reasons people visit.

### The Beach

Well, of course. The city is named for its miles of sand, after all. Daytona makes almost every list of the country's best beaches and it's easy to see why. It's uncommonly wide so even when it's crowded it doesn't feel like it. The sand is white and clean, the surf moderate, and nearby parking abundant. An inexpensive trolley will carry you for miles up and down the beach, so you can pick exactly the right spot.

We don't usually think of beaches as wheelchair accessible, but vehicles with handicapped plates or tags can drive and park on the beach for free (others pay a small daily fee), and lifeguards and beach patrol can provide disabled visitors with a free "surf chair" that's ideal for sand and shallow water. [Phone (386) 676-4160.]

The beach actually stretches for miles in both directions from the center, from Ormond Beach to New Smyrna Beach, but if you want to get right to the focus of things, there's a large, inexpensive parking garage at Atlantic Avenue and Earl Street in the heart of Daytona Beach. A walkway over the street will take you to Ocean Walk Shoppes, a downtown shopping mall, and a quick walk through that leads you to the beach.

You'll come out near the Bandshell. This has been a local landmark since 1938. It hosts concerts year-round that range from rock to big band and blues to barbershop in an open-air theater that seats more than 4,000 people. Here you're at the north end of the beach's famous Boardwalk.

Except it's made of concrete.

*Daytona Beach © Johnlric/Dreamstime.com*

That's all right, I suppose. The maintenance costs are probably lower, but I'd prefer the atmosphere of the real thing, Coney-Island style. It's a great place for a stroll. Head for the Main Street Pier, about one-third of a mile (550m) away. There's plenty to gawk at. Volleyball courts. Plaques commemorating the days of racing on the beach. A singularly ugly clock tower memorializing Sir Malcolm Campbell, who set a land speed record on the beach in 1935 at more than 276 mph (440 kph).

And a rock with a hole through it, sitting on a pedestal. There is no plaque on the monument to explain why it's here. This provides a good opportunity for Dad to invent a fantastic story about the significance of the rock to tell the kids.

Further along are the arcades, go-kart track, swimwear shops, souvenir stands, carnival games, and snack concessions you'd expect from any self-respecting boardwalk, concrete or not. You can also rent deck chairs, bicycles, even ATVs (All Terrain Vehicles), if you want.

If you continue to walk, you'll soon come to the pier. Nearby is the Daytona Slingshot, which is like a bungee jump on steroids. Two people with more nerve than all but the most intrepid travel writers are loaded into a padded ball that's suspended by big bungee cords between two towers. Then they're fired aloft. I don't know why anyone would want to do this, but if you try it, please write and tell me.

You can take a more sedate ride on the Skyride to the end of the pier and back, or you can be really boring like me and just walk out there. You can only go about halfway for free, then pass through the bait shop, where you can rent a fishing pole, if you're so inclined, and go the rest of the way, to see if you can hook your dinner. But the signs firmly remind you: No Shark Fishing.

Or you can just pay $1 and walk to the end of the pier without being required to fish.

There's more, of course, enough to keep you busy for your whole vacation. But now let's look at the other big Daytona draw.

## Daytona International Speedway

Florida is crazy for auto racing, especially stock car racing (NASCAR is an acronym for National Association of Stock Car Automobile Racing), and its epicenter is in Daytona. Racing is in people's blood here. There has been racing on the beach since 1903, and by the 1920s, Daytona Beach was where drivers like Sir Malcolm Campbell came to try their fastest vehicles.

The races have been popular from the beginning—so popular that promoters used to put "Beware of Rattlesnakes" signs all around the track to discourage people who wanted to watch without paying.

"Big Bill" France, the owner of a local auto repair shop, was one of the spectators who saw Campbell's record run, and the sight inspired him to begin racing and promoting races himself, culminating in late 1947 with his central role in forming NASCAR. He opened a new 4.1 mile (6.5km) track on a stretch of beach a few miles south of Daytona a year later, and in 1959 opened the famous Daytona International Speedway.

Now the Speedway is rivaled only by the Indianapolis Motor Speedway as the heart of auto racing in the United States. But you don't have to attend the Daytona 500, or any of the other races held here to get an inside feel for the place. **DaytonaUSA** *[International Speedway Blvd. Open Daily until 7* *p.m. Adm.]* is the next-best thing to driving in the big race.

This place is huge (60,000 square feet or 5,575 square meters), and you don't have to be a big racing sophisticate to enjoy it. If you do follow NASCAR, your first stop will probably be to get up close to the most recent winning car from the Daytona 500—it's driven in straight from Victory Lane, all the dirt and grime from the race intact. In fact, you can see what it's like to drive on the high banks of the track yourself in one of the Acceleration Alley simulators, so realistic it's scary.

In another corner, a motion simulator lets you feel the same kinds of G-forces, twists, and turns on the 31-degree banked turns that NASCAR drivers do, and five or six times a day, you can be part of a real pit crew and see if you can get a tire changed and your car back out on the track in a 16-second pit stop: This is the real thing, not a simulation. There's lots more to see and do—static displays, movies, and very interactive experiences.

You can also get out on the track. The track is in use for racing or testing about 300 days a year and you can sit in the stands and watch, if there aren't ticketed events taking place. Better yet, you can take a guided ride around the track at speeds that don't even frighten a travel writer. If that's too tame for you, you're at least 16 years old, and you have a considerable bulge in your wallet you'd like to reduce, sign up for a three-lap ride with a professional driver at speeds of over 150 mph (240 kph). Other programs (costing in the $500 to $2,000 range) let you actually drive the track in a real stock car.

But you don't have to spend that much to have a great time here. There's so much for race fans to do that you'll be glad to have skipped a day at the beach. Where else but Daytona could there be anything like this?

## Other Daytona Attractions

You're not finished with Daytona yet, I hope. You still haven't eaten an alligator—a chocolate one! That's one of the endless ways to satisfy your sweet tooth at **Angell & Phelps Chocolate Factory** *[124 S. Beach St. Closed Sun. Free.]* in Daytona's business district. This family-operated business has been a local institution since 1925, although why somebody would start a chocolate factory in a hot climate before air conditioning is more than I can explain. But I'm glad they did!

You can join one of the free hourly tours and see how creams and molded pieces are made, watching through the large windows as candy makers operate the equipment, some of which is more than 70 years old. And you get free candy at the end of the tour. It's like a real-life "Charlie and the Chocolate Factory."

We just missed the tour on our visit, but still watched the operation from the windows. One candy maker saw us looking hungrily at their work and took pity on us. She grabbed a big tray of chocolates and popped out the door, smiling and insisting, "Here, help yourself!" That's real Southern hospitality. There's also a very good café attached to the factory, where sometimes a candy maker will stroll through the dining room bearing a tray of complimentary goodies. As one of our sons said, "Disney World calls itself the happiest place on earth, but maybe *this* is!"

You'll find more familiar sorts of Florida attractions, too. Waterparks? Sure. Try the **Daytona Lagoon** *[601 Earl St. Open daily. Adm.]*. Lighthouse? Florida's tallest is six miles south of the Beach, the big, red 175-foot (54m) **Ponce de Leon Inlet Lighthouse** *[4931 S. Peninsula Dr. Open daily until 5 p.m. and until 9 p.m. in summer. Adm.]*. Elegant houses? Try the winter home of John D. Rockefeller, **The Casements** *[25 Riverside Dr., Ormond Beach. Closed Sun. Open until 9 p.m. Tu-Th. Free.]*.

The fossil skeleton of a prehistoric giant ground sloth, and art from around the world, are at the **Museum of Arts and Sciences** [1040 Museum Blvd. Open daily. Adm.] and both the **Bulow Plantation Ruins State Park** *[Old Dixie Hwy. north of Ormond Beach. Open daily. Adm.]* and **Tomoka State Park** *[North Beach St. 3 miles north of Ormond Beach. Open daily. Adm.]* offer outdoor hiking and picnicking near the ruins of an 1821 plantation or the burial mounds of one of the earliest Native American settlements in eastern Florida. You can even attend a Daytona Cubs minor league baseball game at **Jackie Robinson Ballpark** *[105 E. Orange St.]*, the historic field where Jackie Robinson broke professional baseball's color barrier in 1947. It's downtown, on City Island—within sight of the candy factory.

When you get tired of Daytona—no, that's not possible—when you decide to leave Daytona, your next stop might be one of the greatest destinations in the world. I don't mean Orlando, terrific as that is, because there are great theme parks all over the world. I don't mean even better beaches than we've seen, because there are hundreds of marvelous beaches. But in all the world, there is only one place like this, the place from which humankind has made its most distant and dangerous journeys—Kennedy Space Center.

# DESTINATION
## The Space Coast

If we're paying special attention in this book to the things that make Florida so different from everywhere else, we've hit pay dirt. There is one place in Florida that can't be duplicated anywhere else on earth, a few square miles along the Atlantic Coast, just an hour's drive from the playgrounds of Daytona Beach. This is a place where all human lines of knowledge intersect: science, technology, history, philosophy, mathematics, and more, a place where some of the most inspired ideas of the Twentieth Century became reality. This is a place from which, after a million years of looking at the stars, mankind reached out and began to try to touch them.

### Kennedy Space Center

The Space Age didn't really begin here. That happened in a remote area of what was then the Soviet Union, closed entirely to outsiders. But from Cape Canaveral, Florida, in full view of the world, scientists and visionaries took the small steps and the giant leaps that first allowed human beings to walk on the surface of a world not their own.

From the time I was a boy I've been fascinated by space exploration, watching black and white television pictures of the launches of America's first earth satellites, following every faltering step of the beginnings of manned space travel. It was inevitable, I suppose, that I would end up living in the city where the airplane was invented: The Wright Brothers' bicycle shop was about three miles from where I'm sitting to write this chapter. My adopted state produced John Glenn, the first American to orbit the earth, and Neil Armstrong, the first man to walk the moon. So I couldn't wait to visit the Kennedy Space Center on our first family trip to Florida.

It doesn't disappoint.

You can't take A1A all the way down from Daytona because it peters out temporarily through the Canaveral National Seashore and you're shunted back to U.S. 1. That's okay. Just take

> **Tip:**
>
> Get there early, especially at peak times, when slugabeds might have to wait up to an hour to get the first bus. "Peak time" here means around Christmas or during spring break. The rest of the year you'll seldom have to wait long at all.

it south to Route 405 and turn east. You'll pass the Astronaut Hall of Fame—more about that later—and cross the Intracoastal Waterway (called the Indian River here) on the NASA Causeway, soon arriving at the KSC Visitor Center. The awe begins here.

You can see stunning movies and simulations in one of KSC's numerous theaters, including two huge Imax screens, but the heart of the visit is the bus tour around the complex. Buses leave every ten to fifteen minutes, and stop at the Launch Complex 39 observation gantry (the Space Shuttles lift off from Pads 39A and 39B), the Apollo/Saturn V Center where you can stand beside the mightiest engines ever built and get the full story of NASA's six trips to the moon, and the International Space Station Center, where NASA does all the planning for astronauts who spend months at a time circling the earth.

Each stop is probably worth a day in itself but you can spend as much time as you want at each; buses come by every ten minutes or so. I think the best part of the tour is the second stop, the Apollo/Saturn V Center, where you'll sit in an authentic NASA Apollo control room ... not a reproduction at all, but the real command center from the first trip to the Moon ... and learn all about the most daring exploration in all human history.

There's much more. Just the area around the Visitor Center can fill your day, with exhibits, artifacts, and theaters; rockets and space capsules that have carried

astronauts into space for more than 40 years; a full-size Space Shuttle replica; and even a chance several times a day to meet an astronaut, one of the fewer than 500 people who have ever flown in space. (I've already done that one. I went to high school with a kid who became an astronaut and flew in space seven times.)

KSC also offers a variety of special tours, workshops, and camps for those with special interests. But even if you don't do any of the extras (and they can be expensive), a day at Kennedy Space Center is truly a one-of-a-kind experience, like nothing else in the world. Beaches are everywhere. Theme parks abound. Historic buildings, quaint towns, fabulous scenery are available around the world. But this is unique.

## Other Space Coast Attractions

The Space Coast is filled with other connections to the space program, but the one other must-see stop for space buffs is the **Astronaut Hall of Fame** *[on Rt. 405 just before the Causeway to KSC. Open daily. Adm. but can be combined in ticket for KSC tour]*. Only about 60 former astronauts have been elected by their peers and NASA officials to this select company, although I have to agree with one of our sons, who said that as far as he was concerned, *all* the astronauts ought to be there.

You're greeted with a statue of America's first astronaut, Alan Shepherd, in the rotunda, and a 30-foot-high (9.1m) mural painted by astronaut Alan Bean. Once inside the exhibit hall, you can see glass etchings of the men and women who have been chosen the best of the best. Exhibits include Mercury and Apollo capsules, a Gemini trainer, and a number of interactive displays and simulators that are like a high-quality, hands-on science museum.

Not everything along the Space Coast has to do with outer space, though. There's much else to keep boredom at bay along this 60-mile (90km) stretch.

For example, you can visit the **American Police Hall of Fame** *[6350 Horizon Dr., Titusville. Open daily. Adm]* right across the street from the Astronaut Hall of Fame. In the center is a memorial to all police officers killed in the line of duty, but there is much else, from a reconstructed crime scene and forensics lab, to a jail cell and dungeon, to rather grisly displays of capital punishment like a guillotine, a gas chamber, and an electric chair you can sit in. Brrr! More fun are the rides in a police helicopter that start at as little as $25. There's more aviation at the **Warbird Air Museum** *[6600 Tico Rd.,*

*Titusville. Open daily. Adm.]* at the Space Coast Regional Airport in Titusville for displays of vintage military aircraft.

For outdoor fun, try the beaches and trails at **Canaveral National Seashore** *[headquarters at 308 Julia St., Titusville. Open all year. Adm.]*. Free beach chairs for the disabled are available on request. And the **Merritt Island National Wildlife Refuge** *[5 mi. east of U.S. 1 on Rt. 402. Open daily. Free]* has miles of trails and wildlife observation platforms.

If you have a day of relentless rain, try the **Brevard Museum of History and Science** *[2201 Michigan Ave., Cocoa. Open daily. Adm.]* or the **Brevard Museum of Art and Science** *[1463 Highland Ave., Melbourne. Closed Mon. Adm.]* for exactly the sorts of exhibits the museum names imply.

Also in Melbourne are the **Brevard Zoo** *[8225 N. Wickham Rd., Open daily. Adm.]* and **Andretti Thrill Park** *[3960 S. Babcock St., Open daily. Adm.]* with its four go-kart tracks and other racing activities, kiddy rides, and a huge arcade.

If some people want to go shopping while others are racing go-karts, the place of choice is **Historic Cocoa Village** *[Delannoy Ave., Cocoa on Rt. 520. Open daily.]*. This is not Cocoa Beach, which is on the ocean, 8 miles to the east. This is the restored downtown of Cocoa, now packed with dozens of shops, restaurants, and historic buildings, an easy-going (but potentially expensive!) day out for any confirmed shopaholic.

Don't be reluctant to turn aside from wherever you're headed, though, when you see something that looks interesting. This part of Florida is filled with fun things to discover.

---

### *Recommendations*

&#x221D; Some of Florida's best and least busy beaches are in this part of the state, making it an ideal destination for a holiday on the Atlantic.

&#x221D; St. Augustine has the feel of a European village and is worth at least a day.

&#x221D; Three words: *Kennedy Space Center*. There is nowhere else in the galaxy like it.

&#x221D; Stay off the highways and meander down A1A for the convenience, charm, and relaxed pace.

# 9
# The Southeast

BEFORE WALT DISNEY INVENTED ORLANDO, THIS WAS WHAT MOST Northerners thought of as Florida. Fort Lauderdale was the college spring-break Mecca. Miami was the ultimate place for winter sunshine. Palm Beach was more or less a private club for people with more money than you can imagine—no matter how good your imagination is. But after Walt Disney World opened in 1971 and every other conceivable attraction followed, families thought differently about Florida.

There's just as much reason as there ever was to head for the southeast, however. The beaches are still fabulous, the shops dazzling, and the rowdiest of the spring breakers have been encouraged to move elsewhere. We've had several friends who spend time down here every year, and every year we sigh over the photos they e-mail us from the beach as we sit in Ohio and watch another sleet storm from our window.

Winter in this part of Florida is perfect. The only really popular indoor sport is watching television reports of New England blizzards, so why would you want to stay indoors?! Any time, winter or summer, is great for visiting, however. This is a subtropical climate, so although summers can be very hot and humid, don't let that keep you away. The water, the ocean breeze, and the minimal clothing will keep you comfortable on the beach (as long as you remember to put on sunscreen), and everywhere else is thoroughly air-conditioned. Besides, summer is the wettest time of year in south Florida, usually coming in the form of late-afternoon rains that cool the end of the day, just when you need it most. Daylong rains are rare.

Best of all, some of the very coolest family attractions in the state are in this part of Florida. The beaches down here are the big draw, but there are so many one-of-a-kind places to visit that you'll want to shake the sand out of your shoes and try them out more often than you expect.

# Getting Around

As I pointed out in the last chapter, Florida has a major airport about a coconut's throw from almost everywhere. Palm Beach International, Fort Lauderdale/Hollywood International, and Miami International airports serve this part of the state well, with all major U.S. airlines and many foreign carriers serving each.

> **Tip:**
>
> If your destination is Miami, consider flying into Fort Lauderdale instead. It's much less busy, and they're less than 30 miles (50km) apart.

If you can travel by train, Amtrak stops in West Palm Beach, Delray Beach, Deerfield Beach, Fort Lauderdale, Hollywood, and Miami. There is also a commuter train, the Tri-Rail, that runs between West Palm Beach and Miami. Service is hourly Monday through Friday and every two hours on weekends. It's not especially convenient for tourists but it's inexpensive, and less hassle than driving. Fares depend on distance traveled and range from $2 to about $6 each way. Parking and taxis are available at stations, which are not always near tourist attractions. Miami has a small citywide system of elevated trains that can get you quickly from one end of the metro area to the other without the need to drive, but again, the system is designed more with commuters than with tourists in mind.

Most people drive, either their own cars or rentals, and that provides maximum flexibility. Drivers have the same choices they did further north—I-95, U.S. 1, and Route A1A. And they have a fourth choice, a toll road called Florida's Turnpike. It's a silly name but a useful route for drivers coming from the northwest part of the state. It begins south of Ocala where I-75 turns toward Tampa, runs through Orlando, and approaches the coast near Fort Pierce, running parallel to I-95 the rest of the way to Miami. It carries less traffic than I-95 (which is free), making it a good bet for drivers in a hurry.

But I still like the leisurely pace, greater convenience, and more pleasant scenery of A1A. And there's lots of public beach access from this highway.

# DESTINATION
## The Treasure Coast

The first things your kids will want to know is how the Treasure Coast got its name … and can they get some. The first one is easy. A number of Spanish galleons sank off the east coast of Florida in the 1600s and 1700s, many reputed to have been carrying great wealth. Artifacts and treasure have been found along the coast by archeologists, divers, and amateur treasure hunters ever since.

As to the second question, all I can tell you is that your odds are probably better if you invest in lottery tickets. Nevertheless, you'll see somebody with a metal detector patrolling just about every beach you visit, and they do make finds. Their treasures are more likely to be quarters and earring backs than doubloons and diamond brooches. But renting a metal detector can be a fun beach activity. Just don't get your hopes too high.

There's one place you can go for the real deal, though— **Mel Fisher's Treasures** *[1322 U.S. Highway 1, Sebastian. Open daily. Adm.]*. Mel Fisher was probably the world's greatest treasure hunter, bringing up tons of gold and silver from centuries-old wrecks. His company (Mel himself died in 1999) runs museums and stores here, in Key West, in Kissimmee, and in Henderson, Nevada. You won't be able to afford anything in them, but you can look, dream, and go rent that metal detector, although I'll admit it didn't work for me. I had hoped that having grown up in the same part of the world as Mel (northwest Indiana) might mean we'd have the same gold-finding abilities. Nope. Must have been something else … like talent.

Aside from those lured by treasure, too many visitors skip this part of Florida altogether in their rush to get to West Palm Beach, Fort Lauderdale, or Miami. There are definitely reasons to slow down though, and I'll tell you about a few of the sort you won't find anyplace else.

### The Manatee Observation and Education Center
Everybody gets excited over dolphins, and everybody loves seals. Hardly anybody pays much attention to the lovable and gentle manatee, however. They are delightful, apparently lethargic, animals, mammals who spend their lives in the water but who breath air like us, just as dolphins and whales do. Sometimes they're called "sea cows" and that

# Protecting the Manatee

Manatees are some of Florida's most distinctive and fascinating native creatures. Mostly they are Florida residents, and only very rarely venture farther north than the Carolinas, because they like water that is 72 to 78 degrees Fahrenheit (22–26°C). That's one of the things that keeps a colony in the Fort Pierce area: A power station on Moore's Creek warms the water just enough to provide a snug wintertime environment for them.

Manatees are an endangered species, protected by state and federal laws, and you can do your part in taking care of them by following a few easy rules:

If you're swimming, don't approach or chase them. They are gentle creatures, but you wouldn't appreciate someone coming uninvited into your home and chasing you, either.

If you're boating, be on the lookout for them. Polarized sunglasses can help you spot them underwater. Go very slowly, preferably with a pole or paddle in shallow areas. Motorboats are very dangerous for manatees; individual animals are usually recognizable because of the scar patterns each has from encounters with propellers.

If you're fishing or walking the beach, don't litter. Manatees can easily become tangled in discarded fishing line or ingest plastic bags. Both can be lethal.

seems to fit, because they're large—about 1,000 pounds (455kg)—slow-moving vegetarians. They have faces that look as perpetually sad as a basset hound's and seem to spend much of their time resting and quietly munching on aquatic plants. Still, they seem almost snuggly.

The **Manatee Observation Center** *[480 N. Indian River Dr., Fort Pierce. Closed Mon (Oct-June) and closed Mon—Wed (July-Sept). Adm.]* does not keep this endangered animal in captivity but does whatever it can to protect and promote the welfare of these gentle creatures. The center is located on a small creek that manatees like to enter for food and warmth, and volunteers keep an eye out for them, running a special flag up the flagpole when one comes up to the center, an event that will bring everyone in the neighborhood flocking to the observation decks. Sightings can't be guaranteed when you visit, but are common, averaging one to four times a day, all year round.

Kids find manatees fascinating. If they're resting, manatees can stay submerged for up to 20 minutes, but will surface every 3 to 5 minutes when they're on the move. They're perfectly comfortable living in the salt water of the ocean, but near the center, they return frequently to Moore's Creek to drink fresh water. The center also runs boat tours to see manatees, dolphins, and other residents of the local waters.

## Other Treasure Coast Attractions

I read a lot as a kid, and I have vivid memories of one book about Navy frogmen. I thought it would be exciting to be one, but since I turned out to be a lot better at sinking than at swimming, I ended up a teacher and writer instead. That was probably a good thing for our national defense. I still enjoyed my visit to the **Navy Seal Museum** *[3300 N. A1A, Fort Pierce. Closed Mon. except Jan-Apr. Adm.]*, however.

The museum tells the story of the Navy's underwater demolition teams from World War II onward, and is filled with dioramas and life-sized models, weapons, medals, breathing apparatuses, and biographies of decorated frogmen. Military families and those who enjoy water activities like boating, snorkeling, and diving will find this especially fascinating.

Perhaps the quirkiest of any of the hundreds of museums I've ever been in is located just a few more miles down A1A. The **Burt Reynolds & Friends Museum** *[100 N. U.S. 1, Jupiter. Open Fri-Sun only. Adm.]* celebrates the long career of a rather ordinary actor whose best professional move was probably the thing that jump-started his career, posing for a nude centerfold in *Cosmopolitan* magazine in 1972. (No copies of the centerfold were on display, thankfully.) But the building is filled with props from his films, autographed photos of a fully dressed Reynolds with every U.S. president since Carter, and thousands of pieces of sports and show-business memorabilia, posters, and autographs. The museum even sponsors acting and cinematography classes, occasionally taught by Reynolds himself (he lives nearby) when he's in town.

Cheesy, yes ... but rather fun.

# DESTINATION
## West Palm Beach and Boca Raton

Even if you're vacationing further north or south, here's an area that's worth a day or two as a side trip, while offering enough neat things to do for as long as you'd care to stay. But don't take my word for it: The president of the United States is a much more credible source. During the nuclear war scares of the 1960s, President Kennedy had a bomb shelter built for his family on *Peanut Island*, in the Intracoastal Waterway between Riviera Beach and Palm Beach Shores.

I don't know what attractions were on the island that long ago, but now you can go swimming, snorkeling, fishing, boating, camping—and even visit the old Kennedy bunker.

The Kennedys would have felt very comfortable here, as long as there were no nuclear missiles coming in. The family is annoyingly rich, so they would have fit in well with other habituates of the area—one of the richest in the country.

But more about that later. You don't have to be rich to have a good time here now, and I'm living proof! There are the usual Florida draws here, of course—fabulous beaches, several water parks, numerous boat tours, plenty of opportunities for fishing, diving, and more. But let's focus on a couple of truly amazing places.

### Lion Country Safari

I know this is a book about Florida, but one of the best attractions in the state whisks you to the very heart of Africa. This is a zoo like no other you've ever seen. Here the animals run free in a 300-acre (121-hectare) park, and the visitors are penned up, confined to their cars, as they drive 4 miles (6.5km) through forest and veldt, watching a hundred species of animals in a natural environment. I've been to more zoos than I can remember, and this is the best I've ever seen.

You're given a CD or tape describing the animals found in each section that you can play as you drive slowly through the park. You also are cautioned to keep your windows rolled up and to stay in your car, no matter what. These are wild animals, and having a family member eaten here will put a damper on the rest of your vacation. (If you have a convertible, you can rent a sedan for a nominal fee.) You can stop as often as you like, for as long as you like, to watch the animals—just pull to the side of the road. And you can drive through as many times as you want to with your admission.

Even though some animals might occasionally approach your car, keep your windows closed—they are *not* tame. And signs especially warn you to keep your distance from the rhinoceroses. They are big, sometimes aggressive, and can do serious damage to your car, which would be hard to explain to your insurance company.

In fact, we were stymied by a rhino in the park one afternoon. He stood squarely in the middle of the road, apparently content to remain there all day. I've owned cars that looked like they'd been stomped by a rhino, but this was a rental car and I was taking no chances. *["Mr. Lain, your car was full of dents and holes when you returned it. What happened? A rhinoceros? In Florida? Really, sir, we can't accept a story like that."]* Soon a keeper in a very battered truck came along to nudge the rhino out of the way—it took awhile, because he didn't want to go—so we could go on our way. Herding rhinos with pickup trucks: Now I *have* seen everything.

Besides rhinos, you'll drive past giraffes, herds of zebras, ostriches, gazelles and antelopes of all sorts, water buffalo, elephants, giant tortoises, an assortment of monkeys, and, of course, lions. The park even has its own campground (*outside* the animal enclosure, fortunately) so you can wake to the sound of the lions' roars, which gets your full attention!

That's far from all. The facility also includes its own water park, a large animal contact area (you can pet a tortoise and feed a giraffe), carousel, riverboat, Ferris wheel, train ride, and much more. Practically everything is completely wheelchair accessible. Plan on at least three to four hours here—but there's more than enough to keep your family busy and happy all day. The park is about 20 miles (32km) west of Palm Beach, an easy half-hour drive. The simplest way is to take U.S. 98 (Southern Blvd.) west from A1A, Route 1, I-95, or Florida's Turnpike, to Lion Country Safari Road. There are plenty of signs. *[2003 Lion Country Safari Road, West Palm Beach. Open daily. Last admission 4:30. Adm.]*

## Loxahatchee Everglades Tours

I try to lead my readers to only the classiest attractions—the top museums, the most elegant galleries, the most picturesque parks, and, of course, the very finest swamps.

Don't scoff! This is one of Florida's must-do's! I wasn't sure whether to put this here or down further in the chapter with Fort Lauderdale, because it's really between the two. But in this case, sooner is better.

The Everglades is the country's most amazing ecosystem. Covering millions of acres and taking in a national park and several wildlife and nature preserves, this unique area is a World Heritage Site. There's nothing else like its austere beauty and enormous variety of wildlife. The Everglades stretches a hundred miles (160km) from Lake Okeechobee to the tip of the state, and is up to 60 miles (97km) wide, an enormous river of sawgrass, sedge, and cypress.

You'll find dozens of places where you can take tours of this marvelous wetland, and you absolutely must do so, because you'll never see anything like this again in your life. I'll tell you here about one knowledgeable and reliable tour operator, but if you don't go to this one, be sure to find a tour elsewhere, one that is sensitive to the fragile ecology of the area.

**Loxahatchee Everglades Tours** *[15490 Lox Road, Boca Raton. Open daily. Adm.]* isn't

> ### Tip:
>
> Always take an Everglades tour early in the day. The surface temperature can be as much as 120 degrees Fahrenheit (49°C) in the afternoon, and the alligators seek cooler spots where you won't see them. Even in the morning, however, you'll want sunscreen, a hat, and a bottle of water.

exactly on the so-called "beaten path," but you shouldn't expect it to be—it's at the edge of the swamp! However, it's an easy drive from Boca Raton. Route 7 (it's also U.S. 441) runs north-south along the western edge of all the major cities along here, from West Palm Beach to Fort Lauderdale. Just south of Route 798, Lox Road angles off to the west. (Some maps call it Loxahatchee Road.)

It's an unpromising road, trafficked mostly by gravel trucks going to and from a local quarry, punctuated with speed bumps that slow the vehicles and flanked by a tired looking canal. You'll pass an informal dump or two and some run-down property, but carry straight on. It's just 6 miles (10km).

The road ends at the entrance to the Loxahatchee National Wildlife Refuge. But just before you enter, you'll see a gray concrete-block building on your left. That's the place. You'll usually buy your ticket from the concession stand outside. Inside is a small exhibit area with coral, press clippings, and lists of all alligator attacks in the state since 1986 (about 300) and circumstances of people killed by gators since 1957 (about 21).

But the trip into the swamp is perfectly safe. You'll be on an airboat, well above the water. This company uses boats that are tiered, so everybody has an unobstructed view, something that's not always true on other tours, and low-power motors that disturb the wildlife and vegetation as little as possible. Tours run from 1 to 3 hours in length and leave hourly beginning at 10 a.m.

Everybody will love the tour. We saw dozens of gators, some small and some that were just huge. (You can estimate how long a gator is even if all you see is his nose sticking out of the water: They run about one foot of length for every inch of snout.) We also saw the most astonishing collection of birds I've ever seen outside an aviary, an assortment of snakes, a fine variety of turtles—it was like an aquatic version of the Lion Country Safari above, except humans were definitely the intruders in this environment. It was one of the coolest tours I've ever taken.

### Other West Palm Beach and Boca Raton Attractions
I like the juxtaposition of returning from a tour of the swamp to talk more about the elegance, refinement, and opulence of this area. That's part of the wonderful variety that characterizes Florida.

Palm Beach, the city that lies between the ocean and the Intracoastal Waterway (here known as Lake Worth), has been a playground of the rich for more than a hundred years. Gilded Age magnates built their mansions here and parked their lavish yachts in ocean and lake. West Palm Beach, on the other side of the lake, was once swampland, fit mostly for housing the workers who served in the mansions and hotels.

If you have people who like to shop in your family, the ultimate destination on this vacation will be Palm Beach's **Worth Avenue**. But I'll warn you: Before going there, put your credit cards in an envelope and mail them to yourself, so they will be out of reach for a few days. The skeptical will certainly call this street a bastion of capitalistic excess: Nowhere else in America can you spend as much money, at as many opulent stores, more quickly. Fortunately, window shopping is free.

Oh, there are low-end chain stores like Neiman-Marcus, Brooks Brothers, and Armani—the sorts of places your chauffeur shops. But there are countless one-of-a-kind boutiques and galleries that will burn a hole in a Rockefeller credit rating faster than you can sign a check. It seemed too much of a cliché to be true, but there really *was* a Rolls-Royce parked in front of Tiffany's when we were there!

And where do people who shop in places like this live? In places you can't go into. But you can get a taste of the true hyper-wealth of years past with a visit to the **Flagler Museum** *[One Whitehall Way, Palm Beach. Closed Mon. Adm.]*. Flagler was the partner of John D. Rockefeller in Standard Oil, and this was his winter home, a mansion even more opulent than Rockefeller's that we visited in the previous chapter. The museum is expensive for as much time as most families will want to give it but is filled with luxurious appointments and remnants of the Gilded Age for those who might be interested.

If you're staying in the area and are interested in some of the more conventional attractions, the **South Florida Science Museum** *[4801 Dreher Trail N, West Palm Beach. Open Daily. Adm.]* has galleries on Egypt, outer space, an aquarium, and a miniature golf course with a science theme. The **Boca Raton Children's Museum** *[498 Crawford Blvd., Boca*

*Raton. Open 12-4 p.m. Tues-Sat. only. Adm.]* has some good hands-on exhibits for your youngest vacationers, but is open limited hours. The **Palm Beach Zoo** *[1301 Summit Blvd., West Palm Beach. Open daily. Adm.]* offers a more typical zoo experience than Lion Country.

## DESTINATION
## Fort Lauderdale

You wouldn't think so, but Fort Lauderdale can be hard to find, because it is a city thoroughly encased by suburbs that seem almost as large as itself, and that's not even considering Miami, just a half-hour away and twice its size, with suburbs of its own. I don't know why so many people leave the crowded cities of the North to come to the busy places here. Except for the wonderful beaches. And the ocean. And the warm winters. And the endless attractions. And—oh, never mind.

The only people who run out of things to do in Fort Lauderdale are the ones whose ashes are being scattered over the ocean from an airplane. It would take a separate book to list all the terrific beaches and water parks, but I'm going to show you some less common attractions I think will be a hit with some members of your family, the sorts of things you're not likely to stumble across in Liverpool or Osaka or Des Moines.

### Wannado City

I really didn't want to go here; I thought it had a silly name. Far worse, it is tucked into one end of a suburban shopping mall, and I would rather slam my finger in a car door—twice—than go to a mall. I didn't expect it to make the book; a lot of the places I visit never do, because I don't think they have enough appeal. But I was intrigued by what I'd read about it and wanted to see for myself how bad it was.

My mistake. This is a great place.

Wannado City is a high-energy place where kids aged 4 to 12 can explore in an often very realistic, hands-on way more than three dozen types of jobs and careers. This is more than pretend, because everything possible is done to make each experience as lifelike as it can be. Surgeons remove a lifelike dummy's appendix with real (but blunted) surgical instruments under the hum and beep of real heart monitors. Newspaper reporters see their stories printed in a full-sized newspaper. Actors perform on a fully equipped stage in front of a live audience. Pilots fly real flight simulators in a real airplane fuselage.

Kids get paid in the local currency, "wongas," which they can deposit in a bank, get a working ATM card for use in the city, and spend for snacks or attractions.

Adult helpers are everywhere—teaching, guiding, encouraging. Kids can try any or all of the jobs, which may take 15 to 30 minutes each for the full experience. Police officer, EMT, fire fighter, TV news anchor, nurse, chef, store clerk, circus performer, lawyer, archeologist, fashion designer, dentist, miner, hairdresser—they're all here, and more.

Staff members work very hard to keep kids happy and safe, and kids 8 and up can be left on their own while parents shop, sit in the coffee shop, or maybe even take a nap from all the stimulation. No child is allowed to leave without the adult he or she came in with.

It's not cheap. Admission for kids is about $30, with adults about half that, but you can spend a very full day here. Adults will be exhausted if they try to keep up, and kids might be so overstimulated you won't get them to bed until 2 a.m. But you're on vacation, after all. This is worth it.

*[Sawgrass Mills Mall, 12801 Sunrise Blvd., Sunrise. Open daily until 8 p.m. Adm.]*

## Other Fort Lauderdale Attractions

Wannado City is a place of such high intensity it appears that adrenaline is being dispensed in gallon jugs. The perfect lower-your-blood-pressure alternative is less than 15 minutes away at **Butterfly World** *[3600 W. Sample Rd., Coconut Creek. Open daily. Adm.]*. This is the largest butterfly aviary in the world, housing more than 3,000 butterflies of over 150 species.

Nestled in a city park a few miles north of downtown Fort Lauderdale, Butterfly World sets the tone for visitors even before they enter, with soft piano music piped throughout and around the facility, and a sign that tells patrons, *"You are about to enter paradise ... a world where dreams come true."* That's a pretty high standard to hold yourself to, but it's accurate if you dream a lot about butterflies and other delicate flying things—it also has the world's largest enclosure of hummingbirds. The unremitting piano interludes can wear you down after awhile; I'd throw in the occasional string quartet or acoustic guitar for variety. But the butterflies, flowers, and hummingbirds are stunningly beautiful, the macaws and lorikeets (who will eat nectar out of your hand) are fun and colorful, and the bug zoo is creepy enough for any kid. It can cost a family of four almost $70 for admission, so you might send rambunctious kids with short attention spans to another activity for awhile. This is a place to savor at a relaxed pace.

Once you've had your fill of butterflies, maybe you'd like to try fleas. No, not the sort you have to scratch, unless you have an itch to go shopping. I'm talking about the largest flea market in the United States, Fort Lauderdale's famous **Swap Shop** *[3291 W. Sunrise Blvd., Fort Lauderdale. Open daily. Charge to park]*.

More than 12 million people a year buy almost every imaginable thing here, as well as go to drive-in movies (14 screens), visit the large farmers' market, watch circus acts, ride the carnival rides, and play arcade games. Outside vendors are hard at work starting between 5 and 6 a.m., seven days a week, and indoor stalls open between 8 and 9 a.m. daily—even holidays.

The venture started in 1963 as just a single-screen drive-in movie theater, which had the misfortune to schedule its grand opening for November 22—the day President Kennedy was assassinated. Despite the rough start, the movie business was successful in the year-round good weather of South Florida, and in 1966, the owners began hosting flea-market vendors on Saturday and Sunday mornings, something that had been tried in California, but never before in Florida. When you see what it's turned into, you'll conclude that it worked out pretty well. You can easily spend an entire day here.

For a more traditional shopping experience, **Las Olas Boulevard** in downtown Fort Lauderdale is what you want, seven blocks of great shops, galleries, restaurants, and nightspots just a block north of the New River and the picturesque **Riverwalk**. Las Olas isn't as over-the-top expensive as Worth Avenue in Palm Beach, but you can find plenty of places to spend a month's salary in ten minutes, if that's what you're after. There's an extensive mix of places for the rest of us, too.

Florida's Native American heritage is represented best at the **Ah-Tah-Thi-Ki Museum** *[Big Cypress Seminole Reservation. Open daily. Adm.]*, where the history and culture of the Seminole tribe are on display through tribal artifacts, a living village, and many demonstrations. The reservation is about 50 miles west of Fort Lauderdale on I-75, then 17 miles north of Exit 49 on County Route 833. Closer in is the **Seminole Okalee Indian Village and Museum** *[5716 Seminole Way on Route 7, Hollywood. Closed Mon. Adm.]*. This is actually on the grounds of the Seminole Hard Rock Hotel and Casino, but the tribe offers many heritage exhibits and demonstrations, as well as alligator wrestling and snake shows.

You can visit the **Bar-B-Ranch** *[1300 Peaceful Ridge Rd., Davie. Open daily. Fee for horse rental.]* for horseback riding. Most non-Floridians don't realize that few states have more cowboys and do more cattle-raising than Florida, and this gives you a taste of that life. Inexperienced riders can get lessons here, and you can even rent ponies that small children can ride while their parents lead. This is really horse country around here with several other equestrian parks nearby.

If you're visiting the horses, you can also take time to visit Florida's most famous birds at **Flamingo Gardens** *[3750 Flamingo Rd., Davie. Open daily except Mon. June-Sept. Adm.]*, just five minutes from the Bar-B-Ranch. You'll find plenty of flamingos here, but also alligators, birds of prey, otters, bobcats, and much more.

Of course there's a great science museum and Imax theater, the **Museum of Discovery and Science** *[401 SW 2nd St., Fort Lauderdale. Open daily. Adm.]* near the downtown Riverwalk. And just north of Flamingo Gardens is the **Young at Art Children's Museum** *[11584 W. State Road 84, Davie. Open daily. Adm.]* with loads of art, music, and learning activities.

I'm a sports fan and know the records of all the sports immortals, but I never realized there was such a thing as the **Fishing Hall of Fame** *[300 Gulfstream Way, Dania Beach. Open daily. Adm.]* until we stayed at a motel nearby. See record-size fish, all sorts of tackle and other gear, learn how to catch the big ones, and learn more about fish than you ever imagined there was to know. Or, if you like to make like a fish yourself, try the **International Swimming Hall of Fame** *[One Hall of Fame Dr., Fort Lauderdale. Open daily. Adm.]* just off A1A near Los Olas Boulevard. The museum has special displays devoted to Johnny Weissmuller, Mark Spitz, and other great competitors, endless displays on Olympic and international events, the history of swimming, and more than anybody without webbed feet can possibly absorb.

Getting out on the water is probably more fun than looking at exhibits about it. Fort Lauderdale is a wonderful place with dozens of companies offering glass-bottom boat tours, ocean charters, diving, snorkeling, surfing, water skiing, even parasailing high above the ocean—something my intrepid sister-in-law and nieces have done but which I will *not* be trying, even for my favorite readers. But I'll watch from the beach if you want to give it a go. Fort Lauderdale's beaches are some of the country's best, and the Beachfront Promenade is a fabulous place to walk along the ocean. You can't go wrong with Dania Beach and its historic wooden roller coaster, the Dania Beach Hurricane, picturesque Hollywood Beach and Boardwalk—there are no bad choices here for sun and sand.

We still have miles of Florida to go, however. Let's get back on A1A and head further south.

## DESTINATION
## Miami and Miami Beach

I'm sticking with my advice to follow A1A, and now we'll take it to the end of the line. It's still a great drive, but more congested now (of course there are no *un*congested streets in the Miami area), running between the ocean and the Intracoastal Waterway—Biscayne Bay here. The street, called Collins Avenue once it reaches Dade County, takes us past endless numbers of elegant hotels and condos, classic resorts like the Eden Roc and Fontainebleau, shops and restaurants, and not very much access to the beach: Most places along here are privately owned, although there are a few public parks along the way. But even in heavy traffic, it won't take long to reach one of the world's ultimate beach destinations.

### South Beach and Ocean Drive
*South Beach* is on almost every list of the world's best beaches. It's wide, clean, has terrific access to everything you might need and is open from 5 a.m. until midnight. The beach is 23 blocks long, more than enough for even crowded winter days. South Beach is well patrolled, adjacent Lummus Park is filled with tall palm trees, public toilets are easy to find, and there's plenty of inexpensive parking, both in garages at Seventh and 13th streets, and pay-and-display street parking along Ocean Drive, if you get there early enough. Parking rates everywhere are about a dollar an hour.

You might even spot a celebrity or two on the beach. South Beach is extremely popular for photo shoots, and it's no great trick to spot models and photographers at work. But if all you want to do is lounge on the beach, you're in for a good day. You can rent a beach chair ($15 a day), an umbrella to ward off the intense sun ($12), or even a cabana big enough to hold two beach chairs ($15). Swim, sun, surf, or just sit and watch the enormous gray ships passing silently out at sea.

If you want to get out of the sun for awhile, *Ocean Drive* is one of America's architectural treasures, perhaps the most memorable collection of art deco buildings in the world; the area is on the National Register of Historic Places.

You can spend an entire morning looking at the art deco hotels and condos, most of which have been immaculately restored. When you're tired of walking, you can sit at a sidewalk table and enjoy a cool drink or a delicious brunch or lunch; there are some expensive restaurants here, but dozens of inexpensive ones, too. Be careful where you sit, though—coconut palms cluster here and there along the street and it's not unheard of for a coconut to come down at an inopportune moment.

If this isn't the best people-watching place in the world, only a sidewalk café on the Champs-Élysées in Paris has got it beat.

## Little Havana

Earlier in the chapter I took you on a tour of Africa. Now it's time for another international experience, and once again, you can leave your passport at home—unless you're visiting Florida from abroad, in which case you already have yours in hand. This time we're going to Havana.

It is still illegal for vague political reasons for American citizens to visit Cuba, although no other country seems to have a problem with it. But there's nothing illegal about spending a couple of hours … or a couple of days … in Miami's *Little Havana*.

Centered on Southwest Eighth Street (*Calle Ocho*) and running for about fifteen blocks just southwest of downtown Miami, Little Havana is home to the largest Cuban community outside Cuba, as well as residents from other Latin American countries. You don't have to speak Spanish to get along here … but it will come in handy if you do.

I come here for the food, delicious Latin American specialties that are hard to find anywhere else. But that's just a good beginning to a visit. You'll find exciting street

*View of South Beach from a jetty © Jeff Strand/Dreamstime.com*

parties the last Friday and first Saturday of every month with great food, nonstop entertainment, and cultural performances. Flamenco nights are Tuesdays and Thursdays on Calla Ocho at 16th Avenue.

On a quiet afternoon you can look at the statues of Cuban heroes and religious shrines in the small park at 13th Avenue. An eternal flame honors the victims of the unsuccessful 1961 Bay of Pigs invasion. A bit further on you can stand at the window of the Moore & Bode Cigar Company and watch craftsmen rolling cigars by hand the traditional way, interesting even for non-smokers like me. At Maximo Gomez Park, the old men of the neighborhood meet for games of dominoes each day, and nearby is the *Paseo de las Estrellas*, the Walk of Stars, honoring Latin American celebrities from all walks of life. It's fun to see how many names you recognize.

Travel is all about embracing new experiences and new cultures. This is a wonderful way to do it, right in the heart of Miami. ¿Entiende?

## Other Miami Attractions

When do you suppose the oldest European-made building in the Western Hemisphere was built? You'd have to guess sometime after the arrival of Christopher Columbus in 1492, right?

If that was your guess, you'd be wrong. There's actually a building in North Miami Beach built by Europeans in about 1140. The catch is, they built it in Spain.

William Randolph Hearst was one of the great newspaper tycoons of the late 19th and early 20th cen-turies, and an inveterate collector of art and antiquities. He bought the entire 800-year-old **Ancient Spanish Monastery** *[16711 W. Dixie Hwy, N. Miami Beach. Open daily at 9 a.m. except 1 p.m. Sun. Adm.]* in 1925 and packed it off to the United States. He ran out of money before he could rebuild it, however, and it sat in crates until the mid-1950s. It is now a working church and part of the Episcopal diocese that covers South Florida, and one of the area's most unusual tourist attractions. I've been in many old buildings like this in Europe and this has all the feeling of antiquity you'd expect: old iron gate, red tiled walk and pebbled paths, wonderful early medieval cloisters hidden behind 3-inch-thick wooden doors, worn coats of arms, statues of St. Bernard and several Spanish kings.

While religion is the main business here, of course, the church has a lucrative sideline of hosting weddings and

*Cigar making is still an important business in Little Havana*

receptions. Most of its gift shop and website are given over to that enterprise. But even if you're not getting married here, it's worth a stop if you want to get the feel of old European complexes just like this one. It's best on a rainy, humid morning which provides just the right atmosphere, I think.

You expect to find jungles here in the tropics, and Miami has two great ones. **Monkey Jungle** *[14805 SW 216th St., Miami. Open daily. Adm.]* is another great place where the animals run free—more than 400 primates from 30 different species roaming a 30-acre (12 hectare) park, everything from lemurs to gorillas.

If you like squawking birds more than chattering monkeys, try **Parrot Jungle Island** *[1111 Parrot Jungle Trail near downtown Miami. Open daily. Adm. plus parking fee]* a full-fledged zoo with snakes, gators, monkeys, farm animals, and even parrots. Best, in my opinion, is a rare Liger named Hercules. A liger is the offspring of a male lion and a female tiger and is larger than either. And if you get tired of animals, there's even a steep, 3-story-tall water slide.

Of course there's the more traditional sort of zoo in a city this large, the **Miami Metrozoo** *[12400 SW 152nd St., Miami. Open daily. Adm.]* and you just know a big city on the ocean like this will have a world-class aquarium. That would be the **Miami Seaquarium** *[4400 Rickenbacker Causeway, Key Biscayne. Open daily. Adm. plus parking fee]*, home of Flipper of television and movie fame. I can never resist a dolphin, and this is the place to see them.

The **Everglades Alligator Farm** *[40351 SW 192nd Ave., Florida City. Open daily. Adm.]* is another great place to see gators. It's near Homestead, about 40 miles south of Miami.

If you like to hit all the science museums in your travels as the Lains usually tried to do, the **Miami Museum of Science and Space Transit** *[3280 S. Miami Ave., Miami. Open daily. Adm.]* has great exhibits on Isaac Newton and Leonardo da Vinci, sharks, space travel, even the Titanic.

And if you've already visited the fishing and swimming halls of fame, you might as well go for the trifecta with the **World Chess Hall of Fame** *[13755 SW 119th Ave., Miami. Closed Mon-Wed. Adm.]*. I don't know why all these places locate in South Florida, but if you've got a special interest, you'll be able to find out all about it in Florida.

That's the lure of this part of Florida—there is always something new to see, enough variety to keep you going back many, many times.

## *Recommendations*

∽ Somewhere, somehow, take an airboat tour of the Everglades. It's a unique experience.

∽ Florida has innumerable animal parks. Visit one that is unlike any zoo you've ever been in.

∽ Shopping—even just the window variety—is better in South Florida than almost anywhere else. But leave your credit cards in the hotel safe!

∽ One very important reminder: Sunscreen and water bottles.

# 10
# The Worlds of Disney

IF I HAD A NICKEL FOR EVERY CHILD I'VE MET IN THE PAST TEN YEARS whose dream vacation is a visit to Walt Disney World, I'd have retired to Florida long ago.

That's not a criticism in any way. When I was a kid, Disneyland in California had just opened, and that was *my* dream vacation. I didn't get there, but our family did a lot of other fun things, so I didn't feel especially deprived.

In fact, nobody should feel deprived if they don't make it to Disney. It's an exciting place and there's something there for everyone (quite a lot of things, actually). But I've spent the greater part of this book trying to show you the incredible scope of family fun in Florida. Contrary to popular belief, the state is packed full of great experiences that have nothing at all to do with mice.

Still, I can hardly ignore the place, can I? If your kids' hearts are set on the experience or you're making a stop in Disney World part of a longer trip, I'll show you around a bit in this chapter. There are tall shelves filled with books just about Walt Disney World—strategies for planning your visit, step-by-step directions for getting through the parks most efficiently, tactics for choosing which rides to ride at what times of day; few military campaigns have been planned with such precision.

It doesn't have to be that complicated. I have no quarrel at all with those authors and you can buy as many of their books as you like, but in the next few pages I'll give you the highlights of Walt Disney World, enough for you to be able to decide whether or not you need several hundred more pages of instructions.

## Getting Around

If anywhere is easier to get to than Orlando, I don't know where it could be. Practically every major airline I can think of flies to Orlando International Airport (MCO), a modern, gleaming air hub. The airport is just fifteen minutes from the south end of the city, which is where all the big theme parks are. You can probably be shaking Donald Duck's hand in little more than an hour after the time your airplane's wheels touch the ground.

Amtrak trains stop in Orlando, although downtown Orlando is 20 miles (32 km) from the Disney complex and there's no public transportation to get you there, but rental car agencies are nearby. Some trains also stop in Kissimmee, less than 10 miles (16 km) from the park. Several rental car agencies are within a half mile of this station, too.

If you're driving, you'll find that so many roads lead to Orlando that it might as well be Rome. Interstate 4 cuts through the heart of the city and goes within minutes of all the big parks. Because Walt Disney World is so spread out, exits 64, 65, and 67 all lead to various parts of the park. It's virtually impossible to go astray. I've never been anywhere that's as clearly and carefully marked with road signs.

Florida's Turnpike cuts across the state just south of Orlando and crosses I-4 about 10 miles (16km) north of the Disney Complex, an easy connection for anyone driving from the north on I-75. The other major north-south route, I-95, is only a half-hour's drive east of Orlando.

If you're staying at a resort on Disney property, getting to the park is the easiest thing in the world. A Disney bus will pick you up at the airport and take you straight to the resort. After that you can use Disney's buses, boats, or the monorail to move around the parks. Of course, since Orlando public transportation is limited, that means you're pretty much tied to the Walt Disney World complex—a fact that might not have gone entirely unnoticed by Disney officials.

If you've driven to Walt Disney World, just park your car at the resort and use Disney transportation in the parks. Now, of course, you're able to go at will to other attractions.

If your accommodations are not on Disney property, you'll have to drive and pay to park, about $10 a day. Many area hotels and motels offer free shuttle service to the big theme parks, though.

## The Basics

"Insider" books about Disney World comprise an extensive sub-category of publishing in themselves. I don't consider myself a particular insider, but I can give you the fundamentals that will make your planning easier and your trip more fun. Here are some of the things you'll find helpful; you won't need a lot more unless you're going to be pretty relentless visitors.

## What Will It Cost?

There's no way to sugar-coat this: A lot. At the time this book went to press, a one-day visit to one park cost almost $70 for everyone age 10 and more. Kids 3 to 9 paid nearly $60. So a family of four, with kids 8 and 12 would pay almost $260, plus $10 parking and any food or souvenirs they bought. In fairness, though, you could spend an amount approaching that to go to a major league baseball game or any number of other activities.

Each park you visit will probably take pretty close to a full day, although sturdy travelers might get to two if they're choosy about what they want to do. Your ticket limits you to just one park a day, however, unless you buy a separate multi-park option. If you want more Disney immersion than just a day gives you, how about a four-day ticket? Prices for these run over $200 and $165. Add a "Park Hopper" pass so you can move from park to park as you please at about $45 each, and the Water Park and More option to get access to the other facilities at about $50. Those are set prices, whether you by a one-day ticket or a four-day (or more) ticket. That family of four is now paying $1,154 just on admissions.

A lot of people think it's worth it and I'm certainly not going to argue with them. There's nothing else remotely like the complete fantasy experience you get at Walt Disney World.

## When Should You Come?

Disney World is never *not* busy. The peak time, as you'd expect, is around the Christmas and New Year's holidays. The park is also very busy in the spring, from President's Day (the second weekend of February) through Easter, because winter and spring breaks are scattered through the period and kids are out of school. If you're looking for slower times, check the Wonderful Weeks page on Disney's website. Just do a search for it in the box on the Disney homepage.

One Disney official suggested, "Post-Thanksgiving weekend up until the week before Christmas tends to be a good time for several reasons: We're dressed up for the holidays, with many of our special holiday entertainment features taking place; weather can be very pleasant; and it is a less busy time. Post-New Year's until mid-February is another time to come when it is less busy."

Because of changes in school calendars, late summer ... after mid-July ... has also become a slower period, although the weather will be at its hottest then.

### Where Should You Stay?

Disney has 24 themed resorts and hotels on the property with amenities and prices ranging from fairly inexpensive to places that would stretch a Rockefeller budget. Staying in a Disney property has benefits. You can get into one of the parks an hour before it opens to the public—the park changes every day—or can stay for up to three hours after a park closes to the public.

There's no need to pay to park, since you can get from your resort to any of the parks by bus or monorail. You get priority in making reservations at Disney restaurants and for meals with Disney characters (I'll talk about that in a few minutes), and a bus will even pick you up at the airport, deliver your luggage straight to your room, and take you and your belongings back to MCO at the end of your stay.

On the other hand, you can easily pay less (or more, if you insist) at a local hotel or motel. There are more of them than I have the energy to count and that means prices are very competitive. Many places offer free shuttles to the park. But you give up the extended hours and discounts that resort residents get, and if you drive your own car, you have to pay to park each day.

Disney resorts are fantasy worlds in themselves, with African, Polynesian, New England, sports, pop culture, and more motifs, each done with typical Disney thoroughness in design, décor, cuisine, and every other imaginable way. Most have fine restaurants and all have snack bars or food courts, video arcades, outdoor recreational facilities, and swimming pools and some offer private beaches, boat rentals, suites, and even kitchens.

Whether to choose a Disney resort really comes down to what you're planning for your vacation. If all you plan to see is the Disney complex, the convenience of staying on the property probably trumps other considerations. If you're going to be driving to many of the other area attractions, there are other possibilities for your stay.

### Types of Tickets

You can get just about any sort of ticket you can imagine for Walt Disney World—except cheap. And even that's possible in a relative sort of way. Pricing options are complex.

Let's start with the *basic one-day, one-park ticket*. That goes for almost $70 for visitors age 10 or more, and close to $60 for kids 3 to 9. Younger kids enter free. A two-day ticket costs about double and a three-day ticket not quite triple the base price.

After that, things get better. A four-day ticket adds only about $10 to the cost of a three-day, and you'll pay only an extra couple of dollars per day for each day after that. So tickets for four or more days are the best value.

*Tip:*

If you're traveling with pets, you can leave them at kennels near park entrances. You'll need proof of appropriate vaccinations. Only service dogs are allowed inside the parks or resorts.

Tickets are good for only one park per day. If you expect to do more than that, however, each person would need to buy a *Park Hopper* ticket for about $45 more. That's a flat price, whether you're using a one-day ticket or a ten-day ticket.

Want to cool off at a Disney water park or challenge the arcade at Disney Quest at the end of the day? Then you'll add the *Water Park Fun & More* option for about another $50 per ticket. Again, that's a flat fee regardless of the duration of your admission ticket.

Obviously these things can add up. But if this won't be your only visit to Disney World, see the sidebar on page 124 *Investing in Disney Futures* for a way to save big.

Auto clubs, travel agents, and Disney itself offer a bewildering variety of other discounts to members, to Florida residents, to people who only want to use Epcot after 4 p.m., and to almost anyone else with the inclination to navigate the maze of possibilities. A good travel agent, or several hours in front of the computer screen, can unearth more of these than I can possibly print.

## Getting Around the Complex

It's easy to get from one place to another in Walt Disney World, although "easy" is not always the same as "fast."

You can drive from one park to another, of course, and if you pay to park at one theme park, you can park at another on the same day for free by giving your first parking pass to the parking attendant at the gate of the second park.

Disney's parking lots may take up more space than some of the world's countries. Each lot is named for a character,

animal, or something similar. Make careful note of where you park, or you'll spend the rest of your vacation looking for your car.

A tram will pick you up in each parking lot and deliver you to the park entrance or, in the case of the Magic Kingdom, to the Transportation Center, from which you can take a ferryboat to the Magic Kingdom or a monorail to either the Magic Kingdom or to Epcot. When you return to your car, you'll catch the tram in the same place it dropped you off earlier.

If you're taking a bus to somewhere else in the complex, you'll find a bus hub in the same area.

The best and quickest way around the park is the monorail that connects the Magic Kingdom, Epcot, and several resorts. You can also take a boat from some resorts to the Magic Kingdom or MGM parks, or between Epcot and MGM, and buses connect everything in the park. Sometimes you have to take a bus to Downtown Disney and transfer to another bus, however, so travel time can approach an hour.

All transportation inside the park is free.

If you have a chance to ride the monorail, do it. It's quick and fun. The Walt Disney World complex has 13 miles (21 km) of monorail track, and they zip along at 40 mph (64kph), providing marvelous views, especially pulling into Epcot.

## Layout of the Parks

As you enter each park, you'll slide your ticket into a card reader and press your finger against a glowing blue light that scans your fingerprint. That means tickets aren't transferable. If Uncle Ralph and Aunt Dottie have unused days on the tickets they bought last summer, you can't use them unless you also bring the fingers they scanned.

Just inside the entrance to each park are a variety of services you should know about. First you'll find a rack with free maps in six languages, a printed entertainment schedule that lists the times and locations for each of the days' shows, parades, character appearances, and other activities, hours of operation for rides and restaurants, and more.

There will be a Guest Relations office where you can get information about absolutely anything in the Disney complex, upgrade your ticket, get maps of other parks, or just have questions answered. You'll also find a place to rent strollers, wheelchairs, and power scooters nearby.

Look for the Information Board. It will provide updates and additions to the entertainment schedule that you won't find out anywhere else.

Parks are divided into distinct themed areas, each with its own selection of rides, shows and attractions, shopping, and food. Restrooms are everywhere and the best thing about them (other than the obvious relief they provide) is that they're air-conditioned and offer a little respite from the Florida heat.

Each park has a focal point—Cinderella's Castle in the Magic Kingdom, the Geosphere at Epcot, the Tree of Life in Animal Kingdom, and the Sorcerer's Hat at MGM. From there you can go quickly to any of the park's theme areas, or you can hit them all by following a circular route around the park. (Epcot, with two key areas, is slightly different.) The maps are very clear. Exits are adjacent to the gates you came in.

## Rides and Shows

I can't begin to list all the rides and shows in the park. To begin with, they change to some degree each year. Besides, this chapter is an outline, not an exhaustive guide. Dozens of books (or, more cheaply, scores of websites including Disney World's own) can give you those details. But they're all free once you're in the park. Rides range from ones so mild a timid 2-year-old will enjoy them to a few so terrifying that lion tamers and astronauts won't try them.

Disney is a very safety conscious place, though, and when an attraction is restricted to riders of a certain height or excludes people with specific medical or physical conditions, follow the rules. Some of the rides put extreme stresses on the body, and nobody's health is worth the thrill of a three-minute ride.

Shows in the parks are justifiably popular, done with the same care and professionalism as everything else. For some, like the ones in front of Cinderella's Castle in the Magic Kingdom, all you need to do is join the crowd. Others, like the auto thrill show and Indiana Jones stunt show at MGM have enclosed seating areas. Use *Fastpass* (see below) to guarantee a spot, but still get there early. Go to the most popular rides, or the shows you're most interested in, as soon as the park opens, when crowds are smallest.

If you like 3-D movies (and who doesn't!), you'll find several of the best you've ever seen.

## *Fastpass*

This is Walt Disney World's "virtual queue." Instead of waiting in line at the most popular attractions, guests can insert their park tickets into nearby Fastpass machines and be issued a ticket with a return time, usually a window of 15 minutes to an hour. They can then wander off and enjoy other parts of the park, returning during their designated time window and get into a separate, much shorter line for what is usually just a 5- to 10-minute wait for the attraction. The service is free.

A good strategy is to go straight to the ride you most want to try as soon as the park opens. Get a Fastpass ticket, then join the Standby line, which will probably be at its shortest then. You'll have a short wait for the ride and by the time you come out, your Fastpass ticket might have reached its assigned time so you can ride again right away.

It's important to get Fastpass tickets early in the day, because when the park is busy, sometimes all boarding times for popular rides have been assigned by early afternoon. Then your only hope is to wait in long Standby lines.

The downside is that you can't gather up a fistful of Fastpass tickets all at once. Times vary according to how busy the park is and how the machines are programmed each day, but once you have a Fastpass ticket for one attraction, you might have to wait up to two hours to get another.

Attractions that use the Fastpass system are designated on the map you get when you enter the park,

> **Tip:**
>
> On some rides, you can move more quickly to the front of the line by using the "Single Rider" option. Groups are broken up and individuals are seated wherever there is just one space available in a car. It's always lots quicker than standing in the regular line.

and are strongly recommended for the most popular rides like *Expedition Everest* in Animal Kingdom, *Soarin'* and *Test Track* in Epcot, *Tower of Terror* in MGM, and *Splash Mountain* and *Space Mountain* in the Magic Kingdom.

### Character Dining

Would anybody in your family like to have breakfast with Snow White, tea with Alice and her Wonderland friends, or an evening barbecue with Mickey himself? This is the place. All four Disney parks offer many opportunities for special meals with the most popular characters, and so do many of the resorts.

You have to reserve a spot months in advance, especially for any meal held in Cinderella's Castle where they recommend calling six months ahead. The cost of meals range from $12 or so for a child's breakfast to about $200 for mother and daughter to have tea with Disney princesses.

Meals and characters are too many and too changeable to list, but updated information is always available on the park's website. Telephone reservations are accepted 180 days in advance.

### Disney at Night

Daytime-only visitors to the parks miss one of the most memorable sides of the Disney parks, the nighttime spectaculars. Every night, the Magic Kingdom, Epcot, and/or MGM host extravaganzas with fireworks or lasers, music, and enough adrenaline-producing spectacle to make it hard to go to sleep for hours. The *SpectroMagic Parade* in the Magic Kingdom is the most fabulous hour in the park, and concludes with fireworks over Cinderella's Castle, a real fairytale ending to a day.

At Epcot, *IllumiNations* is a nightly fireworks and laser show that takes place at the World Showcase lagoon with walls of fire and brilliantly illuminated international pavilions. At MGM, you'll see *Fantasmic!* each night at the special theater at the end of Sunset Boulevard. There's limited seating for this one because it's in its own theater, but the lasers, fireworks, and dancing fountains make it worth standing in line to see.

The nighttime shows are popular, and it can take a long time to get out of the parking lot or back to your resort afterwards, so it will be a late night for the little ones. But you can sleep late in the morning. It's worth it! There's not a show or parade at each park every night, so you'll want to check the schedule on the Disney website before your trip so you'll know when you want your late nights to be.

## Autographs

You'll see Disney characters everywhere in the parks, and kids (and adults) love to line up and have their photos taken with them. They are incredibly patient and kind with little ones, no matter what the provocation. In every line, half the kids, it seems, will be carrying autograph books. I can't connect emotionally with an autograph from a fictional character, but I'm sure that to a little kid, an autograph from Mickey Mouse or Snow White means as much as my Ernie Banks and Fred Astaire autographs mean to me.

So join the fun. One park employee (they call them "cast members") told me the autograph craze began in the early 1990s and has accelerated ever since. Some kids bring elaborate scrapbooks with pictures of characters on each page, and spend their whole vacation trying to get signatures on each picture. Others just buy the simple blank autograph books that are now sold in all the park gift shops for about $9.

### Health and Safety

The Florida heat and sun can be fierce. Orlando temperatures can reach the mid-90s (35°C) by April and linger into October. That means there are two absolute essentials for any trip to Walt Disney World: plenty of sun screen and plenty of water.

On one trip in early May, I saw at least a half dozen people in the parks with serious, painful sunburn; some were kids and some were parents, but all were at serious risk of having their vacations ruined by the unseasonably early heat wave. You can buy ointments that will take some of the sting out of a bad burn, but it's much better to avoid it in the first place.

I don't like to slather my body with goo any more than anybody else, but it's sure preferable to the alternative. Use a high SPF sun block (at least 30) on every bit of exposed skin before you step out the door of your lodging in the morning. Do this even on cloudy days, because clouds do little to block the sun's most harmful rays. Take the sun block with you and reapply it every few hours.

It's very easy to get dehydrated in big amuse-ment parks. The sun beats down relentlessly, and heat bounces back up

**Tip:**

International visitors should know that many Disney employees ("cast members") are multilingual. Those who speak languages other than Eng-lish have little flags on their name badges that represent the langu-ages they speak. Maps and other publications are available in English, Span-ish, French, German, Portuguese, and Japanese.

from the pavement, cooking you twice as fast. So each person should take a bottle of water. Water fountains are everywhere in the parks but, frankly, that's just not enough. Each person in your group will probably pour down at least a half gallon (2 liters) of water on a hot day, and you want to make it easy for them to do it. You can go broke buying beverages in that quantity. The water is free: just keep refilling your water bottles at the drinking fountains.

The parks are crowded and sometimes families lose track of each other. When you arrive at a park, decide on a meeting place. Be specific. Don't just say you'll meet next to Cinderella's Castle in the Magic Kingdom, or the Sorcerer's Hat at MGM. They're big structures. Pick a specific spot. Then tell kids that they can ask any cast member for help in getting to that place if they get lost. Show them how to recognize cast members by the clothing characteristic of each park, or by the name badges they all wear.

## Accessibility

Few places I've ever been make more provisions for special needs visitors. Virtually all buildings are fully wheelchair accessible, most rides are available to wheelchair-bound visitors as long as they can transfer, most shows are captioned or provide assistive listening devices. There are even Braille guidebooks and audio guides you can borrow from Guest Services; Braille maps of the parks are placed in prominent places. Special viewing areas for parades are set aside in each park for guests in wheelchairs. Every Disney cast member I saw made every possible effort to accommodate guests with disabilities with kindness and dignity.

In truth, I saw the same attitude toward special needs visitors in all of Orlando's big theme parks, not just in Walt Disney World. Disney just seemed to make more of a point of it.

# The Magic Kingdom

This is the heart of the Disney universe, all the things Walt Disney built and honed and promoted over his long career, worlds straight out of his imagination, and the imagination of anyone who ever went through childhood. Of course you can see, just below the surface, the corporate Disney, clever ways to make kids want to buy things, the easy availability of a hundred ways to get into your wallet.

But suspend your cynicism. Sure, it's a business like any other: It exists to make money for the people who own it. But it's no more true here than it is at a major-league baseball stadium, at your favorite local restaurant, or, for that matter, at the store that sells you a refrigerator. Disney is selling things people want—a world of perpetual childhood, of imagination, of freedom from the worries of everyday life. If you make the decision to go to Disney World, don't analyze it, just enjoy it.

Ponce de Leon was right—the Fountain of Youth *is* in Florida. It's just in Orlando instead of St. Augustine.

If you've parked in the parking lot (for goodness sake, write down where you've left the car and tuck it in your wallet!), you'll take a tram to the Ticket and Transportation Center, where you can board a monorail or a ferry-boat to the Magic Kingdom. If you take the ferry, go straight to the other end of the ship when you board. You'll have the best view of Cinderella's Castle drawing closer, and you'll be among the first off.

You'll enter the park at *Main Street USA*, a sort of idealized small town that might have been plucked out of 1902 Iowa or some-thing. There you stand a good chance of meeting your first Disney character face to face in the town square.

Wander among the food and shopping areas, ride a horse-drawn tram-whatever you do, you'll inevitably be making your way

> **Tip:**
>
> Park attendants do check your bags and backpacks when you enter any of the parks, but regardless of what you've heard, they don't keep you from bringing your own food and beverages into the park to save money. You can even bring in small coolers (maximum size 24" long by 15" side by 18" high—or 61x38x46cm) to keep things cold. You can also use your own stroller instead of renting one.

toward the biggest piece of eye-candy in the park, something that doesn't look a bit like 1902 Iowa: *Cinderella's Castle*.

Each of the Disney parks has a centerpiece like this, but Cinderella's Castle is more than just representative of the Magic Kingdom: It's symbolic of the whole Disney empire. It's a beautiful and fanciful piece of architecture and if you can't take a gorgeous picture of this building, federal law requires you to turn in your camera. This is also the focal point of the nightly fireworks shows.

One of the classiest of Disney's character meals, Cinderella's Royal Table, is in the castle, as is a small, six-person guest suite originally built for Walt Disney himself, who died before the park was finished. Now the chance to stay there is used as a prize in Disney promotions.

From the castle, you can head off to any of the other Magic Kingdom areas:

- Experience the Old West in *Frontierland*
- Walk the streets of early America in *Liberty Square*
- See pirates and take a jungle cruise in *Adventureland*
- Ride a magic carpet in *Fantasyland*
- Meet Mickey Mouse at home at *Mickey's Toontown Fair*
- Look into the future in *Tomorrowland*

I can't possibly list all the great things to do in the Magic Kingdom. You want big rides? Try *Space Mountain* in Tomorrowland or *Splash Mountain*, one of the world's great water rides, in Frontierland. Tamer thrills? Maybe the *Jungle Cruise* in Adventureland or the *Indy Speedway* in Tomorrowland. Fun rides for little ones? *Dumbo* in Fantasyland or *Aladdin's Magic Carpets* in Adventureland will do it. And everyone will enjoy the train that circles the park, giving you a glimpse of everything.

Of course there are countless shows. You can meet all the presidents of the United States in Liberty Square's *Hall of Presidents* or sing along at the *Country Bear Jamboree*, two of the shows featuring Disney's famous animatronics, lifelike robots that are programmed down to the last flicker of an eye. I was amazed at the lifelike reactions of the individual

*Visiting Cinderella's Castle in the Magic Kingdom is a dream come true for many kids*

# Investing in Disney's Futures

If you're planning a future trip to WDW, here's a clever way to save money. Let's stick with that family of four I described earlier — Mom, Dad, and kids 12 and 8.

A three-day ticket for each member of the family, with the Hopper and Water Park options included, would cost, at current prices, $1,112, or $372 per day. Tickets will expire 14 days after purchase. The prices break down this way:

| | |
|---|---|
| $ 572 | 3 adult 3-day tickets at $192 each |
| 160 | 1 child 3-day ticket |
| $ 732 | admission total |
| 180 | 4 Park Hopper options at $45 each |
| + 200 | 4 Water Parks & More options at $50 each |
| | |
| $1,112 | total |
| $ 372 | per day for 3 days |

But you can add another option to your tickets. For an additional $125 each, your tickets will never expire. That sounds like a lot, but if you plan to make multiple visits, it can work in your favor. On this trip, instead of buying three-day tickets for each person, get ten-day tickets. Add the Hopper, the Water Parks, and the non-expiration option.

Now the math works like this:

| | |
|---|---|
| $ 648 | 3 adult 10-day tickets at $216 each |
| 177 | 1 child 10-day ticket |
| $ 825 | admission total |
| 180 | 4 Park Hopper options at $45 each |
| 200 | 4 Water Parks & More options at $50 each |
| + 500 | 4 Non-Expiration options at $125 each |
| | |
| $1,705.00 | total |
| $ 170.50 | per day for 10 days |

Next year, or five years from now, you can come back, as long as you keep your original ticket, and spend another three days free — and still have four more days to spend a few years after that, no matter how much prices have increased. That even applies to the 8-year-old who is now in the adult-ticket range. As one Disney employee put it, "We don't charge our guests for their children growing up."

Remember that tickets are not transferable, though, so you can't sell your unused days to your favorite neighbor. The tickets will be rejected at the gate as soon as your neighbor tries to scan his fingerprint.

presidents as they listened to Abraham Lincoln (clearly the star of the show) speak to the audience.

There are plenty of live shows, too, plus parades several times a day and a spectacular parade and fireworks show before closing many nights.

Oh, this doesn't begin to cover the magic of the Magic Kingdom. These are only words on paper; the Magic Kingdom is a full sensory experience. My favorite moments are probably watching little kids' eyes light up as they spot Goofy or seeing them dance down the street to the music that's everywhere.

This is called the Magic Kingdom for a reason. When we watch a magician we know it's really all just an illusion, but that doesn't keep us from being amazed at the trick. The Magic Kingdom is the same way. It's all smoke and mirrors. It's illusion. But it's magic.

## Epcot

As juvenile as my kids think I act sometimes, I'm really a grownup, and as much fantasy fun as the Magic Kingdom is, what's really fun for me is the science, technology, and cultural experiences I can have at Epcot.

Epcot is really an acronym for *Experimental Prototype Community of Tomorrow*, which in Walt Disney's original concept would have been an actual city which served as a sort of proving ground for innovation. Instead, it became a theme park dedicated to innovation and multiculturalism.

Thrill seekers won't be disappointed, though. Some of Walt Disney World's best rides are here, including a hang glider ride above California in *Soarin'* and the speed thrills of cars pushed to the edge in *Test Track*. And *Mission: Space* is one of Walt Disney World's most intense attractions. As a confirmed coward, however, my own preference is Epcot's tamer side.

Epcot really has two very distinct areas. The one that is immediately around the Geosphere is *Future World*. This is where you'll find the rides I mentioned, plus tamer attractions for smaller kids (or more cowardly writers), another 3-D film,

> *Tip:*
>
> If the weather is extremely hot, these and the many other indoor exhibits at Epcot are great places to cool off.

*This 16 million-pound golf ball is the Geosphere that welcomes you to Epcot*

an animatronic presentation of the history of human communication called *Spaceship Earth* inside the dome, and two pavilions, *Innoventions East* and *West*, that focus on present and future technology in our lives.

This is great stuff, like two big hands-on science museums with tons of things for kids to try out as well as to see. Kids can design their own robots, see how Under-writers Labs tests products for safety (and they can try to break a TV picture tube with a mallet), or learn to drive a Segway, that funny two-wheeled pedestrian scooter. It's not all about technology, either; there's a challenging interactive game that teaches players the principles of entrepreneurship. You can spend a couple of hours in these two exhibits alone. In the adjacent *Club Cool* kids will love the opportunity to try Coca-Cola products from several other countries. Some of the flavors are distinctly odd to American taste buds.

Epcot's second major area is *World Showcase*, surrounding the lagoon beyond Future World. This might be my favorite place in Disney World, and I could spend all day here. In fact, I have.

*Tip:*

One other feature in this part of the park you should know about: Between France and the UK is the International Gateway. This is a separate entrance to Epcot, where you can connect by boat to some of the Disney resorts, and to MGM Studios. If you're staying on the property, or visiting these two parks on the same day, check this out.

Eleven international themed areas ring the lagoon. Each presents a look at a different country's culture, traditions, and cuisine, and (of course) offers opportunities for shopping. It's an effective and low-key way to learn about Mexico, Norway, China, Germany, Italy, the United States, Japan, Morocco, France, the United Kingdom, and Canada.

Each section has buildings characteristic of the country (often scaled-down versions of ones you'll recognize), most offer films, demonstrations, or live performances (the acrobats in China are spellbinding!), and the food is probably the best and most varied in all of the parks. The ever-present background music changes appropriately as you walk your way around the world.

Another touch typical of Disney thoroughness: employees ("cast members") who work in each national section are natives of the country itself.

There's a large outdoor theater halfway around in the American sector that presents free high-energy musical shows several times a day. I found it only slightly strange that on one visit the headliner in this centerpiece of the American display was Petula Clark...who happens to be British. Underscores the focus on internationalization, I guess.

# Animal Kingdom

Does anybody in your family like animals? Silly question, I know, especially if you've got kids...which most readers of the *Family Travel Series* do. Kids like just about every sort of critter, including the slimy sort you wish they wouldn't bring into the house.

Animal Kingdom is a place where they can indulge their interests to the point of satiation, and you can relax because the Disney World folks won't let your kids take any of their animals home with them. But here in Animal Kingdom they can watch them, pet them, and get to know them on a first-name basis, while learning how all of us, finned, winged, two-footed, and four-and-more-footed creatures alike really depend on each other for our survival.

Animal Kingdom is a lot more than a zoo, and it's not just for little kids. It doesn't have as much of the "whiz-bang" of the other parks (except for some of the rides, which have plenty of whiz and all the bang you could want), but like Epcot, visitors are going to learn a lot—often without realizing it—and have lots of fun doing it.

You'll enter the park at the Oasis and immediately meet creatures you won't find in your back yard (the anteater is my favorite) and move along to Discovery Island and the park's focal point, the 145-foot-tall (44m) *Tree of Life*, a tribute to the diversity of the world's varied animal life, featuring the sculptures of 325 mostly endangered creatures. Inside the tree is the 3-D movie *It's Tough to be a Bug*. As you walk around the island you'll encounter exotic animals from all over the planet.

From here you can head directly to any of the themed areas in the park, or just make your way around the loop. A popular first stop for many families is *Camp Minnie-Mickey* for the show *Festival of the Lion King*, which takes place six to eight times a day. It's hugely popular, so get there very early—an hour isn't too much. This part of the park is also the best place to meet Disney characters, and maybe gather those autographs.

> ### Tip:
>
> At Conservation Station, be careful where you put your litter. One of the trash bins has a bit of an attitude and will talk to you, and maybe even chase you across the plaza in front of the station. It's startling at first, then just plain fun.

The next area you'll come to is *Africa* and here's the heart of animal country with *Kilimanjaro Safaris* that take you into the savanna where the animals live free. This is one of the trademark Disney attractions, and provides an experience similar to taking the train through Busch Gardens or driving through Lion Country Safari, maybe with a little more polish. By all means, walk along the Pangani Forest Trail and watch hippos splashing. I can watch the gorillas lumbering through the forest all afternoon.

*Rafiki's Planet Watch*, next to the Africa section, is one of the neatest parts of this park, because you can take a train "backstage" to see where the park's animals are cared for, and on to the Conservation Station where you'll learn about ecology, animal protection and preservation, and get to see the veterinary hospital that takes care of the park's animals. Trains leave every five minutes or so.

The big attraction in the *Asia* section of the park is another of Disney's signature rides, *Expedition Everest*, which will bring you face to face with a Yeti before your terror-inducing plunge down the mountainside. The Disney version of Everest isn't really as high as the original, but it is actually the tallest mountain in Florida, at 199 feet (61m) high. It will feel much taller than that as you go careening down.

Finally you come to DinoLand USA. There are no live dinosaurs here, I'm sorry to report, but there's *Dinosaur*, a scary themed ride, and another popular show, "Finding Nemo—The Musical."

But that's it for the day. This is the only one of the four big parks that doesn't have some sort of nighttime extravaganza lighting up its sky.

## Disney/MGM Studios

Tendrils of the Walt Disney Company reach everywhere. The corporation owns the ABC television network, the cable-TV giant ESPN, book publishers, record companies, more than a dozen magazines, a gang of radio and television stations, and more. But when most of us think of Disney, we don't think of a corporate monolith. We think of movies.

So many of the delights of everyone's childhood have included "Snow White & the Seven Dwarfs," "Dumbo," "Sleeping Beauty," "Peter Pan," "Cinderella," and the many other more recent classic animated films that the company continues to add each year. It's fitting, then, that the fourth major piece in Disney's Florida empire is a theme park devoted to movies.

MGM Studios isn't actually part of the Disney media empire. They're linked here through contract, not ownership. But it doesn't matter; it's an effective partnership and this park provides a very full, very fun day for all ages.

When you step through the front gates of the park, you're suddenly not in Florida any more, but in Southern California, surrounded by the gleaming art deco architecture of *Hollywood Boulevard*, with the park's centerpiece, a 122-foot-tall (37m) version of Mickey Mouse's Sorcerer's Hat from "Fantasia." This is your gateway to the rest of the park.

I like to start by wandering around Echo Lake, maybe stopping somewhere for a cup of coffee, or for an ice cream from the stand in the giant dinosaur named Gertie on the other side of the lake.

Right across from Gertie is the first of several great shows in the park, the Indiana Jones Stunt Spectacular, where you can watch them perform live (and sometimes explain) many of the amazing stunts from "Raiders of the Lost Ark." Both kids and adults will find it thrilling, and kids will like it even more because they blow stuff up.

So here you are, walking along the street when you look up and say, "Wait a minute. I started out in Florida, found myself in Hollywood, and all of a sudden it looks like I've traveled to New York! Am I going crazy?"

I'm not qualified to diagnose your mental health, but chances are you're perfectly sane and have just wandered into the *Streets of America* section of the park—movie sets with such an authentic feel that I kept expecting to get flattened by a taxi as I walked along the street. But look behind some of the buildings: Scaffolding! They're just facades. Hollywood magic. Even better is the San Francisco Street. From a distance it looks like you've got a tall hill to climb. Not until you get up close do you see it's just a brilliantly painted piece of forced perspective.

This corner of the park has one of the best auto thrill shows you'll ever see, "Lights, Motors, Action!" that puts to shame all the movie car chases you've watched over the years.

There's lots to do along *Mickey Avenue*, but my favorite is the Backlot Tour for a behind-the-scenes look at a working movie studio. The tour changes some-times because of projects in production, but you'll probably get to watch (and maybe take part in) the special effects needed in filming a

*Learn the trick and shortcuts of the movie business at MGM Studios*

## Gertie the Dinosaur

What very few visitors realize is that Gertie is Disney's tip of the cap to the very first significant animated film, "Gertie the Dinosaur," by Winsor McCay,

McCay was a newspaper cartoonist and author of the popular early-20th century comic strip called "Little Nemo." Nemo was not about a fish, so there's no Disney connection there, but a little boy who had vivid, adventurous dreams.

About 1909, almost 20 years before Walt Disney's "Steamboat Willie," McCay began using a short animated film about a mischievous dinosaur as part of his live lectures. "Gertie" may or may not have been absolutely the first animated film, but it was undoubtedly the first of any influence, and it paved the way for a new movie genre.

And everyone knows that in 1928 a young artist named Walt Disney introduced a certain mouse, soon to be renamed Mickey, to the world. The presence of Gertie in the park is a nice touch that only a handful of people get, but one that is typical of the sort of thoroughness that is characteristic of Disney world.

naval action scene, be shaken by an earthquake, and feel the heat when an oil tank truck explodes, then wander through the prop warehouse.

Further down the avenue you can listen to a Disney artist talk about how animation is done and learn about the life and legacy of Walt Disney.

Suddenly you're back in Hollywood, strolling *Sunset Boulevard*, heading for the *Beauty and the Beast* live stage show or the *Tower of Terror* ride.

There are more shows and movies at the MGM park than there are rides, but all are some of the best Disney has to offer. There are Muppets, shrunken kids, Star Wars flights, visits to Narnia, Little Mermaids, and more than you can squeeze into most days. Use your Fastpass to get into these, and show up plenty early for the shows. They are wildly popular.

Even the restaurants seem more special in this park, from the upscale Brown Derby (a delicious reproduction of its Hollywood namesake) to the Sci-Fi Drive-In Theater Restaurant, where you can sit in your convertible and eat while you watch old movies on the big screen—just like high school!

# Other Disney Facilities

I hope you're not tired yet, and have time left on your ticket. There's still plenty to do. It seems like you can get to a water park in less than ten minutes from anywhere in Florida, but Walt Disney World has two superb ones, *Typhoon Lagoon* and *Blizzard Beach*.

Pictures can make it look that way, but there isn't really any snow at Blizzard Beach, that's just its premise, that a freak blizzard hit central Florida and left all these fanciful slide— and toboggan runs. The park has Summit Plummet, the tallest water slide in the United States, a 120-foot (36.7m) chute where you can get your body up to highway speeds.

Typhoon Lagoon is built around the idea of a ship stranded on a mountaintop by a typhoon. Its center-pieces are its huge surf pool and shark reef (the kind that won't chomp your leg, fortunately).

The *Disney Wide World of Sports Complex* includes Major League baseball spring training games in March and a variety of sports tournaments and clinics year-round, but what most vacationing families go for is the fishing, boating, golf, horseback riding, or the chance to ride in (or, for several hundred dollars more, to drive) a NASCAR race car at over 160mph (260kph). It's much more of a make-your-own-fun place than the main parks.

## Downtown Disney

Officially, Walt Disney World has four theme parks and two water parks, but you could almost add a fifth park— Downtown Disney, except you don't have to pay to park and it doesn't cost anything to go and walk around.

This is a fine place for shopping (some stores don't even have a Disney slant to them) but it's even better for eating, with some very fine—and also some affordable—restaurants.

It's a still better place for nightlife. The center of the complex, *Pleasure Island*, is home to seven themed night-clubs from comedy to 70s and 80s dance mixes to Top 40. At night you pay for access to the Island (it's included in the Water Parks and More ticket option) and some, but not all, clubs have age restrictions.

Another entertainment option is the stunningly beautiful modern circus troupe, Cirque du Soleil, which has a perma-nent theater here. Admission to these performances is definitely *not* included in your Disney ticket: Performance

**Tip:**

If you plan to be out late, remember what I said about babysitting earlier in this chapter. If you're staying at one of the Disney resorts, you can arrange it through your Guest Services desk.

tickets start at more than $50 and top out around $120.

The place the kids will want to head for, though, is *Disney Quest*. At first glance it looks like just a five-story video arcade, but it's really a virtual, interactive theme park. It costs more than $30 per person, but it, too, is included in the Water Parks and More ticket.

I'm not sure I can do justice to the place. There are video games, simulations, and Virtual Reality experiences of every description, a carnival gone mad. Try Astro Blaster, sort of a bumper cars on steroids where you not only bump into other players, you can fire asteroids at them with your air cannon.

You can play a VR version of every imaginable sport, sometimes on a big screen that makes everything larger than life-size. But not everything is high tech; I even found a place with midway oldies like skee-ball.

This place is all about over-stimulation with video screens and music and game sounds and kids' voices and all sorts of colored and strobe lighting. But the fourth floor is quiet, the lights don't flash, and there are comfortable chairs where parents or little kids can get away from the racket. And there are even computer terminals here where you can check your e-mail, surf the internet, or play quiet video games well suited for little ones.

You'll also find a well-stocked art area where kids (or grownups) can create their own pictures, and 12 to 15 times a day, anyone with the interest can take a 30-minute class taught by a Disney artist on the principles of cartooning and how to draw Disney characters. The Disney people think of Disney Quest as another sort of theme park, and I don't think I can argue with them.

Downtown Disney is easy to walk through, but you can also take a free water taxi from one part of the neighborhood to the other. There are three main areas: The *West Side* is home to Disney Quest, Cirque du Soleil, and a variety of shops and restaurants. *Pleasure Island* is mostly nightclubs and is pretty quiet until late afternoon except for the Irish pub at one end.

*Downtown Disney at night © Rajesh Pattabiraman/Dreamstime.com*

And the *Marketplace* has many more shops and restaurants, including my favorite, the Lego Imagination Center, with some of the most amazing constructions you can imagine made of the tiny colorful bricks. You can even rent a boat at the Marketplace to go cruising in Village Lake.

Locals sometimes complain that Downtown Disney and its counterpart at Universal Studios—City Walk—have ruined downtown Orlando as an entertainment center. People who visited Orlando a few years ago and enjoyed the clubs and boutiques in the Church Street Station district downtown now find the area just a shadow of itself. But that's the price, I suppose, of being a city that has defined itself as a tourist hub.

In this chapter, I've tried to give you as clear an overview as I could of the Disney universe; *world* is too small a word for all it encompasses. Florida has so much more to offer than just this, even though it's the first thing most kids think of when somebody mentions a Florida vacation. I really do urge you to try out the rest of Florida, too—there is so much from Pensacola to Key West to see and do that is completely unlike anything you'll see anywhere else. But if Disney is your destination, I can promise you a great time.

There's just one more thing I want to say about Walt Disney World, and this is the place to do it, because to omit it wouldn't be quite honest, or give you as clear a sense of what I think as you deserve. Here it is: Before I went to Walt Disney World, I really, really did *not* want to like the place. It seemed to me to represent everything about corporate dominance I'm skeptical of, with a million and one ways to separate you from your money, to sell you things you don't want or need, to fill your kids' minds with commercials and demands for products—impersonal consumerism run amok.

Walt Disney World *is* big and bloated. It *is* a corporation firmly fixed on the bottom line. But it works. It's fun. It sends out tons of good, positive messages about acceptance, tolerance, diversity, patriotism, and respect.

We're willing to pay for our fun, whether it's going to a basketball game, buying a book, seeing a movie—or going to Disney World. As long as we believe we get fair value for what we spend, it's an even exchange. Of course you're going to be immersed in Disney culture here. But you know that going in.

Walt Disney World is a big, corporate entity, but it's a humane place. Children, adults, special needs visitors are all accommodated in every possible way, and with care and dignity. Sure, it's a fantasy world, but one where people are kind and endings are happy. We can all use a little more of that. Is it Disney magic? I think it really is like that magic trick I described earlier: Even when you know how the trick is done, and that it's not really magic but just a trick, you still watch, amazed.

That's magic indeed.

## *Recommendations*

∞ Decide before you go what your highest priorities are in each park and do those first. The lines won't get any shorter as the day progresses.

∞ Use Fastpass as much as you can.

∞ Sunscreen and water—early and often.

∞ You don't all have to go to the same park. If your time at Disney is limited, one parent and child can go to Epcot and everybody else can visit MGM.

∞ Try to catch at least one of the nighttime shows; they are spectacular.

# 11
# Orlando Beyond Disney

newspapers across the country: *Disney Not the Only Attraction in Orlando!* I know it's shocking, but I've been there. It's true!

Okay, okay. I'm over-dramatizing again. But Disney World is so well marketed and such a firmly fixed icon of American popular culture that it really does take an effort of will not to have images of cute talking mice and flying elephants pop into your mind at the very mention of the name of the city.

Truth of the matter is, though, that Orlando has a lot of other attractions, some of them going head-to-head with Disney World and coming off very well. You can spend your whole vacation having a fun time in the city without going anywhere near Disney World.

To begin with, there are three more theme parks that some members of your family might like as well as anything Disney serves up. Add another first-rate water park, a street that has some neat museums and some delightfully tacky places to spend an hour or two, and even Walt Disney himself could have had a great vacation without using his own parks.

If you've got sturdy shoes on now, I'll walk you around some of the other reasons why Orlando is the center of the tourist universe. I'll just plunge straight in, since my advice in the last chapter about how to get to Orlando and where to stay when you get there still applies ... except you're not likely to be staying at a Disney resort if you're not going to any of the Disney parks.

## SeaWorld

I'm not going to say this is my favorite park in Orlando. That depends on the day of the week, the direction of the wind, the phase of the moon, what I had for lunch on Tuesday, and a host of other factors. SeaWorld is a less intense experience than many of the others, though, and sometimes that's just what you need.

Does that mean that kids who want to do nothing but ride roller coasters will be bored?

They shouldn't be. Sea World has coasters that will get the adrenaline pumping just fine, especially *Kraken*, which flips you upside-down seven times, drops you over 150 feet (46m), twists you

around (in several unpleasant ways, and hits speeds of 65 miles per hour (105kph). Ride aficionados also like *Journey to Atlantis*, a combination roller coaster/water ride with some nifty special effects.

This park is more about animals than rides, though, and is, frankly, lower key that some of Orlando's other parks. While Disney and Universal offer animal shows of various sorts, but animals are really the signature attractions here.

The unquestioned star of the park is Shamu, the orca—the killer whale.

Shamu isn't really a specific whale, just a generic name used in marketing all three SeaWorld parks. (There are others in San Diego and San Antonio.) It doesn't matter a bit what the names are of the actual whales that perform several times a day in Shamu Stadium; they put on a terrific show. Watching a 30-foot-long (9.5m), 2,700-pound (1,227kg) whale leap from the water and turn a back flip is not something you'll soon forget.

They're incredible beasts, called killer whales because they're at the very top of the food chain; *nothing* preys on an orca. Yet tiny trainers who wouldn't make a decent hors d'oeuvre for a whale like this stand on the tips of their snouts, or ride their backs as they have the orcas fling hundreds of gallons of water onto the audience with a flip of their tails.

There are plenty of other shows, too. Everybody loves dolphins, sea lions, and penguins. This is the place to find them. You can even feed a dolphin in *Dolphin Cove*, watch the gentle manatees up close in the *Manatee Rescue* pool, pet stingrays at the *Stingray Lagoon*, or walk through a clear underwater tunnel surrounded by sharks.

For a view of the entire area, ride to the top of the 400-foot (122m) *Sky Tower*. Or pick an oyster at the bottom of a huge tank and send a pearl diver down to get it for you at *The Oyster's Secret*. An adjacent shop will pry open your oyster and retrieve the cultured pearl inside, and even create a unique piece of jewelry for you on the spot ... provided a bit more money changes hands.

What's a theme park without a spectacular nighttime show? SeaWorld has one with fountains, fireworks, shooting walls of flame, and more. This is not an every-night event, though. It's usually performed during the summer and at other times of the year when the park is busy. Check Sea World's website for details of performances during your stay.

Because the park is part of the Anheuser-Busch Company, you can expect to meet Clydesdale horses during your stay. And because of that ownership, you can get tickets here to Busch Gardens, about an hour away in Tampa, and be whisked over there by shuttle. If you plan on visiting that park anyway, getting a combined ticket for both here can save you $25 per person. You can also get a four-park pass that covers SeaWorld, both Universal theme parks, and the Wet 'N Wild water park at a savings.

Next to SeaWorld you'll also see the entrance to Discovery Cove. This is a more hands-on animal experience that allows you to swim with dolphins, snorkel with exotic fish, hand feed rare birds, and more. Only a thousand people a day are permitted in the park, and reservations are required. Prices start at more than $250 and include passes to SeaWorld or Busch Gardens.

But you might not need all the add-ons. SeaWorld in itself is a great day out, with more to do than you can squeeze in, and an unprecedented chance to meet some of our aquatic cousins up close.

## Universal

We're not finished with theme parks yet, not by a long shot. We have to chat about Disney's biggest competitor. Actually, parks in the Six Flags group probably draw a few more people in their 29 affiliates internationally than Universal does in its five. But Six Flags doesn't even try to butt heads with Disney and Universal in Florida; they have nothing at all in the state.

*There's no bigger star at SeaWorld than Shamu, the killer whale*

So what does Universal offer that allows it be taken seriously along side the Disney empire? Quite a lot, actually—two extremely well done theme parks that out-do the Mouse in some respects, and a water park that does very nicely without the built-in advantage of Disney's on-property parks. Universal is accessible and more central for visitors who aren't in Orlando solely for Disney, as well as far more compact.

Disney can feel overwhelming, and that's deliberate; Disney World really is an entire world of its own: You never have to leave, and everything is done to make sure you never want to. Universal has a more human scale. It's straightforward and less intimidating ... except for some *very* intimidating rides.

But I'm getting ahead of myself. Let's look at the Big Picture first.

### Universal Basics

Universal's two theme parks, *Universal Studios* and *Islands of Adventure*, are adjacent to each other and you can walk between them in five minutes, which means you only have to park (and pay) once. You lose out on the Disney monorail ride, but gain time and park access. The water park, *Wet 'N Wild*, is a very short drive away down Universal Boulevard.

Moreover, Universal has its own "downtown" shopping, dining, and entertainment area called *City Walk*, which may not be as large as Downtown Disney, but which is a lot closer—right at the entrance to the theme parks, in fact.

Universal's properties are much closer to the center of Orlando than Disney World, so it's easier to stay off-property and to visit other area attractions. Unless your accommo-dations are some distance away, it's not even necessary to get on I-4; surface streets will get you there easily. Signs into the park are good, but are less helpful when you leave, unless you're going to I-4.

Let's review a few other things you need to know about Universal before we go into the parks themselves.

*Tickets and Pricing:* No theme parks anywhere are cheap, and certainly not in Orlando. But you're paying for a full day and your ticket covers everything except food and souvenirs. You can easily spend just as much at an older-style amusement park where you have to pay individually for each ride and each show.

Universal can be a good value, however. The basic one-day ticket is good for both theme parks and costs about $80. (Kids 3-9 pay about $10 less.) That's more than $30 less than a ticket to one Disney park with the Park Hopper option, and it takes only minutes to get from one Universal park to the other. It's possible to buy a ticket to just one Universal park, but most people don't bother—it only saves about $10.

There are other ways to save—combination packages with hotels, auto club membership, multi-park tickets, on-line promotions ... maybe hair and eye color, for all I know. The only people who really have to pay full price are spur-of-the-moment walkups, and who visits a theme park at the last minute anyway?

*Accommodations:* Universal doesn't have Disney's array of two dozen resorts, but they have three of their own. One has a Polynesian theme, another is a Mediterranean-style village, and the third is a Hard Rock Hotel. None is particularly cheap, with rates starting at more than $200 a night and soaring upwards from there.

All offer children's activity rooms and babysitting for pre-teens, and plenty of other upscale amenities. Ticket discounts and other benefits can make stays at these resorts more affordable than other up-scale hotels. You can also get pet-friendly rooms at Universal, something not available at Disney resorts. The biggest perk for Universal resort guests is probably the fact that they can go to the head of the line for any attraction in either park.

There's probably less reason for most people to stay at a Universal resort than a Disney one, though. Universal is just a minute or two away from Orlando's International Drive, which is more thickly populated with hotels and motels than just about anyplace else you'll ever find, many good ones with prices that can be just one-fourth of what you'd pay at a Universal resort—and which provide shuttle service to the park.

*Layout of the Parks:* You'll park in a parking garage for the Universal complex. It's huge, of course, but escalators and people movers help keep people flowing toward the ticket booths. You can leave and return the same day for one fee (about $11) by giving your original parking pass to the attendant when you re-enter. Parking is free after 6 p.m., a plus if you're only coming to hit the City Walk restaurants or clubs.

Guests enter both Universal Studios and Islands of Adventure by going through City Walk. Bear right for Universal Studios and left for Islands of Adventure. Ticket booths and self-service kiosks are at the entrance to each park, and once you have your ticket the process is the same as at Disney: have your card scanned, put your finger on the biometric reader, and in you go.

Once you're inside, you'll find maps in English, French, German, Japanese, Portuguese, and Spanish. You can also rent strollers, wheelchairs, and power scooters just inside. Bags will be checked as you enter and it's okay to bring in food or non-alcoholic beverages, but unlike Disney, coolers are *not* permitted in Universal parks.

Both Universal Studios and Islands of Adventure have a central lagoon with several themed areas surrounding it. Not surprisingly, the areas are called Islands in the Islands of Adventure park. Each area has rides, shows, shopping, and dining.

Here is a totally useless fact. I never realized this until five minutes before I wrote this paragraph, then thought about it and it's true: At all the Disney theme parks, I inevitably go clockwise around the center, while at both Universal parks, it's always counterclockwise. It's odd, I can't account for it … and it really doesn't matter which way you go.

*Rides and Shows:* Both parks have numerous themed rides, shows, and roller coasters, and they're mostly very well done, with lots of special effects. Universal Studios has more themed rides, which sometimes include a moderate roller coaster, and Islands of Adventure has more conventional roller coasters—although the terror they can induce is anything but conventional! Remember that ride restrictions are there for your safety and that of your children. Some rides are extreme: don't try to circumvent the rules.

As with all theme parks, these change a little every year, with new attractions being added and older ones cycled out. The problem (both here and at Disney) is that attractions and references in shows can be based on movies like "E.T."

*The Hulk Coaster at Islands of Adventure will flip you over seven times. Better go before lunch!*

that are so old that most kids haven't even seen them. That may not matter a lot, since most are pretty exciting for their own sake, but it can feel like a bit of a time warp for adults sometimes.

Naturally there's a big nighttime spectacular, *Universal 360*, a fireworks, movie, and laser extrava-ganza in the Universal Studios lagoon each night during the summer.

*Express Plus:* The counterpart to Disney's Fastpass, Universal's *Express Plus,* has no time limit between attractions and no return time to make you wait until later to go to the head of the line. You just pick the ride you want and go straight to the Express entrance with no waiting. You can use it once on every major ride in the parks.

There's gotta be a catch, right? Yeah, there is. You have to buy it and depending on the time of year, it can cost from about $25 to more than $50 a day. So it's more useful than Disney's Fastpass, but it can cost a family some serious money. Which is better? I suppose it depends on which you have more of on your vacation—time or money.

*Accessibility:* The Universal parks also get high marks for the way they cater to guests with special needs. Special wheelchair seating areas are provided for all shows and some rides have special accessible entrances for wheelchair-bound riders. One ride is not accessible— *Pteranodon Flyers* at Islands of Adventure.

Shows in both parks are sign-language interpreted (Guest Services can provide a schedule of when) and captioning and assistive listening devices are available. Service animals are welcome throughout the parks.

That's the overview. Now let's have our tickets and fingerprints scanned, push through the turnstile, and get into the park for some serious fun!

## Universal Studios

Universal Pictures has been making movies since 1912, so let's start with this park. And if that's our approach, there's no more obvious place to start than the *Hollywood* section. A stroll down Hollywood Boulevard feels like the real thing, with Schwab's Pharmacy, Mel's Diner, and a Walk of Fame with the stars of entertainment's biggest names. The *Horror Make-Up Show* here is a great behind-the-scenes look at how to get an ax sticking out of someone's head, but the simulated blood and violence here might be too intense for young children.

If you bear to the right and stroll down Sunset Boulevard (yes, there's one at Disney's MGM, too—try not to think about it), you'll come to *Woody Woodpecker's KidZone*, a neat place for your youngest traveling companions. There's a playground and kid-sized roller coaster here, a chance to sing along with Barney, and meet other cartoon characters. But the best part, I think, is the Curious George playground. Kids (and maybe parents) will get soaked here with all the fountains, waterfalls, hoses, water cannons, and cascades, ideal for a hot Florida afternoon. And when the bell rings, watch out! The big bucket on top of the fire house will tip over, sending a veritable flood into the square below. No showers necessary tonight!

Next stop is the small area, *World Expo*, with the Men in Black ride, and then what I think is the most picturesque area of the park, *San Francisco/Amity*. Wouldn't your friends back home love to see a photo of you with your head in the jaws of an enormous man-eating shark? Wouldn't you like to drink a "Fear Factor" smoothie full of worms and bugs? Haven't you always wanted to go through a big earthquake or watch ghouls dancing about with electric guitars? Then this is the place for you.

> *Tip:*
>
> Watch for opportunities to create your own special effects photos at several places in the park–places to put your camera so it will capture not only the "real" view, but also a small painted "background" a few feet away. Your photo might look, for example, like you've taken a picture of a movie theater with the Hollywood Hills and famous Hollywood sign behind it.

*The movie set for Amity looks too peaceful for an attack from the shark Jaws. Just watch!*

The *New York* section has the park's most popular attraction, *Revenge of the Mummy*, which incorporates great special effects, some really scary moments, and a good roller coaster. Waits for this can be really long, so if you didn't buy Express Plus and want to cut your wait, you can join the Single Rider line. Your group will be broken up into separate cars but the line does move faster.

I've spent a lot of time in New York City (the real one, not the Universal or Disney models) and can confirm the authentic feel of the place. But be sure to look behind some of those realistic buildings. You'll often find just scaffolding holding up a block of store fronts. That's life in the movies. If you feel up to it after being in a San Francisco earthquake a little while ago, you can go through a tornado here in the *Twister* ride.

The *Production Central* section contains working studios and soundstages, but there's also a themed ride based on Nickelodeon cartoons and a pretty good 3-D movie starring the animated monster Shrek—meet him personally in the souvenir shop across from the movie…a bit of clever planning.

Now let's walk past the Hard Rock resort and NBA City restaurant (where, ironically, the outdoor basketball court was closed on a recent visit) over to a park with a very different feel to it, the Islands of Adventure.

## Islands of Adventure

If you've come to Orlando looking for big rides, this is one-stop shopping. Disney World has as many good rides, but they're scattered through four different parks. Nowhere else in Florida do you have as many motion-sickness-inducing thrills all in one place.

Islands of Adventure seems tame enough when you enter and stroll through the Port of Entry with its fanciful buildings and shops. Then you notice a mass of green twisted metal on your left, with screaming people being shot along it at improbable speeds and suddenly things don't seem so tame any more. Instead of going left, maybe we'd better turn right and work up to this.

If that's what you do, the first "island" you arrive at will be tame indeed: *Seuss Landing*, featuring the whimsical landscapes and characters of the beloved children's author. There's nothing scary here at all, but some easy rides on an elevated trolley, in a flying fish (red fish, blue fish, other-colors-too fish!). It's a delightful place for little kids, or for anybody who once was one.

> You will like it, yes you will.
> No big rides to scare or chill.
> Just a silly, smiley spot
> Before the action gets too hot.

Don't get complacent; the next island, *The Lost Continent*, will snap you back to whatever passes for reality in this place. On one side see the waterfall flowing from the mouth of the mysterious face carved into the mountain. (Your family gets one extra point for decorum if none of the kids—or Dad—makes jokes about the mountain throwing up. There's a decent stunt show here and a pretty good themed ride, but most people come for the roller coasters, *Dueling Dragons*, twin high-speed coasters that give every impression that they are going to collide but manage to miss each other by inches.

The next island is *Jurassic Park*, where you can go exploring a primeval landscape, or ride a short, tame sky ride above the island. If you're brave enough, try the *River Adventure* ride and dodge raptors, drop 85 feet (26m) in the dark, and get soaked at the end. On a hot day, cool off in the *Discovery Center*, an effective blend of fantasy and real science. You'll learn real things about fossils and biochemistry—and also watch baby dinosaur eggs hatch.

*Tip:*

Introduce yourself to the fountain in front of the Sinbad stunt show amphitheater. It will talk back to you—and probably squirt you. It sounds like it has the same odd voice as the talking litter bin in Disney's Animal Kingdom.

If you escape from rampaging dinosaurs, cross over to *Toon Lagoon*, the most colorful place in the park. Cool off in a fountain and walk among gigantic renditions of comic-strip characters—even some that feel a bit dated. ("Gasoline Alley," for example, has been published since 1919 and has outlived three of its principal artists. I have no information on the health of the current one.) The biggest attraction here is *Ripsaw Falls*, an extremely popular water ride that compares favorably with Disney's Splash Mountain. You've taken showers that have left you drier than this ride will.

We're almost all the way around, now, just one island to go—*Super Hero Island*, home of Spider Man, Dr. Doom, and the Incredible Hulk. Two of the best rides in the park are here, *The Amazing Adventures of Spider Man*, a wild, special-effects, 3-D experience, and that twisted mass of green metal we saw when we came in—the 60 mph (100kph) *Incredible Hulk Coaster*. If you can survive the first ten seconds, you'll be just fine....

*Tip:*

You'll find continually updated signboards all around the park that list wait times for all the major attractions so you can see where the queues are shortest.

If that's not enough for you, just wait. Universal has announced that they're adding one more "island" here, *The Wizarding World of Harry Potter*, due to open in 2009. Plans call for the attractions here to draw extensively from all the books and movies, and the art director for the Harry Potter films is on Universal's design team.

*Seuss Landing at Islands of Adventure is a fun and peaceful place for little ones ... and their parents*

There's no after-dark spectacle here. If your knees haven't buckled on the coasters, you'll have to stroll over to the Universal Studios park next door—or maybe stagger if the rides have had the desired effect.

## Other Universal Attractions

No self-respecting Orlando mega-theme park would be happy with just that, however! You might still have some time left on your vacation, or extra energy to burn off ... or unspent money left in your wallet. So naturally there's more to offer.

If Disney has a "downtown," Universal has to have one, too. Their version is called *City Walk* and its great advantage is its proximity to the parks. You don't have to drive or take a bus. In fact, you can't avoid it unless you plan to abandon your car. It's comfortably sandwiched between the parks and the parking, for your shopping convenience. It's not as big or, in my opinion, as good as the Disney equivalent, but it has its high spots.

You will find some interesting shops here, but also seven or eight good restaurants (counting the Hard Rock and NBA over the bridge), twenty movie screens, and half a dozen or so nightclubs, some of which welcome kids. Clubs have cover charges, or you can buy a *Party Pass* for about what the cover charge for two clubs would be. Visitors who purchase a multi-day ticket to the theme parks get a free Party Pass.

The newest attraction is a permanent home for the Blue Man Group show, competition for Disney's Cirque du Soleil. Prices are in the $50-$70 range.

Anyone in Florida who doesn't operate a water park feels left out, so naturally Universal has one, too. *Wet 'N Wild* is off the main Universal property, about two miles (3km) away at the intersection of Universal Boulevard and International Drive.

This is the place for nearly vertical water slides—one of 76 feet (23m), another of 250 (76.5m)! There are several inner tube rides that will make you wish you were back at Islands of Adventure on something tame like the Hulk coaster, and lots of things for kids, like a giant bubble to slide on, and scaled-down versions of the big attractions.

Had enough? Phew! I have ... at least for now. I'm sure I'll be back, but let's see what else Orlando has to offer.

## I-Drive

If you refer to this by its proper name, International Drive, everybody will know you're a first-time visitor to Orlando who has been here less than fifteen minutes. Call it *I-Drive*, like everybody else does.

There's nothing the least bit subtle about I-Drive. It's all about tourism, from the huge convention center to the nearly 100 hotels, to the garish souvenir shops, to the endless line of cars that parade along the street 24 hours a day. This sounds like an exaggeration, but it's not, believe me: You can have a marvelous vacation filled with fun attractions, great food, plush accommodations, and boutique shopping and *never* leave I-Drive.

And it's just as easy to find cheesy attractions, fast food, budget accommodations, and outlet malls on the same street. Whatever you want, except snow, is available on I-Drive. But, come to think of it, you can find an iceberg here, and that's nothing but densely compacted snow. So I guess you *can* find anything on I-Drive.

I-Drive meanders for almost 15 miles (24km) southwest of central Orlando, roughly from Universal to Disney World. Most of the places you'll want to go are on the northern portion of the road—north of Highway 528, the expressway to the airport. Certainly there are reasons to go south from there—SeaWorld, hotels, golf courses, some outlet shopping, and eventually Disney World (although I-4 is a better route to WDW). But the northernmost five miles (8km) of I-Drive is much more densely packed with goodies.

## Getting Around, Looking Around

Driving is the obvious way. Don't expect it to be quick, because the Drive is packed with cars from all over North America. That means you'll never whiz past your destination, because nobody whizzes anywhere on I-Drive. Traffic notwithstanding, it's an easy street to drive on because there are plenty of places to pull off, to turn around, or to park and walk.

If you're staying at a hotel on I-Drive, you can make your life even easier by leaving your car in the parking lot and hopping aboard the I-Ride Trolley. These big green motorized trolleys prowl the upper ten miles (16km) of I-Drive daily from 8 a.m. to 10:30 p.m., all the way from the Universal resorts and the huge Prime Outlets Orlando mall at the north end of the Drive to the huge Orlando Premium Outlets mall a few miles from Disney, stopping at more than 40 places along the way.

It's cheap at just $1 per ride (just 25 cents for passengers age 65 and more), and an unlimited ride, one-day pass is just $3. Multi-day passes are an even better value. Kids age 12 and under ride free if they're with an adult. Trolleys run about every 20 minutes and all have wheelchair lifts.

I-Drive is worth a pass through even if you're not staying here because, if nothing else, the architecture is often kitschy and fun. You'll see gaudy souvenir shops that look like castles and pirate ships, or just painted in color combinations that will make your eyes ache. Along with plush hotels that would look at home in the ritziest parts of Miami Beach, you'll spot one that looks like a pink castle. They probably call it coral, but it sure looks pink to me.

The goofiest places to me are the miniature golf courses. I counted five places to play mini-golf along here and I could easily have missed some. Want to play golf amidst bubbling volcanoes or scurvy pirates or wild jungle animals or with glow-in-the-dark balls and holes? Of course you do, and this is the place for it.

Would a building sinking into the earth get your attention? What about one that's upside down? Got one of each here and I'll talk more about 'em in a minute. Trains, helicopters, and sinking ocean liners are all part of the I-Drive package.

And if you're looking for the *ultimate* emotional experience, you can choose between exchanging vows at the Wedding Chapel or having yourself hurled skyward in a giant slingshot. Even if you don't stop anywhere at all, I-Drive is a world all its own—practically a theme park itself to rival Disney or Universal. Now let's stop a few places.

### Shopping

Yes. Anything you want to buy. No need to say anything more. Okay, then, just this: There are approximately 500 stores on I-Drive, from Armani and Burberry to souvenirs so tacky and embarrassing that you just have to wonder why somebody even thought of them in the first place. You'll find four major shopping complexes on I-Drive, and a plethora of strip malls, small shopping centers, and stand-alone shops that can occupy a determined shopper for weeks and put a hole in a credit card that an oil tycoon couldn't fill.

### Dining

Yes. Anything you want to eat. No need to say anything more.

Oh, I'm not trying to be annoying. It's true. Just go there and you'll see what I mean. Choices range from some of Orlando's most elegant "white tablecloth" restaurants to every fast food chain you can think of. Speaking of which, the world's largest McDonald's restaurant is right here, at the intersection of I-Drive and Sand Lake Road. If you like dinner theater, you can choose your theme from among pirates, detectives, country jamboree, magic, and more.

### Attractions

Without a doubt, the building on I-Drive that's most likely to cause whiplash as you do a quick double-take is **Wonder Works** *[9067 International Dr. Open daily until midnight. Adm.]*. It's upside-down! The backstory is that scientists made an artificial tornado in the Bermuda Triangle, which raged out of control, plucked up the building, and eventually dropped it here. It's a silly story, but they needed a premise of some sort for an upside-down building, didn't they?

Silly stories notwithstanding, inside is a pretty classy hands-on science center that kids will be able to enjoy all afternoon. They can design their own roller coasters, play a giant piano with their feet, lay on a bed of nails, learn how to land the space shuttle, and put themselves inside a giant bubble. Even kids who hate math will be fascinated by the section that teaches them about probability theory by trying to find one purple bead in a bottle con-taining one million beads. And everyone will be fascinated by the incompre-hensible optical illusions of artist M.C. Escher.

Just up the street is another odd building, this one looking like it's sinking into the Florida swamps. This is another branch of **Ripley's Believe it or Not!** *[8201 Inter-national Dr. Open daily until 1 a.m. Adm.]*. This has a collection of oddities similar to other branches, in this case including a car made out of matchsticks, some shrunken heads, and, well, more than you can believe.

Across the street, one building houses two attractions, **Air Florida Helicopters** and **Train Land International** *[8990 International Dr. Closed major holidays. Adm.]*. Helicopter tours start at about $25 per person for an eight-mile (13km) ride over SeaWorld, and go into the hundreds for longer trips. Train Land costs much less and has the country's largest collection of G-gauge model trains. If you're a train enthusiast or model train hobbyist, the layouts are well done and interesting. Casual visitors might find the $8 admission a lot for just a quick walk-through.

You'll find a couple of amusement parks on I-Drive, but **Magical Midway** *[7001 International Dr. Open daily until late (varies seasonally). Adm.]* will provide some serious thrills. Highlights include a slingshot that will fire you 180 feet (55m) into the air at the speed of a roller coaster drop, then jerk you back to earth again, then throw you upwards, back and forth until you sit suspended in space. Why *do* people do those things on purpose? You can also ride to the top of a 230-foot (70m) tower and be spun around at highway speeds, or drive high-speed go-karts on elevated tracks high above the midway. There's lots more, too, if your heart can take it.

If you want to fly without leaving the ground, you can try the **Skydiving Wind Tunnel** *[6805 Visitors Circle. Open daily. Adm.]* where for less than $50 you can simulate freefall in a vertical wind tunnel.

**Tip:**

The big blue building with the Titanic sign on I-Drive is only the ticket office. The exhibition itself is in an adjacent shopping center whose best days appear to be behind it.

Few ships have captivated the public like the *Titanic*, and **Titanic, the Experience** *[8445 International Dr. Open daily until 9 p.m. Adm.]* will satisfy anyone's curiosity. With more than 200 artifacts from the ship itself and movie props from the films *Titanic* and *A Night to Remember*, the museum tells the story of the great ship from its construction to the salvage operations after its discovery on the ocean floor. It's all very well done from the grand staircase to the iceberg that brought the ship down.

Orlando isn't one of those places that's got something for everyone. It's more like seven or eight somethings. I've never heard of anybody who traveled here and spent the entire time watching TV in their hotel room: Orlando is a place to experience. Crowded, commercial, over-hyped, tacky—and more fun than you can handle. There's nowhere else like it.

## *Recommendations*

✏ One man's opinion: The Shamu show at SeaWorld is the best animal show in Orlando.

✏ Roller coaster fanatics might not get any farther than Universal's Islands of Adventure. It's the best concentration in a coaster-crazy city.

✏ I-Drive. No need to say anything more.

# 12
# The Bay Area

MY FIRST EXPERIENCE OF FLORIDA WAS THE TAMPA BAY AREA AND, best of all, my employer paid the bills, because I was attending a job-related workshop. It didn't take me long to return, though, at my own expense with the entire family along. The workshop gave me a chance to get familiar with the area and some of the attractions (one of our sessions was held at Busch Gardens, for example), and I got good advice about where to go from my grandfather, who lived in nearby Largo. Now, as a grandfather myself, I get to be the one dispensing good advice.

Finding fun and interesting places to go with your family in the Bay Area is even easier than in most other parts of Florida, because everything is so close together. In the Panhandle or along the Atlantic Coast you might have to drive some distance to get from one attraction to another (although along A1A that's no burden), but everything in this chapter is close to everything else. With truly pathological determination, you could easily drive past all of them in one day, although that wouldn't leave you any time to actually visit any of them!

Like everywhere else in Florida, the Tampa Bay area has water parks, aquariums, and lush state parks about every three miles along any road you happen to choose. If that's what you're looking for, you won't have any trouble finding them, and you'll have a great time. But this is an area that's especially rich in less ordinary attractions. Combined with miles of beaches bordering the warm waters of the Gulf of Mexico, the Bay Area produces a family destination that is utterly compelling.

## Getting Around

You're going to need a car to get the most out of your stay. Buses and trams run within and between major cities and trolleys patrol the beachfront in places, but they're not a good option for sightseers. So if you don't drive to Florida, you'll have to rent a car.

Air travelers can shop for good airfares, too. Tampa International (TPA), St. Petersburg-Clearwater International (PIE), and Sarasota-Bradenton International (SRQ) airports all serve this area. Major mainline international carriers and discount airlines both provide plenty of choice from almost anywhere.

If you'd rather take the train, Amtrak offers rail service to Tampa from anywhere along the U.S. Atlantic Coast.

The most convenient way to drive into the Bay Area is down Interstate 75, which goes straight into Tampa, then continues down the Gulf Coast all the way to Naples. There it turns east across the Everglades, ending in Miami. But I-75 isn't what you want for seeing the attractions in this chapter. It stays too far from the coast.

Unfortunately, the Gulf Coast doesn't have the equivalent of A1A on the eastern side of the state. Some highways run a few miles along the shore, but there's not a single, mostly picturesque route on the Gulf side the way there is along the Atlantic. Still, you'll go through some very pretty scenery and over some spectacular bridges from time to time, although you might also have to deal with traffic congestion, as well.

# DESTINATION
## Tampa

Tampa and Miami are similar in size, between 300,000 and 400,000 people, but Tampa has always seemed more manageable and approachable to me. Miami, even though it's only a little bit larger, seems glitzier, faster-paced, and more self-conscious. Maybe that's why I like Tampa—it's more like a place real people live. It's not that I don't like Miami. I do! But I feel more relaxed in Tampa.

"Relaxed" doesn't mean bored, though. There's enough to do here to keep you away from the beach for your whole vacation, if you want, although I don't know why you would. Tampa has an easy-going, tropical feel to it that makes you want to walk a little slower and enjoy the palm trees and southern sun. (Unless you're caught in rush-hour traffic trying to cross the Bay—then it's just like any other traffic jam.)

*Downtown Tampa © Roza/Dreamstime.com*

Besides the usual big-city array of museums, galleries, historical sites, and urban bustle, all of which I enjoy wherever I travel, Tampa has a few experiences that are sure to please some or all members of your family.

## Busch Gardens

Ask ten people to name a major theme park in Florida and they will probably answer that big one over in Orlando eleven times. If you're spending your holiday in the Tampa Bay area, though, there's no reason to make the 80-mile (130km) trek just to buy a pair of mouse ears. You can have a fabulous time right on Tampa's north side. Busch Gardens has everything you want from a theme park: exciting rides, exotic animals, fun shows, and endless amounts of food. They even have a kennel if you're traveling with a pet.

I don't suppose it matters when you see the animals or watch the shows, but there are a few rides at Busch Gardens that you definitely want to tackle on an empty stomach. First among those is probably *SheiKra*. Choose your own adjective for this one: thrilling, terrifying, heart-stopping—they all fit. This is not a ride for the timid. Climb slowly to a height of 200 feet (61m), pause for a moment, then hurtle straight down—90 degrees—at a speed of 70 miles per hour (113 kph), into a rolling loop, through a tunnel, then through the water, the longest three minutes of your life. I can hardly bear to watch it.

There are plenty of other exhilarating rides, plus the much tamer *Skyride*, that takes you high above the park for a seagull's-eye-view of everything, and the *Serengeti Railway* that meanders through the animal area of the Serengeti Plain. The train runs every 10 to 45 minutes, depending on how busy the park is and, like practically everything else at Busch Gardens, is wheelchair accessible.

> **Tip:**
>
> The Serengeti Railway is also a great way to rest your legs and get from one part of the park to another, since there are three stations located in different areas of the park.

Everyone will enjoy watching the African animals roaming free, seeing shows that range from rock-and-roll to pirate adventures to sing-alongs, with special activities, animals, fairy-tale shows, and rides for the youngest family members in a dragon-themed play area. You can meet animals and their keepers up close throughout the park, and I counted at least thirteen places to find meals and snacks.

The admission price is steep—around $60 for visitors age 10 and above, and about ten dollars less for kids 3 to 9—so you'll want to spend the day to get your money's worth and parking is extra. All attractions, rides, and shows are included in the admission price. You could easily spend as much money going to three separate attractions in a single day. In fact, there's more than enough for a single day here. I haven't even mentioned King Tut's Tomb, posing with the gigantic Clydesdale horses, and much else. And I guarantee—you'll be just as exhausted after a day here as you would have been if you'd made the 80-mile trip to that *other* theme park.

I should also mention that Busch has its own water park called *Adventure Island* adjacent to the amusement park. Admission is separate, and you can't possibly do both in one day.

Busch Gardens is located at Busch Boulevard and 40th Street on the north side of Tampa, 2 miles (3km) east of I-275 and 2 miles west of I-75. *[Busch Blvd., Tampa. Open daily. Adm plus parking]*

## Ybor City

If Busch Gardens is fast-paced and modern, historic Ybor City on Tampa's south side is about history, elegance, and gentility. I'm not very genteel and I'm certainly not elegant, but this is my favorite part of Tampa. This is the place to walk streets that ooze 19th century charm. If you've been to New Orleans, it will remind you of the French Quarter with its old buildings, wrought-iron balconies, and countless restaurants, shops, and nightclubs. But its main street, 7th Avenue (*La Septima Avenida*), is more benign than Bourbon Street, because you won't have to worry about blundering with your kids into a strip club.

Ybor City is just south of Exit 1 on I-4. Go south on 21st Street and two minutes later you're in the heart of the area. You'll find inexpensive parking garages at 7th Avenue and 13th Street, as well as at 5th Avenue and 15th Street. This is an area to explore on foot.

> *Tip:*
>
> Don't be confused by the surfeit of numbered streets. In Tampa, numbered streets run north-south. Numbered avenues run east-west.

Ybor City has a definite Latin flavor, because it's been home to endless numbers of Central and South American immigrants, and is the locus of Tampa's cigar industry; it was once the cigar capital of the world. In fact, it's named for the 19th century cigar maker who made this area (pronounced *EE-bore*) the focal point of the industry.

But there are more flavors here than just Latin spice. This is a very cosmopolitan area. Much like New York's Lower East Side, this has been the first stop for wave after wave of immigrants of a multitude of ethnicities, and there is still a very strong Irish and Italian presence in the area. That's the biggest difference between Ybor City and Miami's Little Havana. The mix of nationalities makes Ybor City feel a little more accessible to most visitors.

You get the feel of the diversity of the area in all sorts of ways, but especially from the restaurants. Italian. Irish. Cuban. Colombian. Spanish. Creole. Greek. French. Japanese. Then add delis, diners, vegetarian, barbecue, and seafood places, and coffee shops, and ice cream parlors, and goodness knows what else!

It's a pleasure to walk through the neighborhoods here, looking at the shops and numerous art galleries. Look for the gallery of Arnold Martinez at 9th Avenue and 9th Street. This local artist creates local scenes using paints made from coffee, tea, tobacco, beer, and wine. The gallery is near the **Ybor City State Museum** *[1818 E 9th Ave. Open daily. Adm.]*, a good local history museum that focuses on the immigrants, architecture, and cigar-making history of the 30-square-block area. It's a popular destination for school field trips, and one afternoon the ranger on duty (the museum is classified as a state park) told me the kids just lap up the information but at the end, after the discussion of the area's importance in the cigar industry, one wide-eyed child always asks, "But isn't smoking *bad?*"

"I'm never sure how to answer that," she said. "I usually just say that people didn't understand that in those days."

You can do some serious shopping, too, not just along 7th Avenue, but throughout the neighborhood, and at Centro Ybor, the four-square-block center-city mall and entertainment complex that runs from 7th to 9th Avenues and 15th to 17th Streets. If there are any kids (or dads) who don't care for shopping, there are plenty of other things to do, including a 20-screen movie complex and a large **Gameworks** at 8th Avenue and 17th Street, with its tons of video games, snacks, and even (for dad) a bar. It's a great attraction for kids and is clean and very well supervised.

Don't miss a ride on the streetcar! It's a must-do if you're visiting Tampa. You can take a relaxing ride through the area and down to another shopping and entertainment neighborhood at the seaport. Trolleys begin running at 11 a.m. on weekdays, 9 a.m. Saturday, and noon Sunday, and run as late as 2 a.m. on weekends, though earlier on other days. You can also connect to a line that runs through downtown Tampa. It's inexpensive, just $2 a ride, but discounted all-day passes are available on board. It's definitely the best and classiest way to get around.

## Other Tampa Attractions

Sometime when I have a free week or two, I'm going to make a list of all the science museums I've visited. The **Museum of Science and Industry** *[4801 E Fowler Ave. Open daily. Adm.]*, not far from Busch Gardens, isn't the best I've ever been to. It is fairly expensive (adults about $20, kids under 12 a little less) and the exhibits are not as wide-ranging as at many other places. Still, they have some good ones, like a high-wire bicycle you can really ride, two huge dinosaur skeletons, and Disasterv-ille, where you can undergo hurricane-intensity winds and experience what it feels like to be in the basement of a house being ripped apart by a tornado.

What makes MOSI worthwhile is *Kids in Charge*, its adjacent hands-on science center for children. Kids can explore physics, biology, and engineering first-hand in ways that will keep everybody entertained. This isn't a half-day attraction; two hours will be plenty. But it's a great place to get out of the heat or rain and see some neat things.

Lots of people go to Florida to retire, but the most interesting retirement community in the state is probably **Big Cat Rescue** *[12802 Easy St. Closed Sun. Adm.]*, where more than a hundred lions, tigers, leopards, and other big cats live out their lives in safety after retiring from circuses, zoos, and other exhibitions. Access is by guided tour only, at 9 a.m. and 3 p.m. (9:30, 11:30, and 1:30 on Saturday), and kids under age 10 are admitted only on separate 9 a.m. Saturday morning tours. The sanctuary is on the northwest side of the city, just south of Citrus Park Drive (Rte. 589). Tours are more than $20 per person, but Saturday kids' tours are about half that.

You'd expect a zoo and an aquarium in any respectable large Florida city, and Tampa won't disappoint. The **Lowry Park Zoo** *[1101 W Sligh Ave. Open daily. Adm.]* and the **Florida Aquarium** *[701 Channelside Dr. Open daily. Adm.]* have all the usual land and sea critters.

Museum goers have lots more choices, of course. The **Children's Museum of Tampa** *[7550 North Blvd. Open daily. Adm.]* turns corporate sponsorship into an art form, with play and simulation areas sponsored by McDonald's, Allstate, Verizon, ReMax, JPMorganChase, and much of the rest of the Fortune 500 list, it seems. But the sponsorships do help keep the admission price low.

You can also check out the **Tampa Museum of Art** *[600 N Ashley Dr. Closed M. Adm.]* along the river downtown; the **Henry B. Plant Museum** *[401 Kennedy Blvd. Closed M. Adm.]*, an opulent Victorian mansion; or the **Tampa Bay History Center** *[225 S Franklin St. Closed Sa-Su. Free.]* for a view of local life through the years.

## DESTINATION
## Clearwater

If you're in Florida to escape from big-city intensity, maybe even as laid-back an urban area as Tampa isn't for you. Fortunately, you have a lot of excellent choices, and one of the nicest is just a short drive from Tampa, making it an ideal place to establish a home base, yet remain close enough to sample the delights of Tampa whenever you want.

Clearwater is right on the Gulf, giving you miles of beach and endless numbers of gulf-view accommodations to try. This is a great place for scuba diving, fishing, parasailing, and other water sports, but I'll take you to a few other spots that assorted Lains ... and thousands of other people ... have enjoyed.

### Clearwater Beach & Pier
Clearwater Beach is across a short causeway from the mainland—a long stretch of beautiful white sand that just invites digging your toes into. The beach and pier are a short walk from the shopping and restaurants along Mandalay Avenue, and you can find an apparently limitless number of inexpensive places to stay along Coronado Drive south of the pier.

The 1,050-foot-long (320m) pier is the center of activities, though. During the day it's a fine place for walking or fishing. From the far end you get a wonderful view of the entire sweep of beach. But the place really comes alive after dark with the nightly **Sunsets at Pier 60** festival. Patterned after a similar festival in Key West, this is a certain good time for everyone in the family, with music, food, games, and craft vendors. My favorites are the street entertainers and it doesn't seem to matter where I go, whether having dinner at a sidewalk table in Paris or a beach in Clearwater, a juggler throwing flaming torches around always seems to turn up next to me.

But it's all great fun and I've yet to have my hat flambéd. It's bound to be safer than the beachside bungee slingshots the kids will flock to! There's even a great playground for small kids, with a slide that brings you right out through the mouth of a big shark.

> *Tip:*
>
> If you're in the area in the Fall when the stone crabs are in, have some! They're as sweet as honey and just not the same anyplace else. The first time we had them was in Clearwater Beach after we left the Sunset Festival one evening. They're best served cold with a creamy mustard-based sauce for dipping.

## Clearwater Marine Aquarium

Because there seem to be almost as many aquariums in Florida as there are McDonald's restaurants, most of which have generally the same sorts of things as the rest, I don't spend a lot of time describing them. There is always an exception.

The Clearwater Marine Aquarium doesn't even look like an aquarium. Instead of a modern, multistory, glass-fronted building with gleaming stainless-steel signs or a 40-foot-long (12m) neon marlin above the entrance, this looks more like an old wastewater treatment plant.

It is.

It's by far the neatest old wastewater treatment plant I've ever been in however (not that there have been a lot of them…), not because of the way it looks, but for what they do there. It's unlike any other aquarium I've ever visited. It's a rescue aquarium—a hospital, as its director calls it.

Life in the sea is dangerous. Great sea turtles get hit by motorboat propellers, paralyzing their hindquarters. Diseases decimate large populations of sea life. Animals become entangled in nets. This is where volunteers bring them to be cured, to have time to heal, or even to live out their lives in safety.

The star of the facility is probably the bottlenose dolphin Winter. Found tangled in a crab trap when she was just three

*The dolphins at the Clearwater Marine Aquarium love to chat with visitors*

months old, with tail fins so badly damaged by the cables that her tail fins were practically cut from her body and soon fell off. Winter would have quickly drowned or become prey except for the CMA, which has cared for her since, and which will fit her with a prosthetic tail when she's ready. She will never be released to the wild as is the goal for most of their animals, but Winter is happy, friendly, comfortable with humans—and spoiled rotten!

Lots of other dolphins are in and out. Our guide introduced is to several, including Nicholas and Indy, who spend most of their time roughhousing with each other in the tank. She just called them "the boys," and that fit, because they really did remind us of the after-dinner antics of our own boys.

The CMA is more that just dolphin encounters, though. You'll meet fish, river otters, and a number of large sea turtles, as well as smaller loggerheads and hawksbills. During the Red Tide infestation several years ago, the facility cared for more than 50 sea turtles.

The aquarium is at the first exit from the causeway after you leave the mainland. There's an admission fee, but less than half of what you'd pay at most of the glitzy aquariums. Don't begrudge the fee, and leave a little extra if you can. This is a special place, and they do good work here. *[249 Windward Passage, Clearwater. Open daily. Adm.]*

## Other Clearwater Area Attractions

If you're staying in this area, you'll certainly enjoy an afternoon in **Tarpon Springs**, just 15 miles (25km) or so north of Clearwater on Alt. U.S. 19. The town is known for two things. One is Greek food. The area was heavily settled by immigrants from Greece and the community retains a large measure of its authentic Greek heritage. You may pass the same men I did last time I was here, sitting over glasses of wine in a back booth in a restaurant, arguing quietly in Greek with much arm waving and finger pointing.

And if you love Greek food as much as I do, there's probably no better place in the country to come other than a few places in New York and Chicago. I've eaten very well here. Waiters chat and joke with the customers here in a very Mediterranean way.

The other attraction is sponges. This was and is the sponge capital of the country, and as you stroll the Sponge Docks along the Anclote River that leads to the Bay, you'll pass sponge boats with freshly arrived sponges hanging like bananas from every available space. The boats go out to the sponge beds, 8 miles (13km) and 160 feet (50m) down. There's little risk of depletion, though. They all grow back in just three years.

There's plenty of shopping here (and not just for sponges, although they're certainly plentiful), a rather tired-looking free sponge museum with a gift shop chock full of more types of sponges than you knew existed, and an aquarium, all along about a four-block stretch of Dodecanese Boulevard, the main street through the area.

In downtown Tarpon Springs, just a mile or so south of the docks, it's worth a brief stop to look at beautiful **St. Nicholas Greek Orthodox Cathedral** *[36 N Pinellas Ave, Tarpon Springs. Open daily. Free.]*. It's cool and dark on even the most sultry Florida day. Don't miss the tiny room off to the left of the entrance, filled with icons and votives.

For a taste of old-fashioned Florida tourism, **Weeki Wachee Springs** *[6131 Commercial Way, Weeki Wachee. Open daily. Adm.]* with its famous mermaid show, is less than 30 miles (50km) up U.S. 19 from Tarpon Springs. It includes a water park and all the usual theme park attractions, but the heart of the park is its famous mermaid show, which has been running for more than 60 years.

If a cruise is to your taste, you'll have no problems filling your heart's desire. Try **Captain Memo's Pirate Cruise** *[25 Causeway Blvd, Slip 3, Clearwater. Cruises daily. Adm.]* from Clearwater Beach. The 2-hour cruises cost about $25 for kids and about $10 more for adults, but are good fun aboard the captain's big red pirate ship. There are usually three sailings per day, including a sunset cruise. The **Sea Life Safari** *[Cruises daily. Adm.]* leaves up to three times daily from the Clearwater Marine Aquarium and picks up additional passengers from the Clearwater Beach marina (slip 58) 15 minutes later. This is more educational, as you'd expect from the CMA, and is the only cruise licensed to use a trawl net to bring up small sea life that the onboard marine biologist will talk about before releasing back to the sea.

# DESTINATION
## The Best of the Bay Area

The Bay area is so densely packed with things you'll want to do that you'll probably start planning your next trip here even before you finish this one. We're not finished yet. Some of my favorite places in this area are still to come.

## St. Petersburg

When two major cities are so close together, it's common for people to sort of mentally incorporate one into the other. One gets left out. People think about Minneapolis and forget St. Paul. Dallas, but not Fort Worth. San Francisco but not Oakland. That's St. Pete's fate, forever in Tampa's shadow.

It's too bad because there's some cool stuff in St. Pete and it deserves to be more than an afterthought. And so much of the best attractions are clustered together, making them easy to get to. Tampa should be so well organized!

Let's start in the heart of downtown.

Find someplace to park east of 4th Avenue near Williams Park in the center of downtown—it's easy, there are long-term meters and lots everywhere. Just about everything we're going to do here is going to be on or near 2nd Avenue North.

Once you park, it's easy to get around on the Looper, an inexpensive trolley that covers the entire downtown. It costs just 25 cents to ride and runs about every 15 minutes every day from 10 a.m. to 5 p.m. (midnight on Friday and Saturday).

Check out the current exhibition at the **Florida International Museum** *[244 2nd Ave N. Closed M. Adm.]*. They do just one exhibition at a time and sometimes they will offer something somebody in your family will be excited by, like Princess Diana's gowns, 45 years of Barbie dolls, baseball artifacts, recovered items from the Titanic, or pictures from the Hubble Space Telescope. At other times the show will be student metalwork or early American silver. If only part of your group is interested, this might be a place to split up, since some of the shows are relatively expensive.

Walk (or ride the trolley) east on 2nd Avenue. You'll pass the **St. Petersburg Museum of History** *[335 2nd Ave. Open daily. Adm.]* with a fine array of local historical exhibits and photographs. The **Museum of Fine Arts** *[255 Beach Dr NE. Closed M. Adm.]* is just beyond it.

The fun spot is at the end of 2nd Avenue, and the trolleys stop right in front of the entrance—the **St. Peters-burg Pier**. *[800 2nd Ave NE. Open daily. Free.]*

This is no rickety wooden fishing pier. At the end of the pier is a five-story inverted pyramid that is a complete shopping and entertainment complex. If you're hungry, there are several family-friendly sit-down restaur-ants, some with both air-conditioned indoor seating and patio tables overlooking Tampa Bay, as well as a food court with all the burgers, pizzas, and typical mall fare your kids can manage.

Shoppers can find cloth-ing and several specialty

> *Tip:*
>
> If you drive, there are inexpensive parking lots along 2nd Avenue near the pier. A free trolley shuttles visitors between the lots and the end of the pier.

shops here. And there's even a small, inexpensive aquarium right in the complex. My favorite thing to do, though, is just to sit on the patio overlooking the Bay and watch the people and the boats drift by. The building is wheelchair accessible and even has lifts into difficult places. If you want something more active, you can fish off an adjacent pier, or rent bicycles and do some exploring.

Just 1 mile north of all the attractions we've talked about on busy 2nd Avenue are two more places worth a visit. Just drive, walk, or bicycle straight up 4th Street. While the places are not associated with each other, they share a building and a parking lot.

The first is St. Pete's classy children's museum **Great Explorations** *[1925 4th St. N, St. Petersburg. Open daily. Adm.]*. Kids find a lot of cool things to do here, like building towers, machines, and race cars. When I visited, I couldn't stop playing with the device that lifted a bowling ball which dropped, creating compressed air that fired a tennis ball clear to the ceiling. There's a huge roomful of great experiments like that, plus play firefighter, veterinarian, and market areas, giant puppets, and much more. I think this is my favorite of the many children's museums in the state.

Right next door is a much more sedate experience. Florida has limitless numbers of tropical and botanic gardens, but this is one of the best and most manageable. The **Sunken Gardens** *[1825 4th St. N, St. Petersburg. Open daily. Adm.]* is a hundred-year-old, city-owned slice of paradise. The Garden of Eden must have looked like this. Paths meander through lush ancient palms in endless varieties, spectacular flowers, and ferns. Ten minutes into the garden and you start wondering if you might not spot a dinosaur around the next bend in the path. We never have, but we have spent the occasional fascinating, restorative hour here.

By the way, I don't want you to be confused. I said the previous two attractions share a building, yet the street address of one is 1825 and that of the other is 1925. That is correct. It makes no sense and it's not my fault. It's just the laid-back Florida way of doing things, I guess.

You might be tempted to visit the **Salvador Dali Museum** *[1000 3rd St. S, St. Petersburg. Open daily. Adm.]*. I've recommended Dali museums in Paris and London with enthusiasm. I'm less keen on this one, but it's a good place to see a selection of the surrealist's work, although there is less

*The Sunken Gardens in St. Pete have a primitive, primeval beauty.*

of his sculpture here than I expected. I found the exhibit on his influence on film greats like Hitchcock and the Marx Brothers to be the best part of the exhibition, as well as a selection of his own films. (Note: There is some nudity in his films, which are shown in a curtained-off gallery.)

## Gamble Plantation

For our next stop, let's get in the car and drive across the spectacular Sunshine Skyway, the world's longest cable-supported concrete bridge.

The first time we drove across this bridge, 5 miles (8km) long and almost 200 feet (60m) high, Barb kept her eyes closed. The boys and I thought it was fabulous. In the nearly 30 years since that first trip, Barb's gotten braver and takes in the extraordinary view now. But it's possible to avoid the bridge by taking I-75 east of the Bay.

That's pretty boring, though.

When you get to the other side, you're just minutes from one of the most interesting stops I've ever made, the **1844 Gamble Plantation.** *[3708 Patten Ave, Ellenton. Open daily. Free, but charge for tours.]*

You will see reminders of and references to the Civil War throughout the South, but here you have the rare opportunity to walk through an authentic pre-war plantation. Most places like this were either destroyed during the war or fell into ruin in the hard times that followed. Fortunately, this one was preserved, and family members lived on the estate until about a hundred years ago.

Most people nowadays think Southern plantations were like Tara in *Gone with the Wind*, but this is much more authentic. Of course there were enormous, elegant mansions in some places, just like there probably are today in your hometown. Most plantations were simpler—larger

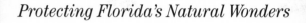

## Protecting Florida's Natural Wonders

One of the things I like about Florida is the number of places that seek to preserve the environment and to protect animals. I've talked about places like Big Cat Rescue, the Clearwater Marine Aquarium, and the Suncoast Seabird Sanctuary in this chapter, as well as numerous similar facilities elsewhere in the book, dedicated to rescuing or rehabilitating animals or environment.

It's a good lesson to talk about as part of your trip, and something to take note of as you visit places like the sponge beds, the Everglades, the Sunken Gardens, and the dozens of other specialized animal and nature preserves that fill the state. Will these animals or this environment be here for the next generation to enjoy the way you are?

Suggest that the kids gather information about the subject at every appropriate stop. They will be able to use it for reports in school next year, and be able to talk about it first-hand to their classes.

and more complex than an average farm—but not Margaret Mitchell's showplace, either.

At one time, this plantation covered 3,500 acres (1,400 hectares) and was worked by almost 200 slaves, although the estate's second owner, John Patten, was known for his fair treatment of blacks and native Americans.

You can wander around the grounds for free, but on the inexpensive guided tour you can go through the house (only the first floor is wheelchair accessible) with its period furniture and 1850 décor, and hear the fascinating stories of how a previous owner used the house to store manure, why house slaves were expected to whistle while they worked (so the master would know they weren't eating his food), and the fascinating story of Judah Benjamin. Benjamin, a one-time U.S. senator (only the second Jew to hold such a high office) was for a time the Confederate States' secretary of war. He hid out here after the Civil War, eventually escaping to England and becoming a highly prominent barrister.

*What could be more relaxing than a sunset along Clearwater Beach?*

The rangers and volunteer guides are master storytellers and make the place come alive for visitors.

### Other Bay Area Attractions

Like pretty much everywhere else in Florida, you really can't go wrong with the beaches here. *Treasure Island*, part of St. Pete, has a justly popular wide, wide beach, although otherwise it's an endless string of motels. It lacks the pure white sand of places like Clearwater, a few miles up the coast, but look closely—it's mostly shells, crushed to powder by eons of pounding surf. Mobility-impaired visitors can get free use of one of the big-wheeled beach wheelchairs you sometimes see.

There are motels, condos, and rental apartments everywhere along the coast. We've stayed in *Indian Rocks Beach*, but it's hard to go very far wrong if you're on the water. One reason we liked it was because it was close to the **Suncoast Seabird Sanctuary** *[18328 Gulf Blvd, Indian Shores. Open daily. Free.]*, another great animal rescue facility, which cares for sick and injured wild birds, healing and releasing them whenever possible.

One of the best beaches and most beautiful views is at **Fort De Soto Park** *[3500 Pinellas Bayway S, Tierra Verde. Open daily. Free.]*, at the tip of the peninsula just south of St. Pete. This is a great place to spend a day away from some of the crowded roads lined with motels and fast food places.

Yes, the area can be crowded and touristy in some places. But the Bay area offers so many unique attractions, gorgeous beaches, and memorable experiences that it's easy to see why so many people want to go there.

## *Recommendations*

∞ Enjoy beach life at sunset, whether it's at a festival like Clearwater's, or on a quiet, secluded stretch of sand. Florida is never more beautiful. Take photos!

∞ If you visit only one aquarium in Florida, make it the rescue aquarium in Clearwater. It's not fancy, but it's memorable.

∞ Even if you're enjoying a beach holiday, get into one of the cities for an afternoon, especially Tampa's Ybor City or to the attractions in downtown St. Petersburg.

# 13
# Southwest Florida

MOST OF THE PLACES IN THE PREVIOUS CHAPTER WERE, TO ONE extent or another, dominated by Tampa. There's nothing wrong with big cities—I've lived near a big one (not now, though; Dayton, Ohio, doesn't really qualify), spent weeks at a time in another one, have kids in another, written books about several, and always have a good time in a sprawling metropolis. Sometimes, though, I want to have my fun a little less surrounded by crowds.

That's why, after reveling in the pleasures of the Tampa-St. Pete area, I'm ready to drive down the coast where things are a little quieter.

You might not think so at the height of the mid-winter tourist season, when the roads and restaurants are crowded with Ohioans from just down my street, as well as with Canadians, New Englanders, Wisconsinites, and natives of just about anywhere that gets Toyota-sized piles of snow. Busy highways notwithstanding, it's still possible to find a quiet, sunny stretch of beach where you can bake yourself to a nice medium-well while reading about the arctic temperatures just a two-hour flight away. But only the most mean-spirited of people send postcards back to their shivering friends telling them how lovely the weather is.

Come to think of it, I do that sometimes.

So follow your iniquitous author to some of the places down the Gulf Coast that are worth sending postcards home about, and that, except at season's height, can provide you with a little more elbow room.

## Getting Around

Drivers have no particularly scenic highways to follow easily along the Gulf Coast, the way travelers down the Atlantic side do in A1A. Interstate 75 is a thoroughly generic highway, and U.S. 41 will more often take drivers through the cities rather than along the beach. Both have occasional picturesque stretches, and sometimes you'll find adjacent streets like McGregor Boulevard in Fort Myers that are stunningly beautiful. Most of the time, though, the roads down here are just a way to get from wherever you are to wherever you want to be, rather than destinations in themselves.

Like most places in Florida, it's easy to fly into this area. Sarasota-Bradenton International (SRQ) is at the north end of our chapter, Fort Myers-Southwest International (RSW) is in the middle, and even little Naples Municipal Airport (APF) at the south end offers a handful of commercial flights a day (although they tend to be rather expensive compared to other places). You can also check prices into Tampa (TPA), about 50 miles north of Sarasota.

Unless you take the train into Tampa, rail travel is not so good. Amtrak stops in Sebring, about 90 miles (145 km) east of Sarasota, and passenger rail gets even farther away as you go south. There's no other really useful public transportation from city to city along the Gulf Coast, so you're limited to your own car if you drive, or a rental if you fly in.

This area has several places that are too good to miss, though, so let's start at the top and work our way south. I've got some real treats for your family at every stop.

## DESTINATION
### Sarasota

One of the advantages of writing travel books is that I have an excuse to visit an awful lot of really cool places and try out new destinations. A disadvantage, though, is that I often find it difficult to get back for another visit to places I really like, because I'm busy working on a book about a new destination. So I was pleased when Interlink decided it wanted a Florida book for the *Family Travel Series*, because I knew I'd have a perfect excuse to go back to Sarasota, and one of my favorite attractions anywhere. That will be the first stop in this chapter.

### The Ringling Estate
In a lot of ways (in too many ways, some friends might say), I'm still just a big kid. When I read the newspaper I turn to the comics first, I'd rather eat ice cream than chateaubriand, and I absolutely love circuses. If you or any of your fellow travelers likes circuses, too, *this* might be the highlight of

the trip: the home of the man who built what was justifiably called The Greatest Show On Earth.

In 1884, five of the six Ringling brothers from Iowa started their own small circus, rather than go into their father's harness-making business. John was the financial brain of the partnership, and they made money hand over fist. The Ringlings ran a different sort of company, allowing no con men or short-change artists to work for them, and by 1907 had bought out all their major competitors, including the famous Barnum & Bailey circus. Today, the Ringling Brothers Barnum & Bailey Circus is still the gold standard of the entertainment world. In 1909, John built a winter home in Sarasota, which grew into the spectacular 66-acre (27-hectare) estate we're visiting in this chapter.

The estate includes three of the most fabulous spectacles in Florida, and a single ticket, priced at about half of what I expected (and students are much less!), includes admission to all three. Spending half a day here won't be too long, and it's easy to spend much more.

You'll enter through the Visitors Pavilion. Do spend five minutes and watch the short film that introduces you to the estate; it's shorter and more useful than most of its kind.

Now I'll walk you quickly through the place, and I'm going to start with my own favorite part of it, the **Circus Museum**. Go straight ahead as you leave the Pavilion. The Circus Museum is in two buildings on your right just a short stroll away.

> *Tip:*
>
> If it's a hot day, you have little ones, or just want to get off your feet for a few minutes, take the trams that run continuously around the grounds. They're free and convenient.

I prefer to start in the Circus Museum building itself, the further one from the Pavilion. You won't find actual performances here, but the building is jam-packed with costumes, props, wagons, posters, clown gear, and explanations of everything you can imagine. You can watch wood carvers at work, making the meticulously detailed and realistically painted props you see at the shows. There's even a play and activity area for younger kids. I could spend my day here—but if I did, I'd miss something even neater.

The building next door is the Tibbals Learning Center, and it contains the most amazing attraction of all—the

*The terrace of the Ringling mansion in Sarasota looks out over the Gulf*

Howard Brothers Miniature Circus. Covering almost 4,000 square feet (370 sq meters), this is an unbelievably detailed scale-model replica of the 1938 Ringling Brothers circus, with each of its more than 35,000 pieces carved by master woodworker Howard Tibbals. The precision is amazing, from the miniscule spangles on performers' costumes to the tiny tent stakes anchoring the big top to the little knives and forks in the mess tent. It is a work of art on a grand scale and Mr. Tibbals, who has a workshop right in the building, keeps adding to it.

But I've got to move on before I begin to rave.

If circus is a little too pop culture-ish for you, our next stop, straight across the estate, is about as high culture as you can get. The lovely coral-colored **Museum of Art** is one of the finest of its kind in Florida. It now belongs to the state of Florida, and the building is a work of art in itself, two parallel wings of galleries with a stunningly beautiful loggia and courtyard between them.

The pride of the museum's collection is its array of Old Masters. Start with the North Galleries and you're immediately swept away by the most wonderful assortment of Rubens' works. As you wander through the museum, each room is more splendid than the last, and you don't need a guided tour to appreciate it, although everyone who works there will happily talk about their favorite pieces. That includes one guard we stopped to chat with, who led us to a painting of a church interior that made the most amazing use of light and shadow. We thought his opinion was worth listening to: He had moved to the area just a couple of years before from the place he'd spent his entire life—about three miles from our house in Dayton!

There's more than just paintings. Even kids will be awed by the sculpture, the silver, the enormous tapestries, the building itself.

You want more for your admission ticket? Sure, we can do that. How about a tour of John and Mable Ringling's house **Cà d'Zan**. (It means, appropriately enough, "House of John" and is pronounced *Kah-duh-Zahn*.) I could learn to live like this.

To begin with, the house itself is a work of art, partly modeled after Mable's favorite hotels in Venice. Tours of the downstairs portion of the house are free, but you can wander about on your own, if you like. They also offer a fairly expensive tour of the private quarters upstairs and the 60-foot-high (18m) tower. It costs more than admission to the entire estate, so most people pass, but it's available if you want it.

I don't think I could stand any more opulence than you get on the standard tour anyway. The whole place is magnificent—the plush carpets, the colored marble tiles, the crystal chandeliers, high ceilings, lush furniture, and the line of thrones (it seems fitting) for family members. You'll only see a few of the 32 rooms (and fifteen bathrooms! Who needs fifteen bathrooms?), then walk out onto the expansive terrace overlooking the Gulf. John's yacht and Mable's gondola used to dock right here. How convenient for them! What a place. There are a couple of restaurants on the grounds, an education center, and the Historic Asolo Theater, built in Venice in 1798 and moved here in the 1950s.

As you'd expect, the grounds are something special here, too. You'll discover a variety of formal gardens on the estate (Mable's Rose Garden is my favorite), a fabulous banyan tree, and the Dwarf Garden, ringed with little statues of dwarves that are variously cute and grotesque. You'll never want to leave the estate. And you won't have to—until the grounds close at 6 p.m. *[5401 Bay Shore Rd, Sarasota. Open daily. Adm.]*

### Other Sarasota Attractions

Right across the street from the entrance to the Ringling Estate is history and design of a very different sort, the **Classic Car Museum** *[5500 N. Tamiami Tr, Sarasota. Open daily. Adm.]*. In fact, if you want to pair it with a visit across the street, it opens at 9 a.m. daily, an hour before Ringling, and stays open until 6, an hour after the Ringling buildings close. Even visitors who don't know a steering wheel from a hub cap will enjoy a stop here. The collection of about 100 automobiles includes historic and rare cars of all sorts.

Are you a pop music fan? Paul McCartney's Mini Cooper and John Lennon's Mercedes are here. So is President Franklin Roosevelt's limo. They have cars so tiny you wonder how the driver folds himself in; cars so large they could host a football game. I even found an old Studebaker just like my first car. Our guide (who, it turned out, had lived not far from me when I was growing up in Crown Point, Indiana!) pointed out dozens of unusual cars and knew the history of every car and every company represented in the museum. They even have a working collection of old arcade games visitors can play.

Like just about every other city and village in Florida, Sarasota has an aquarium, but the **Mote Marine Aquarium** *[1600 Ken Thompson Pkwy, Sarasota. Open daily. Adm.]* is a cut above most, because it's also a major research facility founded by shark expert Dr. Eugenie Clark. Take the causeway out to Lido Key and follow Rt. 789 north toward Longboat Key; the aquarium is just before you cross over to Longboat. Not surprisingly, the emphasis here is on sharks, but there's much more, including a touch pool for kids who seldom have a chance to handle living sea creatures.

The **Sarasota Jungle Gardens** *[3701 Bay Shore Rd, Sarasota. Open daily. Adm.]* has been a fixture here since the 1930s and offers the same sort of lush tropical flora and native birds and reptiles as similar parks.

# DESTINATION
# Fort Myers

Once you've had enough of Sarasota, if that's possible, your next move might be a move farther south.

It's an easy 75-mile (120km) drive to Fort Myers along either I-75 or U.S. 41. I'm more likely to use the latter, because I hate interstates, and other highways provide more opportunities for diversion.

Besides, the best attraction in Fort Myers is close to Route 41. As soon as you get into the city look for the side-by-side homes of two of the most famous of all Americans: Thomas Edison and Henry Ford.

## The Edison and Ford Winter Homes

It was no accident that two of the greatest geniuses in all of American history ended up as next-door neighbors. Thomas Edison, the world's foremost inventor, began wintering here in 1886 when most of the area was wilderness. It was a welcome change from the bustle of his New Jersey lab and the warm winters were good for his health. He built laboratories down here, too, where he could continue his work with fewer distractions.

Henry Ford was 16 years younger than Thomas Edison, and regarded the older man with something akin to hero-worship. Ford claimed that Edison was the first person to encourage his own creative work on a gas-powered automobile, and Ford considered Edison a mentor and father figure. When it came up for sale in 1916, Ford bought the property next door to Edison's home in Fort Myers, where they wintered together until Edison died in 1931. After Edison's death, Ford never returned to his own winter home.

It's interesting to take a tour of the houses, properties, and gardens. Edison electrified the entire complex 25 years before the nearby city had electricity. But the best part of the tour is a chance to see Edison's laboratory, the place where many of Edison's 1,093 patents were born. (He had, in fact, at least one patent a year for 65 straight years!) His cot is here, where he took cat-naps to refresh his brain as he worked around the clock. Most of the work done here was botanical; Edison was trying to develop a domestic source for rubber.

The adjacent museum is a tribute to the innovative minds of these men, filled with their inventions and adaptations of technology, from Ford's automobiles to Edison's movie projectors, infant furniture, rubber plants, turbines, and phonographs (including one with Edison's teeth marks in it: he was so deaf he would sometimes bite his gramophone so he could feel the vibrations and "hear" the music).

And you can't miss the majestic banyan tree, the largest in the country. It's hard to believe that when Edison planted it in 1925 it was just 4 feet tall and 2 inches in diameter (1.2m and 5cm).

*A statue of Thomas Edison stands amid the roots of a single banyan tree, largest in America*

## The Majestic Banyan Tree

We had to have an old hickory tree in our front yard cut down not long ago, and spent quite a bit of time deciding how to replace it.

If we lived in Florida, it would have been easy: I'd want a banyan tree.

What a specimen this is! The banyan (which is a sort of fig tree) actually drops roots from its branches and when they grow down to the ground, they take root there and thicken into what look like additional trunks. One spreading banyan tree can produce hundreds of these tendrils, creating what is practically its own tiny forest.

The tree is native to India. Thomas Edison planted the first banyan tree in America, a gift from his friend Harvey Firestone, and if you see it on his Fort Myers estate, you'll never forget it. It had, last time we were there, more than 320 roots, and the number increases each year. The tree and its roots measure more than 400 feet (122m) in circumference and cover a full acre. Only the giant sequoias of California can rival this tree for magnificence, I think.

Edison was a man of technology, but you can't help but notice as you leave the estate and head toward our next destination that he was a man of aesthetic genius as well. Take McGregor Boulevard south. This marvelous 14-mile (22.5km) drive between rows of almost 2,000 towering Royal Palms was Edison's idea, too. It is one of the most beautiful city drives in the country. *[2350 McGregor Blvd, Ft. Myers. Open daily. Adm.]*

### Sanibel Island

The old tongue-twister *She sells sea shells by the sea shore* doesn't specify who the "she" is, but if she had a good stock of shells, the unidentified Miss must have been working on Sanibel Island, just south of Fort Myers.

## A Breathtaking Exhibit

Without any possible doubt, the most unusual museum exhibit I've even seen involves Thomas Edison and Henry Ford. Unfortunately, it's not here in Fort Myers, but 1,300 miles (2100km) north, in Dearborn, Michigan.

How much regard did Henry Ford have for Thomas Edison? So much that when it was clear that Edison was near death in October 1931, Ford asked Edison's son to capture Edison's last breath in a test tube, then seal it at once.

If your next family vacation takes you to the Detroit area, be sure to visit the Henry Ford Museum in Dearborn, where you can see the test tube. It looks empty, but still—reputedly—contains Edison's last breath.

In fact the island is packed with shell shops, but it's hard to see why anybody would buy anything in them—the island includes some of the best shelling territory in Florida because of the angle it presents to the tides.

The beach here runs on and on, and is busy with shellers, visitors and locals alike, every time the tide goes out, all doing what's called the Sanibel Stoop as they comb the sands for especially beautiful specimens. And they find them. My mother, never an early riser, used to get up early on visits here, just to beat the competition to the beach, and her home in Indiana is filled with hundreds of shells.

My favorite time of day is the evening, though, as things get dark and quiet, waiting for the old 1884 lighthouse to light up. The island has only been significantly settled since the late 19th century, and the causeway to the mainland wasn't built until 1963, so the island hasn't had as much opportunity to be overrun with development as some other places in Florida.

In fact, it's easy to get around the island. The main east-west road is Periwinkle Way, which jogs right and becomes Sanibel-Captiva Road and runs the entire length of the island. Gulf Drive runs across the lower portion of the island near the shore, and aside from the side streets where people live, that's about it.

This isn't the place to go for fancy hotels and miles of designer stores. The shops on the island run more to crafts,

Sunset over the beach on Sanibel Island
© Photographer: Maunger/Dreamstime.com

jewelry, and, yes, shells. Accommodations are mostly small motels, inns, and cottages, and restaurants are usually quiet spots run by locals, rather than national burger chains. Life is slower paced here. If you tire of the beach, you can visit the "Ding" Darling **National Wildlife Refuge and Bird Sanctuary** *[1Wildlife Dr, Sanibel. Closed F. Adm.].* **The Bailey-Matthews Shell Museum** *[3075 Sanibel-Captiva Rd, Sanibel. Open daily. Adm.]* is the place to find some of the most unusual and dazzling shells you can imagine. You can rent a bike or a boat, or visit the **Sanibel Historic Village** *[950 Dunlop Road, Sanibel, Closed Sept-Oct., Open W-Sat, Adm.]* to see how early residents lived.

Oh, and after you've collected a bushel or so of shells, remember to re-read the Chapter 6 sidebar on how to clean them.

### Other Fort Myers Area Attractions

Want more? No problem. How about an eco-tour to see manatees at **Manatee World** *[5605 Palm Beach Blvd, Ft. Myers. Open daily in winter. Adm.]* about six miles east of the city on State Rte 80. The tours are available in the winter months only, because the area is popular with the animals who come here to stay warm. Tour hours are irregular, so phone (239) 694-4042 first.

Kids might like the **Imaginarium** *[2000 Cranford Ave, Ft. Myers. Open daily. Adm.],* another good children's museum, or the **Southwest Florida Museum of History** *[2300 Peck St, Ft. Myers. Closed M. Adm.],* with old railroad cars, fire trucks, and Native American artifacts. And of course there are the beaches and water sports of Gasparilla Island north of Sanibel.

## DESTINATION
## The Best of the Southwest

If you want to cover the area south of Fort Myers thoroughly, you'll have to retire to Florida like millions of other devotees have. If you're still too young for that, you'll just have to pick and choose what you're going to do on this trip, then try something else next time. At that rate, you'll be able to manage all the things worth seeing and doing in this part of the state by the time you're 250 years old—if they haven't added anything else in the meantime.

But let's hopscotch our way down the coast and look at some of the stops you might want to make along the way.

## Koreshan State Historic Site

I always feel a bit smug when somebody who knows a place well says "Tell me about something I don't know about," and I can. That happened while I was working on this chapter. A friend who is also a travel agent goes to this part of Florida regularly and I was able to introduce her to this most unusual park.

I try never to travel with too inflexible an agenda, so when I saw a sign for this place just south of Fort Myers on U.S. 41, I turned aside to check it out, figuring it would just be one of those big bronze highway markers. I got quite a surprise. This is a pleasant state park with camping and fishing, but built around what was a late 19th and early 20th century Utopian community.

Its founder, Dr. Cyrus Teed, started a religion in New York in 1869, gathered a group of followers, mostly from Chicago, and moved here in 1894 to found the New Jerusalem. He preached that the earth was hollow and that everyone lived inside the planet. He claimed to have received an "illumination" from a deity who told Teed he was immortal and that he should form his new religion. He changed his name to *Koresh*, Hebrew for Cyrus.

Teed's supporters were no wild-eyed loonies. Many were well educated and some were teachers, musicians, and college professors. They were mostly women. His band of followers went to Florida where they planned for a community of 10 million adherents. They topped out at 250, but their dormitories and community buildings can be toured today. For awhile the community was a vibrant one and their bread was locally famous. Edison and Ford sometimes attended performances by their orchestra or of the plays they presented.

But Teed died in 1908, evidently not immortal after all and, predictably, this dampened enthusiasm for the movement. Some members of the community continued to live here until the death of Teed's last follower in 1982. The land and buildings were left to the state of Florida to be preserved in Teed's memory. *[Corkscrew Rd, Estero. Open daily. Adm.]*

## Naples

There's nothing about Naples you won't like—except the price of property if you decide to move there. The beach is absolutely gorgeous, the shopping area is postcard pretty, fine restaurants abound, seabirds walk right up to you and sit down for a chat, and locals and visitors alike seem to be some of the friendliest people in Florida.

Naples has the **Naples Zoo at Caribbean Gardens** *[1590 Goodlette Rd. Open daily. Adm.]* and the **Aviary and Zoo of Naples** *[9824 Immokalee Rd. Open daily. Adm.]*, but shopping and sunning are the big draws here. From the white sand beaches, to the elegant upscale boutiques of 5th Avenue South, to the craft shops in Tin City (an old fishing wharf), it's a great place to stay, or to make a day trip from Fort Myers, less than 40 miles (64km) north. If you're based in Naples, it's also a great starting point for trips to the Everglades and Lake Okeechobee.

## *Recommendations*

∽ Visit one of the great historic homes in this part of the state—Ringling's to be awestruck, or Edison's to learn more about this authentic genius.

∽ Keep your eyes open for the unusual. Maybe the Koreshan site isn't your cup of tea, but you'll find other surprises.

∽ Shells from Sanibel Island make great souvenirs, lovely gifts, and they're free.

# 14
# The Rest of Florida

Fill in your own accusation.

I plead guilty.

It's just not right to lump all the other wonderful things in Florida together under a generic title like *The Rest of Florida.* Yet, here it is. In this chapter I'm going to talk about several places that really deserve entire chapters—if not whole books—that you can see in Florida. I have a number of reasons for doing this

Chapters 8 through 13 cover the most densely populated and most densely visited parts of Florida—the places most families gravitate to. I've highlighted cities that make a good base of operations and described great things to see and do near each. If you're staying along the beach in Indian Shores, for example, you're within an easy drive of Bush Gardens, Ybor City, or the Ringling Estate. If your condo is in Daytona, an hour's drive will take you to the wonderful past of St. Augustine or the wonderful future of Kennedy Space Center.

The cities themselves offer broad opportunities for sightseeing and recreation—museums, zoos, sports, restaurants, and all the other things that make urban life so exciting—but all are also part of firmly established tourist corridors that multiply the possibilities, rather than just add to them.

For the most part, the places we'll visit in this chapter are destinations in themselves. While a lot of visitors cover the whole Bay Area, for example, not many people tour the entire Panhandle. They're more likely to unroll a beach blanket in Panama City or Pensacola and just nibble at the other attractions in the immediate area; they're less likely to just wander along the coast. Visit Key West, of course, and you're hours from anywhere else.

These are places worth visiting. There is nowhere else in the country remotely like Key West, or like the Everglades. The Panhandle offers some of the state's least crowded beaches, but are the ones most accessible to northerners driving down: Clearwater is more than a 350-mile (560km) drive south of Panama City; Daytona Beach is almost 450 miles (725km) from Pensacola.

So up to now, the focus of this part of the book has been on marvelous places that are quite close to other marvelous places. I just can't leave out some of the other parts of Florida you might want to visit, though, or at least tell you what you're passing through on your way to somewhere else. It's a reasonable compromise for books that are the size, detail, usefulness—and price!—I want the ones in this series to be.

Now let's meander down the state together and stop off at some more special places.

## DESTINATION
## The Panhandle

I suppose it's some comfort to me to note that I'm not the only unfair person when it comes to dealing with the Panhandle. At least one major rental car company ignores this part of the state altogether on the free state maps it provides at other airports in the state. Certainly the Panhandle is not what most visitors, or even most Floridians, think of as Florida.

No wonder! Pensacola, at the western end of the Panhandle, is closer to Louisville, Kentucky, than it is to Miami, at least if you stick to the roads. I've been in Miami, and I've been in Louisville, and they're not even remotely similar.

Visitors come to the Panhandle from places like Louisville to get away from the winter ice and snow, to splash in the warm waters of the Gulf, and to slow the pace of life a bit with some quality beach time. While there certainly are things to see, it's not sightseeing that brings the visitors, it's the warm breezes and salt spray of the shore.

The Panhandle isn't necessarily a balmy midwinter destination, mind you. It will get you away from the ice and snow, but if you want to get some color on the beach, you're almost as likely to turn blue as brown. The average January high temperature in Panama City is just 62 degrees (17C), and the average low is 39 (4C). That's an awful lot better than what I'm watching from my window today, where the Ohio snow is still above my shoe tops, but it falls well short of Miami in the winter. But I'd go today in a heartbeat if I could.

## Getting There

It's easy to get to the Panhandle. Visitors driving from the east down I-75 or I-95 will have to take I-10 west to get here, but Midwesterners who come down I-65 need only a brief detour on U.S. 29 just before they get to Mobile, Alabama, to find themselves in Pensacola.

There is good airline service into Pensacola Regional Airport (PNS) at the west end of the Panhandle, Panama City-Bay County International (PFN) in the middle, and Tallahassee Regional Airport (TLH) at the east end.

Amtrak used to run a train between Jacksonville and Pensacola three days a week. That was discontinued in the wake of Hurricane Katrina in 2005, and Amtrak has not yet determined when or if service will be restored, so here, as in most of the country, if you want to travel by train, you're out of luck.

## Where to Stay

If you're visiting the Panhandle, you're almost certainly looking for someplace near the Gulf. *Pensacola* is at the western edge of the state, and is known for its beautiful beaches, especially along Perdido Key, just southwest of the city. Route 399 takes you across the causeway south of the city and along Via de Luna Drive, with many places to stay on Santa Rosa Island.

After passing through Gulf Islands National Seashore, you'll be routed back to U.S. 98 on the mainland, and, about 40 miles (64km) from Pensacola, you will soon be in *Fort Walton Beach*, another great place to set up shop. U.S. 98 skirts the southern edge of Elgin Air Force Base, so things here are rather busy, but that also means there's plenty to see and do.

The next major destination along the highway is *Panama City*, about 60 miles (96km) further along the coast. On some sections of this drive, routes 2378 and 30A, which overlap or run parallel to U.S. 98, are the roads along the shore. U.S. 98 runs along the shore through Panama City; south of the city, 98 veers east again, but the better choice is the longer route, 30A, which stays close to the water. When you come to the end of the land, 7 miles (11km) from where the roads diverge, you can turn right on 30E and head for the peninsula that juts into St. Joseph Bay (There's a beautiful state park at the tip), or turn left and continue on 30A toward *Apalachicola* and St. George Island.

© *Photographer: Jennifer Boyd/Dreamstime.com*

You'll have rejoined U.S. 98 by the time you get to Apalachicola, and can follow it all the way to *Tallahassee*, the state capital, if you want, about 80 miles (130km).

## Sites and Attractions

You'll find two important military installations in the *Pensacola* area. The Pensacola Naval Air Station is just southwest of the city, and Elgin Air Force Base is just a few miles east, near Fort Walton Beach. The biggest attraction is the **National Museum of Naval Aviation** *[1750 Radford Blvd, Pensacola. Open daily. Free]*, with over a hundred Navy, Coast Guard, and Marine Corps aircraft on display. Enter the base through the west gate, at the end of Blue Angel Parkway (Route 173) and follow the signs. It's a beautiful facility, but I'm spoiled on that sort of thing since I live just 10 minutes away from the much larger National Museum of the Air Force, which is the world's largest military aviation museum.

A much smaller, privately owned museum shows a different side of conflict. The **Civil War Soldiers Museum** *[108 S Palafox St, Pensacola. Closed Su-M. Adm]* is a block south of U.S. 98 downtown. The museum was begun with the personal collection of a local physician, so its emphasis on medical care and equipment during the war isn't surprising. More history is available just a few blocks southeast at **Historic Pensacola Village** *[205 E Zaragoza St, Pensacola. Closed Su. Adm]*, twenty historic buildings packed with artifacts of centuries past.

There's the pleasant **Zoo** *[5701 Gulf Breeze Pkwy, Pensacola. Open daily. Adm]* southeast of the city, not far from the historic **Pensacola Lighthouse** *[2081 Radford Blvd, Pensacola. Tours Su 12-4, May-Oct.]*.

In *Fort Walton Beach*, try the **Emerald Coast Science Center** *[139 Brooks St. Open daily. Adm]* for giant bubbles and other kid-fascinating exhibits, or **Florida's Gulfarium** *[1010 Miracle Strip Pkwy. Open daily. Adm]* with dolphin and sea lion shows, plus penguins, otters, and more.

If your destination is *Panama City*, look in at its aquarium (You're in Florida. *Everybody's* got an aquarium!) **Gulf World Marine Park** *[15412 Front Beach Road. Open daily. Adm]* with all the standard attractions. For more fur than fins, try **ZooWorld** *[9008 Front Beach Road. Open daily. Adm]*.

There is no specific big-name attraction I can send you to in *Apalachicola*, but if you're staying there, or on nearby *St. George Island* (one of the prettiest in the state), you'll enjoy walking around this historic town. This laid-back village has a population now of less than 2,500, but it was once one of the largest ports on the Gulf of Mexico, and contains scores of historic homes and buildings and beautiful walks.

*Tallahassee* is the state capital, so naturally has a variety of historical and cultural attractions including the **Capitol Building** *[S Dubal St. Closed Sa-Su. Free]*, the **Old Capitol Museum** *[Monroe St at Apalachee Pkwy. Open daily. Free]* and the **Museum of Florida History** *[500 S Bronough St. Open daily. Free]*. Other popular attractions include the **Riley Museum of African American History & Culture** *[419 E Jefferson St. Closed Sa-Su. Adm]*, and the **Mary Brogan Museum of Art and Science** *[350 S Duval St. Open daily. Adm]*. Maybe the coolest is the **Tallahassee Antique Car Museum** *[3550-A Mahan Dr. Open daily. Adm]* with Abraham Lincoln's horse-drawn hearse, dozens of classic cars, and large quantities of sports artifacts, old toys, bicycles, and much more.

# DESTINATION
## Central Florida

Contrary to popular belief, central Florida really does consist of more than just Orlando surrounded by endless, uninhabited swampland. In fact, when I was a kid my parents considered moving to central Florida—Sebring, I think—for reasons I don't remember. Maybe they were planning to leave me behind and that's why I didn't get many details.

Except for Orlando, inland Florida, as far from the ocean as you can get (which isn't really all that far), is the closest thing you can get to what Florida was like before the tourist boom. Towns are smaller, a little sleepier, and a little quieter. If you stay off the interstate highways and roam through the state on U.S. 27 or 441, you'll see glimpses of the Florida my grandparents knew.

The kids won't be interested in that, of course. Bucolic hideaways hold no attraction for them. That's okay. If you're driving through this part of the state, there are several places worth a stop.

### Getting There

Because Florida is so narrow, almost every major airport in the state, except those in the Panhandle, is within an hour or so of the central part of the state, and Amtrak runs more than a hundred miles through the east-central section of the state from north of Orlando to Okeechobee before returning to the Atlantic coast.

Driving is the way to go, of course, as it is almost everywhere else. U.S. highways 27 and 441 run through the heart of the state until they reach the Everglades and veer east.

### Where to Stay

You can find more places to stay in the Orlando area, of course, than in some entire states. (I think that's an exaggeration—but it might be closer to the truth than you think.) But aside from that, where you stay will depend on what attractions you're visiting. *Gainesville* is home of the University of Florida, and *Ocala* is convenient to many fine parks and recreation areas in north-central Florida.

If you're looking for a theme-park experience but are trying to avoid the crowds of Orlando, you might drive 50 miles (80km) south to *Winter Haven* to visit Cypress Gardens. Auto racing fans converge on *Sebring*, one of

America's premier sports-car racing sites, and *Okeechobee* is a wonderful gateway to the Everglades.

## Sites and Attractions

Whatever the other attractions of a major university might be, most Gainesville visitors are in town for UF football. But before the tailgate party, you might stop for awhile on the other end of campus at the **Florida Museum of Natural History** *[sw 34th St and Hull Rd, Gainesville. Open daily. Free but donation requested]* for its fossil garden, prehistoric skeletons, and butterfly rainforest.

An hour's drive southwest of Orlando is Polk City, home to another nice aviation museum, **Fantasy of Flight** *[1400 Broadway Blvd SE, Polk City. Open daily. Adm]*. This is pricey, but is a chance for aviation aficionados to see the restoration of historic aircraft, try a hang glider simulator, and check out old military war planes.

In nearby Winter Haven is one of the oldest of all theme parks, **Cypress Gardens** *[6000 Cypress Gardens Blvd, Winter Haven. Open daily. Adm]*. Once a large swamp, it was turned into a beautiful 35-acre tropical garden in the 1930s. It has added attractions steadily over the years, and now the gardens are almost an afterthought. Visitors can take advantage of more than 40 rides from heart-stopping roller coasters to cute kiddy rides, from eight shows, a large shopping area, and all the other activities that come with places like this. As always, prices are high, from about $45 for anyone over age 10. (Younger kids and seniors get small discounts.) But tickets are good for two days in a one-week period.

Auto racing fans often think that all roads lead to Daytona (Chapter 8), but if you follow that road 140 miles (225km) further, you'll get to **Sebring International Raceway** *[113 Midway Dr, Sebring. Open daily. Adm for races]*. This is a home of Grand Prix racing in the United States, and its signature event, the grueling Twelve Hours of Sebring endurance race, has been held here since 1952.

# DESTINATION
## South Florida

## The Everglades

In Chapter 9 we took a trip through this unique wetland from Boca Raton. Let me say this again, as clearly as I can: If you're vacationing in Florida anywhere from Fort Meyers or West Palm Beach south, you positively must visit the Everglades. There's nothing else like it on the planet you live on. Yes, the weather might be hot and sticky. Yes, you might be set on by mosquitoes the size of pigeons. But you really won't notice those things, because you'll be fascinated by the endless swamp, filled with more alligators than you can count, by the symphony of bird calls, by the lush foliage, by the complete absence of any sign of human beings. It's like something out of a science fiction novel.

*Swamp in the Everglades © Matej Krajcovic/Dreamstime.com*

Florida's wetlands really begin in a big way at Lake Okeechobee, one of the largest freshwater lakes in the United States. In fact, of lakes entirely within the country, only Lake Michigan is larger. You'll never see the kinds of ships and barges here that you will on the Great Lakes, though. Lake Okeechobee is very shallow, averaging only 9 feet (2.8m) deep.

If it's no good for shipping, though, it's wonderful for fishing, boating, hiking, and camping. The lake is ringed by a number of small towns where you can find accommodation, restaurants, and lake access. Okeechobee on the north side and Clewiston on the south side—both towns of about 6,000—have the most amenities.

But the 'glades seem to go on forever once you get south of the lake. You can drive through the heart of the area on I-75 ("Alligator Alley") from Naples to Fort Lauderdale, or on U.S. 41 ("Tamiami Trail") from Naples to Miami. The latter choice is the better one, since it's more picturesque and has several places to stop, including the **Miccosukee Indian Village** *[Mile Marker 70, U.S. 41, west of Miami. Open daily. Free]*, the **Everglades National Park Shark Valley Visitor Center** *[U.S. 41 25 miles west of Miami. Open daily. Adm]*, and several small towns. All provide wonderful gateways to this unique area. There's even an half-finished, nearly abandoned international airport, started in the 1970s for supersonic jetliners that were never built.

## Key West

Of all the many sins I've committed, perhaps the worst is consigning Key West to a single section of a sort of omnibus chapter. In my own defense, though, the Florida Keys are a destination in themselves. I want to give you a little taste of them here, but if you're heading for the Keys, that's probably the point of your trip. It's certainly possible, however, to make a visit to Key West an overnighter, or even a daytrip, as part of a visit to South Florida. I'll limit myself

*Kayaks await paddlers on the beach at Cedar Key, Florida*
© Stacey Brown/Dreamstime.com

to that idea here, unless you want a book with another hundred pages in it.

The Keys are actually a chain of islands that stretches a hundred miles from the tip of the mainland to Key West, and while you can visit most of the places in this book on a whim, Key West takes more planning.

## Getting There

Driving to Key West is easy. Most of the drive is the 100-mile-long (160km) Overseas Highway, U.S. 1. That's a long way for a side trip. The upside is that it's impossible to get lost or take a wrong turn. Add the distance to your starting point and you have a long, although very picturesque, day ahead of you. Much of the drive is over open water, so you certainly don't want to do this in stormy weather.

If you're starting from Naples, the drive is about 250 miles (400km). Miami is the real gateway to the Keys, but even from there it's 160 miles (260km). You can get a flight from most Florida airports, but that's a bit pricy for most family daytrips.

In Chapter 4, I also told you about a shuttle bus service from major cities to the Keys that offers good service.

I think the best way to get to Key West is by boat; after all, this is a city that's all about life on the water. A ferry from Fort Myers Beach is still expensive but is roughly half the price of a flight, and takes about three and a half hours. Ferries are comfortable, have both open air and enclosed seating, big screen TVs, and a variety of food and beverages. A daytrip by ferry would give you about seven hours on the water and less than six on land, so that might not be the proportion you're looking for, but there are plenty of places to stay, as long as this isn't a spur-of-the-moment trip during the winter when crowds are at their peak.

### Sites and Attractions

There's plenty to do here. You don't want to miss some of the marine museums, for example. There's phenomenal treasure to be seen (and purchased) at the **Mel Fisher Maritime Heritage Museum** *[200 Greene St. Open daily. Adm]* with millions of dollars in sunken treasures salvaged from centuries-old shipwrecks, the **Shipwreck Historeum** *[1 Whitehead St. Open daily. Adm]*to hear the histories of the many ships that foundered on the nearby reefs, and the **Pirate Soul Museum** *[524 Front St. Open daily. Adm]* for artifacts from Captain Kidd, Blackbeard, and other famous buccaneers.

Key West has been a retreat for the famous. Visit the **Ernest Hemingway Home** *[907 Whitehead St. Open daily. Adm]* where the great novelist wrote many of his best-known books, or President Harry Truman's **Little White House** *[111 Front St. Open daily. Adm]* retreat vacation home, not only to the nation's 33rd president but visited by presidents Eisenhower, Kennedy, Carter, and other dignitaries, or the cottage of poet Robert Frost at the **Heritage House Museum** *[410 Caroline St. Open daily. Adm]*. There's even another branch of the **Ripley's Believe It or Not Museum** *[108 Duval St. Open daily. Adm]*.

I won't even begin to name all the boat tours, water sports, and cruises available—they would fill pages. I could say the same thing about festivals—all sorts of art festivals, food festivals, fishing tournaments, even a songwriters' festival. There's always something going on. Not all the festivals are especially family-friendly, mind you. The Fantasy Fest in October, for example, features copious amounts of nudity (which is officially not allowed but commonplace). But most others are just colorful and fun.

Everybody goes to the nightly **Sunset Celebration** at Mallory Square, with music, food, entertainers, and vendors of all sorts. It's a perfect way to end the day.

What have I left out of The Rest of Florida? Oh, lots. But the point is, that wherever you go in this marvelous state— along the coasts, through the middle, along the islands— whether it's tourist destinations, or places you've never heard of, you've got far more good choices than you can possibly take advantage of. It's why *everybody* comes to Florida.

During our endless summer days of childhood, there was always one back yard in every neighborhood where all the kids hung out. It had the best swing set, swimming pool, sandbox, or place to play ball. That's why everybody hangs out in Florida now—it's the best back yard in America!

## *Recommendations*

> ∽ Remember that Florida is more than just beaches, oceans, and theme parks. Great family experiences abound in every part of the state.

> ∽ Don't just stick to man-made attractions, but seek out Florida's natural landscapes and wonders.

> ∽ I've said this often: Stay off the main highways as much as you can and enjoy the slower, more rural side of Florida.

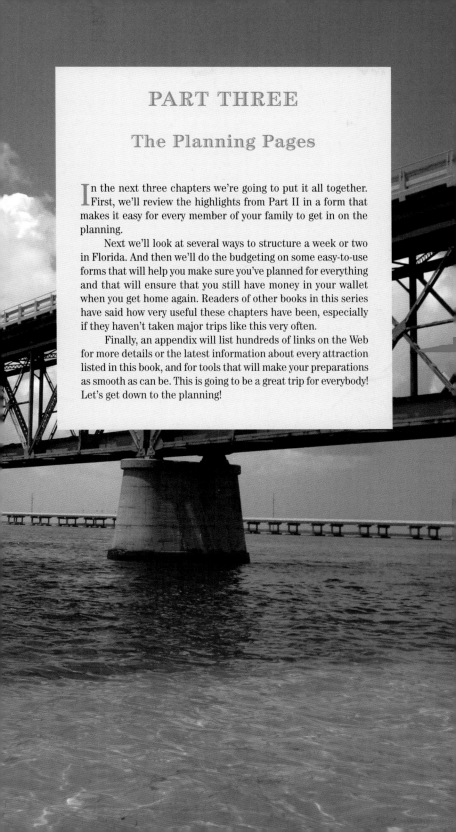

# PART THREE

## The Planning Pages

In the next three chapters we're going to put it all together. First, we'll review the highlights from Part II in a form that makes it easy for every member of your family to get in on the planning.

Next we'll look at several ways to structure a week or two in Florida. And then we'll do the budgeting on some easy-to-use forms that will help you make sure you've planned for everything and that will ensure that you still have money in your wallet when you get home again. Readers of other books in this series have said how very useful these chapters have been, especially if they haven't taken major trips like this very often.

Finally, an appendix will list hundreds of links on the Web for more details or the latest information about every attraction listed in this book, and for tools that will make your preparations as smooth as can be. This is going to be a great trip for everybody! Let's get down to the planning!

# 15
# Top Attractions

WE'VE TALKED ABOUT MORE THAN 200 OF FLORIDA'S GREATEST attractions and experiences in the preceding pages. That's a lot—a whole lot! It's certainly more than you can do in one trip or, probably, five trips…or ten.

This could have been a much, much longer list. I've been scores of places that didn't make it into the book, and considered countless more—probably hundreds. But as I said back in Chapter 7, I've tried to be very selective, in these pages to take you to many places you might not have thought about. If all you want is a beach, you'll find an array of great ones everywhere; water slides are almost as common as ice cream stands. You don't need a book for that.

So I've tried to cherry-pick the state for you and to take you not only to the places you expect, but to those that will stay bright in your mind long after that Mickey tee-shirt has faded from repeated washings. That's true of all my books. Everybody knows about the famous attractions and I take you to them, but often it's the side trip that makes a day memorable. Maybe everyone you know has spent the morning at the Daytona Speedway and the afternoon lounging on Daytona Beach—but how many have gotten a personal tour (with lots of free samples) of the chocolate factory between them?

Now you can.

But just how can you take the more than 200 pages of information that has preceded this chapter and turn it into a trip everyone will enjoy and remember? Let me describe the method that has always worked for the Lains, both when the kids were growing up and the full family was on the road, and even now, when Barb and I mostly travel with just each other.

Our first step in going to a new place is to gather up a few guidebooks we think we can rely on. (Since you're holding this one, obviously you've done a good job so far!) We read as much as we can about our destination so we know what the important attractions are that we'd hate to miss, but also look for the less famous places we think would appeal to one of us. Everybody who is going on the trip does this, whether it was the full crew of five, or just two of us.

Next, we make a list of every single thing that caught the eye of even one of us. I've done that for you, and below is a list of all the attractions I've talked about in this book.

After we had a list of all the possibilities, we voted. Maybe that's not the right word, because it implies something formal and binding. *Prioritized* might be a better way to put it. This can be as simple or as complex as you want, but what we did was to give each member of the family a copy of the list, and he or she marked each item

· I really want to see/do this
· I don't really care about this one way or the other
· I don't find this interesting at all

Being a boring person, I usually numbered items 1, 2, 3, but one of the kids drew smiley and frowny faces, and another one used arrows pointing up, down, and somewhere in between. It shouldn't matter, as long as everybody's thinking seriously about each item.

We also asked each person to mark the one single item that was most important to him or her.

After that was done, planning became simpler. We were able to eliminate many places that nobody had any interest in at all, and to identify a few that were attractive to all or most of us. Then the real planning could begin.

This is an approach that can work well for a trip like this. You can add other items to the list that I haven't covered— I have no way of knowing if you have a grandfather in Sarasota you want to visit, for example—but once everybody has marked the things they most want to do...or to avoid...you can narrow down the list into something manageable.

We talked many chapters ago about the types of vacations Florida offers a family:

- a theme park vacation
- a beach escape
- an urban getaway
- a hodgepodge holiday

Once you look at everybody's list, you should be able to decide, if you haven't done that already.

You should also get a sense now of the geographic possibilities. If nobody wants to do anything but splash in the water and build sand castles, maybe the closest beaches will satisfy everybody. But if beaches are only part of the plan, you'll find good ones near the other attractions that are important to people, no matter what part of the state you end up in.

It might take some negotiation. If one person's ideal vacation simply *has* to include a visit to the Kennedy Space Center and someone else will be inconsolable without a stop at the Circus Museum in Sarasota, it will take some planning since they're 180 miles (290km) apart. But it's manageable. In fact, that was exactly the case the first time the Lains went to Florida. Our solution was to stay near Tampa, to visit the Ringling Estate on a daytrip, and to drive home by way of KSC at the end of the holiday. Everybody was happy.

Of course, if people's No. 1 attractions are in Pensacola and Miami, you're in for a very long or a very expensive vacation unless you can get somebody to wait until next time. That's why narrowing down the geography and selecting a home base is a good idea before you commit to specific activities.

Once you've got that done, you can begin to plan. Have everyone reread the chapter on the area you've selected, and on adjacent areas, too, then list their top attractions and activities just for the parts of the state you'll be staying in or passing through. Now you're ready to nail it down, keeping three principles in mind.

Make an absolute commitment to do everybody's top choice, no matter what. Kids are much more likely to be agreeable traveling companions if they know that what's important to them is important to everybody else. Do these No. 1 activities as early in the trip as you can to make sure nobody is disappointed.

Use the voting as a general guide, but make sure everybody's ideas are included. Don't overplan, because there will be lots of opportunities for surprises you don't want to miss along the way.

Below I've listed all the attractions we've talked about in the earlier chapters. They're grouped according to chapter to make it easy to find the area you plan to stay in. Make copies of these pages for every member of the family to use in voting, or just use them as an outline for good dinner-table discussions. I've put attractions in bold type that I've featured in each chapter; these are the ones that I think offer a little something special, or that have the widest appeal to most families.

But ultimately, it's *all* subjective. You want a holiday your family will enjoy. They are the only ones whose votes really count.

## Chapter 8—The East Coast

### Jacksonville Area

Adventure Landing & Shipwreck Island Water Park, Jacksonville
Angell & Phelps Chocolate Factory, Daytona Beach
Cummer Museum of Art and Gardens, Jacksonville
Jacksonville Beach
Jacksonville Landing, Jacksonville
Jacksonville Museum of Modern Art, Jacksonville
Jacksonville Zoo, Jacksonville
Museum of Science & History, Jacksonville

### St. Augustine Area

Castillo de San Marcos, St. Augustine
Castle Otttis, Vilano Beach
Colonial Spanish Quarter, St. Augustine.
Fort Matanzas National Monument, St. Augustine
Fountain of Youth Archaeological Park, St. Augustine
González-Alvarez House ("Oldest House"), St. Augustine
Lightner Museum, St. Augustine
Marineland, St. Augustine
**Old St. Augustine Historic District**
Old St. Augustine Village
Oldest Wooden Schoolhouse, St. Augustine
Ripley's Believe It or Not! Museum, St. Augustine
**St. Augustine Alligator Farm**
St. Augustine Lighthouse and Museum
Spanish Military Hospital, St. Augustine
World Golf Hall of Fame, St. Augustine

## Daytona Beach Area

Bulow Plantation Ruins State Park, Ormond Beach
Casements, The (Rockefeller Home), Daytona Beach
**Daytona Beach**
Daytona International Speedway
Daytona Lagoon, Daytona Beach
**DaytonaUSA**
Jackie Robinson Ballpark, Daytona Beach
Ponce de Leon Inlet Lighthouse, Daytona Beach
Tomoka State Park, Ormond Beach

## Space Coast Area

American Police Hall of Fame, Titusville
Andretti Thrill Park, Melbourne
Astronaut Hall of Fame, Titusville
Brevard Museum of Art and Science, Melbourne
Brevard Museum of History and Science, Cocoa
Brevard Zoo, Melbourne
Canaveral National Seashore, Titusville
Historic Cocoa Village, Cocoa
**Kennedy Space Center**
Merritt Island National Wildlife Refuge, Titusville
Warbird Air Museum, Titusville

# Chapter 9—The Southeast

## Treasure Coast Area

Burt Reynolds & Friends Museum, Jupiter
**Manatee Observation Center, Fort Pierce**
Mel Fisher's Treasures, Sebastian
Navy Seal Museum, Fort Pierce

## Palm Beach-West Palm Beach Area

Flagler Museum, Palm Beach
**Lion Country Safari, West Palm Beach**
Palm Beach Zoo, West Palm Beach
Peanut Island, Palm Beach Shores
South Florida Science Museum, West Palm Beach
Worth Avenue, Palm Beach

## Boca Raton-Fort Lauderdale Area

Bar-B-Ranch, Davie
Boca Raton Children's Museum, Boca Raton
Butterfly World, Fort Lauderdale

Fishing Hall of Fame, Dania Beach
Flamingo Gardens, Davie
International Swimming Hall of Fame, Fort Lauderdale
Las Olas Boulevard, Fort Lauderdale
**Loxahatchee Everglades Tours, Boca Raton**
Museum of Discovery and Science, Fort Lauderdale
Riverwalk, Fort Lauderdale
Seminole Okalee Indian Village and Museum, Hollywood
Swap Shop, Fort Lauderdale
**Wannado City, Fort Lauderdale**
Young at Art Children's Museum, Davie


*Miami Area*
Ah-Tah-Thi-Ki Museum, Big Cypress Seminole Reservation
Ancient Spanish Monastery, North Miami Beach
Everglades Alligator Farm, Florida City
**Little Havana, Miami**
Miami and Miami Beach
Miami Metrozoo, Miami
Miami Museum of Science and Space Transit, Miami
Miami Seaquarium, Key Biscayne
Monkey Jungle, Miami
Ocean Drive, Miami Beach
Parrot Jungle Island, Miami
**South Beach and Ocean Drive, Miami Beach**
World Chess Hall of Fame, Miami

## Chapter 10—The Worlds of Disney

*Walt Disney World*
Animal Kingdom
Disney/MGM Studios
**Epcot**
**Magic Kingdom**
Downtown Disney

*Waterparks*
Blizzard Beach
Typhoon Lagoon

# Chapter 11–Orlando Beyond Disney

*I-Drive*
Air Florida Helicopters
Magical Midway
Ripley's Believe it or Not!
Skydiving Wind Tunnel
Titanic, the Experience
Train Land International
**WonderWorks**
**SeaWorld**

*Universal*
**Islands of Adventure**
Universal Studios
City Walk
Wet 'N Wild

# Chapter 12–The Bay Area

*Clearwater Area*
Captain Memo's Pirate Cruise, Clearwater
**Clearwater Beach & Pier**
**Clearwater Marine Aquarium, Clearwater**
St. Nicholas Greek Orthodox Cathedral, Tarpon Springs
Sea Life Safari, Clearwater
Sponge Docks, Tarpon Springs
Sunsets at Pier 60, Clearwater Beach
Tarpon Springs restaurants and shopping
Weeki Wachee Springs, Weeki Wachee

*Tampa Area*
Big Cat Rescue, Tampa
**Busch Gardens, Tampa**
Children's Museum of Tampa, Tampa
Florida Aquarium, Tampa
Gameworks, Ybor City, Tampa
Henry B. Plant Museum, Tampa
Lowry Park Zoo, Tampa
Museum of Science and Industry, Tampa
Tampa Bay History Center, Tampa
Tampa Museum of Art, Tampa
Ybor City State Museum, Tampa
**Ybor City, Tampa**

## St. Petersburg Area

Florida International Museum, St. Petersburg
Fort De Soto Park, Tierra Verde
**Gamble Plantation, Ellenton**
Great Explorations, St. Petersburg
Museum of Fine Arts, St. Petersburg
St. Petersburg Museum of History, St. Petersburg
St. Petersburg Pier, St. Petersburg
Salvador Dali Museum, St. Petersburg
Suncoast Seabird Sanctuary, Indian Shores
Sunken Gardens, St. Petersburg
Treasure Island, St. Petersburg

# Chapter 13—Southwest Florida

## Sarasota Area
**Ringling Estate, Sarasota**
Cà d'Zan
Circus Museum
Museum of Art
Classic Car Museum, Sarasota
Mote Marine Aquarium, Sarasota
Sarasota Jungle Gardens, Sarasota

## Fort Myers-Sanibel Area
Bailey-Matthews Shell Museum, Sanibel
**Edison and Ford winter homes, Fort Myers**
Gasparilla Island
Imaginarium, Ft. Myers
Koreshan State Historic Site, Estero
Manatee World, Ft. Myers
National Wildlife Refuge and Bird Sanctuary, Sanibel
**Sanibel Island**
Southwest Florida Museum of History, Ft. Myers

## Naples Area
5th Avenue South Shopping, Naples
Naples Zoo at Caribbean Gardens, Naples
Tin City, Naples
Aviary and Zoo, Naples

# Chapter 14—The Rest of Florida

## *The Panhandle Area*

### Pensacola
Civil War Soldiers Museum, Pensacola
Historic Pensacola Village, Pensacola
Pensacola Lighthouse, Pensacola
National Museum of Naval Aviation, Pensacola

### Fort Walton Beach
Emerald Coast Science Center, Fort Walton Beach
Florida's Gulfarium, Fort Walton Beach

### Panama City
Gulf World Marine Park, Panama City
ZooWorld, Panama City

### Apalachicola
St. George Island

### Tallahassee
Capitol Building, Tallahassee
Mary Brogan Museum of Art & Science, Tallahassee
Museum of Florida History, Tallahassee
Riley Museum of African American History & Culture, Tallahassee
Tallahassee Antique Car Museum, Tallahassee
Old Capitol Museum, Tallahassee

### Central Florida
Cypress Gardens, Winter Haven
Fantasy of Flight, Polk City
Florida Museum of Natural History, Gainesville
Gainesville
Sebring International Raceway, Sebring

### South Florida
**Everglades, The**
Lake Okeechobee
Miccosukee Indian Village, Miami

### Key West
Ernest Hemingway Home, Key West
Heritage House Museum, Key West
Little White House, Key West
Mel Fisher Maritime Heritage Museum, Key West
Pirate Soul Museum, Key West
Ripley's Believe It or Not! Museum, Key West

# 16
# Itineraries

IN OTHER BOOKS IN THIS SERIES I LAY OUT WHAT ARE SOMETIMES fairly detailed possible itineraries, not that I expect anybody to follow them exactly, but to show how a trip can be paced and attractions mixed to provide a wide range of experiences for travelers.

But those books are about individual cities. It's not really practical for me to suggest *Monday: Kennedy Space Center; Tuesday: Edison home in Fort Myers; Wednesday: lay on beach in Pensacola*. You'd have to be as crazy as I am to try something like that. Besides, maybe all you're going to do is spend a week on the beach. You don't need me to tell you: *10 o'clock: apply sunscreen and lay on blanket; 10:30: roll over; 11:00: roll over again; 11:30: reapply sunscreen and roll over again....*

So what can I tell you in this book, that covers such a immense geographical area and includes such a mind-boggling number of very different experiences and activities?

Glad you asked. What I'm going to do here is to suggest that you really do embrace the very thing that boggles all those minds, to take advantage of the very thing that can make a Florida holiday so confusing—too much to do!

I'll take a handful of places you might be using as a sort of home base and show you how you can get the most out of it in a week or so. Even if I don't use the place you're staying as an example, you can easily apply the same approach to just about anywhere in Florida you're staying; that's why I've arranged the book the way I have.

First, though, I want to review some things I've already talked about, and add a few more planning principles that will help you structure your activities.

· Everybody gets his or her first choice, no matter what, and do them early in the trip to avoid disappointment if you have to change plans.

· Don't try to see more than two or three really major attractions in one day.

· Don't overplan. You can't possibly see *everything*, so don't even try. Florida has been here for a long time and it will probably still be here the next time you have a chance to visit.

· Look for things in the same general area, if you can, to save travel time between attractions.

· Vary your activities; don't do two beaches, two science museums, or two state parks on the same day: They'll dilute each other.

· Have a backup plan in case the weather turns nasty on a day you'd planned to be outdoors, or you wake to an especially gorgeous day when you were going to be inside most of the time.

· But unless the weather is *really* foul, don't let it slow you down. If you get wet, you'll dry out again later—I promise.

· Be flexible enough to abandon your plans when your intended destination is closed or you come across something you hadn't known about that people want to do. It happens on every single trip.

· With those ideas in mind, let's see what you can do in just a week in each of these popular Florida destinations. And if one of these isn't where you're headed, that's okay— everyplace else in the state presents similar opportunities. These are just examples.

### Tampa Bay Area

There's so much to do here that a stay of a week will leave you wanting more. Almost every sort of thing Florida has to offer is within easy reach of Tampa. How does a trip like this sound:

Loafing, reading, and playing on the beach. It doesn't matter what beach; you have miles of wonderful places to choose from along here. I really like Clearwater Beach, though, so maybe for this example, I'll set up my base here. There's plenty of room for kites, or some people can try parasailing if they're brave enough. I'll spend at least 3 days of my week here. Look for me every night at *Sunsets at Pier 60*. (3 days)

If I'm in Clearwater, I think I'll spend a morning at the *Clearwater Marine Aquarium* and go for a cruise in the afternoon, either with *Captain Memo's Pirate Cruise* or the *Sea Life Safari*. (1 day)

Tampa is less than 25 miles (40km) away, so we'll have a theme park day and spend it at *Busch Gardens*. (1 day)

Road trip! Sarasota is less than 60 miles (97km) away,

just an hour or so. A day at the *Ringling Estate* with a stop on the way down or the way home at the *Gamble Plantation* will make a wonderful day. (1 day)

Only one more day to fill? I still have too many choices. More beach time? Another day in Tampa visiting museums or *Big Cat Rescue*, with dinner in *Ybor City*? That cluster of museums in St. Pete? Pick one. I'll just have to come back next year and try for some of the places I missed. (1 day)

## Daytona Beach

Would you rather be on the Atlantic side than the Gulf side? That's fine with me. It won't matter; a week's worth of activities still doesn't scratch the surface of the possibilities. I'll show you what I mean. This time we're going to set up shop in Daytona Beach. How would I spend a week in Daytona? Like this:

The beach, naturally. Being lazy by nature, I could easily snooze away my entire week here, as long as somebody turned me from time to time so I cooked evenly. But I won't. I'll spend the same time on this beach that I would have spent on Clearwater Beach, but if that's too much, there's plenty else to do. (3 days)

Even non-racing fans are impressed by *Daytona International Speedway* and *Daytona USA*. After a full morning (and probably more) there, I'll stop for a late lunch at *Angell & Phelps*, tour the chocolate factory, and do some shopping in the neighborhood. If my visit is during April through August, maybe I can catch a Daytona Cubs minor-league baseball game at historic *Jackie Robinson Ballpark*. (1 day)

Anybody based in Daytona is faced with two irresistible road trips, and they're both about an hour's drive away. No need to choose between them—take 'em both! First we'll go an hour north to St. Augustine. We can tour *Old St. Augustine*, try to still the hands of time at the *Fountain of Youth Archaeological Park*, wander through the terrific *St. Augustine Alligator Farm*, or do any of a dozen other things. (1 day)

An hour south of Daytona is *Kennedy Space Center*, the only true spaceport on Planet Earth. The modern technological world sprang from here, and I can't imagine being this close without visiting it. (1 day)

Here's that bummer of a last day again—there's too much left undone! So what will it be? Hop over to Orlando and visit *SeaWorld*? Find a water park to play in? More beach time?

Play the carnival games in the Boardwalk area? Visit one of the great nearby state parks? What ever I choose, I'll regret what I missed. (1 day)

## Fort Lauderdale

I haven't used an example from South Florida, yet, and I should or I'll be in trouble with a lot of friends and acquaintances who make at least one trip here a year a regular part of their lives. I can't blame them. Fort Lauderdale is a lush, beautiful place with enough to keep you busy all winter long, as thousands of "snowbirds" can happily testify. If I didn't have all winter, though, but was just bringing a family for a week, my trip might look like this:

My favorite zoo anywhere, *Lion Country Safari* west of West Palm Beach, keeps visitors confined while the animals roam free. I might spend a whole day there, but if that's too much, I'll drive through Palm Beach and see how the rich people live, and do some gawking in the windows of shops along *Worth Avenue*. (1 day)

No visit to South Florida is complete without a look at the Everglades; the *Loxahatchee Everglades Tours* is not far from here and can provide tours of various lengths. Go early in the day for this, before the heat sets in. In the afternoon, a stop at *Butterfly World* will contrast sharply with the big reptiles. Or we can spend the afternoon cooling off at a water park. (1 day)

I'd start the day at the huge *Swap Shop*. Even though I'm not much of a shopper, this place is fascinating. I've never been anyplace else like *Wannado City*, and kids will go for it in a big way. It will take all afternoon—at least—for this one. (1 day)

How can we be in South Florida and skip Miami? It's only a half-hour's drive. A stop at the *Ancient Spanish Monastery* would give a cultural start to the day, but in any case, I'll want to spend much of the day at *South Beach*. For dinner, I'll head into Miami itself and find something delicious in *Little Havana*. Tuesday and Thursday Flamenco Nights are the best time to go. (1 day)

It's possible I've made those days too full and I'll decide to split some things up, so I won't get my three days of beach time. But however much time I devote to them, I know I'll enjoy the beautiful beaches around Fort Lauderdale. *Dania Beach* with its roller coaster, *Hollywood Beach* and its Boardwalk—there's plenty of fun in store. (3 days)

## Orlando

So you're determined to go to Orlando, despite all the other lures of Florida? You've got a lot of company. About 50 million people a year visit Orlando, according to the Orange County Convention and Visitors Bureau. We're back to having our minds boggled again! It's impossible to imagine that many people ... unless you're in Disney's Magic Kingdom the week after Christmas. It's like the Tokyo subway at rush hour then! Still, all those people have good reasons for being there—the same reasons you're going.

While it's theoretically possible to spend a family week in Orlando and not visit *Walt Disney World*, I'm not certain it's legal, so just to be safe, we'll choose the two parks we most want to see. Or a family can split up and cover even more ground. Some people do more than one park a day, but it makes a very exhausting day. (2 days)

Because they're adjacent, it's possible to visit both *Universal* parks in one day, though it's a push. But that's what I'll do, covering one thoroughly and cherry-picking the other. Roller coaster fanatics will probably spend most of their time at Islands of Adventure. (1 day)

*SeaWorld* is worth a day. The pace will be slower, and at some point I'll need that. (1 day) I said I'd happily make the trip from Daytona to *Kennedy Space Center*, and we're just as close to KSC here in Orlando. It's a must-do for me. Few places stir my imagination more. (1 day)

There's no beach in Orlando, but there are some great water parks and that will get me as wet as I care to be. All I have to decide is whether I want to head back to Disney to use one of their two elaborate ones, or the equally exciting *Wet 'N Wild*, or look for someplace a little smaller. (1 day) Here's my last-day dilemma back again—with a vengeance! I want an extra day at Disney. I want another day at Universal. I want to go to the *Titanic Experience* and to *WonderWorks* on I-Drive. I want ... well, what I *really* want is more time! I'll just have to pick one, and save the rest for next time. (1 day)

That's what *my* one-week vacation might look like in each of four Florida destinations. Notice that I've tried to see and do a lot, but have slowed the pace some days, too. These aren't itineraries I expect you to follow; I'm just showing some possibilities.

You can structure your holiday in any way your family agrees on. You can have tons of fun just driving down the Atlantic Coast, staying someplace different every night and seeing the local attractions along the way. You can have a great time spending all seven days at Disney. You can have a terrific week just camping in the Everglades, as long as you're careful not to become some alligator's midnight snack.

What if you've got more than a week? Good for you. I'm envious. You'll reduce the last-day pressure of having too many good choices because you'll have time to work in more activities. But it doesn't make any difference how long you stay. You will not run out of things to do, I promise.

### *Recommendations*

❧ Plan a slow-paced day occasionally to let everyone sleep late and re-energize.

❧ Don't be afraid to split up if possible when family members want to go different places.

❧ Ask hotel desk clerks, restaurant wait staff, and other locals where *their* favorite family places are in the area. You'll uncover some gems that way.

# 17
# Worksheets

SOMEHOW, ABOUT 2,300 YEARS AGO, HANNIBAL MANAGED TO GET his army—elephants and all—all the way from North Africa, across the Pyrenees, across the Alps, and into Italy to threaten the Romans on their home ground.

His invasion failed because he didn't have the equipment he needed to lay an effective siege of Rome. But here's the little-known fact of the matter: He couldn't get the stuff he needed because he maxed out his credit cards before his trip was over.

If Hannibal had practiced with something really difficult and stressful before he'd tried invading Rome, like traveling with his family, he'd have made it. Not even generals and field marshals face bigger planning challenges than do parents who are trying to organize a family trip. At least soldiers do what they're ordered. Kids? Well....

I'm a compulsive planner, and as much as I want surprises when I travel, I want them to be good surprises. If I run out of money before we run out of vacation, I can't send my kids out to pillage a town for food and someplace to spend the night. So my planning process has always been thorough and relentless. Even now, when our travels consist mostly of just Barb and me instead of five of us, I plan the financial side of a major trip carefully, even if we're more spontaneous in what we do on the sightseeing part of the trip.

The forms in this chapter are the sort of thing we've been using for years, and readers of other books in the *Family Travel Series* have often told me how helpful they are, especially if they haven't undertaken such a large expedition before. The forms are flexible and they will help make sure that you won't have to earn the last two days worth of meals by washing restaurant dishes.

## Travel
First I will provide two forms to help you plan your travel: one for getting a good airfare and one in case you decide to

drive. The services of a travel agent can be helpful if you fly, especially if you're planning a complex itinerary, such as flying into one airport, renting a car, and flying home from another. An agent's services will probably save you more money than the fee the agency charges. Agents have access to more and faster tools than the internet provides.

That said, booking over the internet is easier now than it's ever been, and you can get some great deals provided you use multiple websites.

*Form 1. Flying to Florida:* It's harder than it used to be to get a really cheap airfare, but being flexible in dates and using several search engines (individual airline sites as well as general sites like Orbitz or SideStep) or an experienced travel agent will get you the best deal. It can take a lot of work to do it yourself, but I've sometimes found better fares or better routings than my employer's travel agent could come up with. Be sure you check fares on websites for discount airlines like Skybus or Southwest. They often aren't available on more general travel search engines.

# Form 1—Air travel requirements. Give to travel agent or use with websites.

1. How many people traveling? _____
   ___Adults      ___Children under 18 (ages:_____)
   *There are few age discounts any more, except for infants and, rarely, senior citizens. Active-duty military sometimes get a break. But occasionally you'll find a promotional fare.*

2. Departure date: _____
   Is this date  Fixed or is it  Flexible?
   *If you can travel during Low Season, airfares may be much less than High Season (summer months and holiday) fares. Avoid Friday, Saturday, Sunday flights for better prices.*

3. Length of stay? _____days/weeks
   *Stays of 7 to 30 days usually qualify for the cheapest rates because business travelers usually stay for less than a week. Avoid return flights on Friday, Saturday, Sunday for better rates.*

4. Preferred airline, if any?_____
   *If you or another family member works for an airline, you may be eligible for deep discounts. Do you have a frequent flier account with an airline? Do you have enough miles in an account to get one or more tickets free?*

5. Preferred airports, if any?_____
   *You might save money by driving to a more distant airport where cheaper fares are offered. Price flights from all nearby airports. And not all nearby destinations will have the same price. If you're staying it Fort Lauderdale, check prices into Miami and Palm Beach, too. Fares might vary greatly. That's also true of Tampa, St. Pete, and Sarasota, or other cities that are fairly close together.*

6. Non-stop flight required or connection OK?
   ____ Non-stop only; ____ connection OK
   *Unless you live near a city with non-stop service, this isn't an issue: you'll have to connect. But if there's a choice, the connection might be cheaper. But it might not be. There's a lot of competition on*

*some non-stop routes, especially in the winter (or to Orlando any time).*

**Total Airfare $**_____

*Form 2. Driving to and within Florida:* Gas prices skyrocketed in the United States in 2006, and are still high. (Unless you're visiting from abroad. In that case, you're probably quite pleased at the price.) Still, driving to Florida is the most economical option from much of the eastern United States, and that's how most Florida visitors arrive.

Those costs can be tough to figure, though. The U.S. government uses a rate of just over 50 cents a mile as allowable for business tax deduction purposes, figuring that will take care of gasoline, insurance, maintenance, and other necessary expenses. Since this isn't a business trip, though, we have to come up with another formula. If you're driving your own car, those non-fuel expenses aren't really part of the trip, and if you're driving a rental, they're covered in the rental fee.

The big expense is fuel. The price of gasoline is one factor in that, and so is the type of vehicle you drive. I can't predict either one, so here's the formula I'll give you to figure costs:

Look at the average price of gas for the trip. If you're driving a vehicle that's heavy and uses a lot of gas, like a big SUV, figure 10 percent of the gas price per mile. If you have a small, very fuel-efficient car, calculate your mileage expense at 5 percent of the average gasoline price. This will usually give you a little bit of a contingency cushion to meet unanticipated expenses. So if gas averages $3.50 per gallon, figure the cost of travel at 17.5 cents a mile for a small car, closer to 35 cents a mile for a big van or SUV.

If you're flying to Florida and renting a car once you get there (or renting a car for the drive from home, for that matter), figure fuel expenses the same way, but you'll need to add the car rental fee as an expense. The sidebar in this chapter, *Don't Get Taken for a Ride* has some tips for getting the best rates.

# Form 2—Driving and car rental

1. Round-trip distance from starting point to Florida destination: _____miles

   *Not just point-to-point distance, but include any side trips you plan to take along the way. Add 5 percent to your total—50 miles for every 1000—for unanticipated trips and detours.*

2. Anticipated distance you will drive while at your destination: _____miles

   *Include travel back and forth to the beach, to other nearby attractions, planned trips to out-of-town attractions, and so on. Add an additional 10 percent to your total. Trust me—you'll use it.*

3. Anticipated total mileage: _____miles

   *Add Lines 1 and 2.*

$_____Gas money

   *Use the formula on page 222: Multiply the total on Line 3 above by 5 to 10 percent of the average price of gasoline at the time of your trip. A contingency amount is built into the total*

$_____Auto Rental

   *If you're renting a car, you should be able to determine in advance what you'll pay by following the tips in the sidebar in this chapter. Put that amount here.*

## Accommodations

If you're driving an RV or motor home to Florida, you can skip this section. You know what it costs to drive and about what it costs to park for a night or a week. Let's talk to the people who don't bring their own homes with them.

In Chapter 5, I went over a variety of options for where to stay. You've probably decided by now what sort of accommodations you're looking for, but if you haven't, you might want to review that chapter now. Below, I'll give you two similar forms—one for apartments or condos, and one for hotels and motels.

# Don't Get Taken for a Ride

It's not easy to vacation in Florida without a car, unless you're staying someplace like a Disney resort where they will pick you up at the airport and provide buses to haul you around the property. Few cities in Florida have public transportation that's very practical for tourists, although many places do have beach trolleys that are useful if you're staying right on the coast.

Auto rentals are big business in Florida, though, and because of the competition, you can often get outstanding deals on weekly rentals with unlimited mileage.

You can also get "taken for a ride" in that rental car. Here are a few tips to cut auto rental costs.

Get quotes from several companies. Make sure they're in writing or print the quotation from the website. Some companies will try to change the rate on you at the counter when you pick up the car.

The best prices are usually from companies' own websites rather than general travel sites, but check both. Or use a travel agent, who has access to deals you don't.

Be sure the quote includes all taxes and fees. Demand that there be no hidden charges when you pick up the car.

Take advantage of discounts offered to auto club members, employees of your company, military personnel, or any other group you might be a part of.

Check with your own auto insurer and credit card company to verify that they will cover your rental. Almost all do so. You can save $10 to $25 per day by declining the insurance offered by the rental car company. This is a huge profit center for the rental car industry.

Decline the fuel option and fill the gas tank yourself before you return the car. Rental car companies charge two or three times the price that gas stations charge.

Look over the car before you drive away. If there are any scrapes or dents on the car, insist that they be noted on your rental agreement or you could be charged for them later.

Child safety seats will cost an additional $5 or more per day if you don't bring your own.

Most companies will let both spouses drive the car without an additional charge. If they ask for an extra fee, try to get it waived.

If you can pick up the rental car from a downtown location instead of the airport, you can often save a 5 percent or so airport concession fee.

*Form 3. Apartments and Condos:* These normally will cost more than motels and inexpensive hotels, but can provide vastly more space, plus cooking facilities that will save you more money than the difference. We've taken our family to Florida this way, and it's wonderfully convenient.

Talk to the manager of the facility and get him or her on your side by being friendly and excited about taking your family to this great destination. Prices are always negotiable and it's the manager, not the reservations clerk, who can offer you the best price. Here are some things to ask.

# Form 3—Finding an apartment or condo

1. Hello. I am looking for an apartment in (destination) for ___ people. We will arrive on this date, _____ and will leave on _____, a total of ___ nights. There will be ___adults and children whose ages are _____.

2. We would like a...
     studio apartment
     1-bedroom apartment
     2-bedroom apartment

Please describe the apartment, the building, and the neighborhood:

3. What is the address of the apartment? Is it near public transportation or the beach trolley?
4. How large is the apartment? What floor is it on? How many beds?
5. What kind of bath/toilet facilities are in the apartment?
6. Does the apartment face the street? How quiet is it? Describe the building and apartment security features. (Does it face the beach?)
7. Describe the furnishings and appliances in the apartment. Is there a telephone? A television?
8. Describe the cooking facilities in the apartment. How much storage space is there?
9. Does the apartment have laundry facilities? Air conditioning?
10. Describe the building. How old is it? When was it last remodeled? Is there an elevator?
11. Do you provide cleaning and change the linens? If so, how often?
12. Is parking available? Is there a charge?
13. How far away is the nearest self-service laundry? Grocery store?
14. How do we pick up the keys?
15. What is the best price you can give me, including all taxes?
16. Is there any way to reduce it further? *(like length of stay, weekend specials, bringing our own linens for extra cots, sleeping bags so we won't require an extra bed, cleaning the apartment ourselves and laundering the sheets and towels, etc.)*

17. Are there other dates in about the same time period when the rate would be lower?

18. What credit cards do you accept? How much deposit do you require and when is the balance due?

Thank you. If we decide to rent this apartment, I will confirm this with you within one week.

The Chapter 5 sidebar *How Low Can You Go* explains negotiating strategy in more detail, but you want to give the manager an opportunity to help you. I once had a hotel manager in Chicago's Loop so taken with my family and the kids' excitement about a stay in the "Big City" that he sort of adopted us, referred to me as his cousin, and assigned us a huge upgraded room with a fabulous view, a free rollaway bed, and other perks for less than the price we'd agreed on when I made the reservation.

*Form 4. Hotels and Motels:* Unless you're going at peak season, there's seldom any need to book a motel room if you're just staying for a night or two, then moving on. They're everywhere. Quality hotels are another matter. And if your family plans to stay for several days, booking ahead is a must. You can get your best nightly price, and then often negotiate an additional discount for stays of a week or more, for adjacent rooms, rooms with kitchenettes, or other requirements.

Travel agents have lists of places they recommend to clients, and auto clubs and other organizations publish ratings books of places to stay. I usually use a combination of methods, always including looking at motel websites, where I usually get the best starting price. You can also get some information from user reviews at websites like tripadvisor.com, but remember that people are much more likely to complain about a place than they are to write in and say how good it was.

Asking about the things listed on Form 4 will give you a good idea of what to expect from the places you investigate.

# Form 4—Finding a hotel, motel, or suite

1. Hello. I am looking for a hotel in   (destination)   for ___ people. We will arrive on this date, _____ and will leave on _____, a total of ___ nights. There will be ___adults and children whose ages are _____.
2. Where is the hotel? Is it near public transportation or the beach trolley?
3. Do you have a room or suite with cooking facilities? A refrigerator? Microwave? What else is provided?
4. How large is the room?
5. How is the room furnished? Can we control the heating and cooling in our own room?
6. What kind of bath/toilet facilities are in the room?
7. What is the additional charge for two adjoining rooms connected by an interior door?
8. Are rollaway beds available for extra people?
9. If we don't use a rollaway or bring our own linens for it, is there a deduction? How much?
10. Does the room face the street? Does it face the beach? How quiet is it? Is there an elevator?
11. Does the room have an alarm clock? Coffee maker? Hair dryer?
12. Is breakfast provided? What does it consist of?
13. Is parking available? What does it cost?
14. How far away is the nearest self-service laundry? Grocery store?
15. Can I get a discount for my [*auto club membership or other affinity group*]?
16. What is the best price you can give me, including all taxes?
17. Is there any way to reduce it further? *(like length of stay, weekend specials, bringing our own linens for extra cots, sleeping bags so we won't require an extra bed, cleaning the room ourselves and laundering the sheets and towels, etc.)*
18. Are there other dates in about the same time period when the rate would be lower?
19. What credit cards do you accept? Is the reservation and price guaranteed?

Thank you. If we decide to rent this room, I will confirm this with you within one week.

When you arrive, it's a good idea to ask to see the room before you turn over your credit card. I've been shown rooms that were not clean, that were in bad repair, that had no air conditioning in 90-degree weather. Then it's time to ask for a different one, or just move along to the next place down the street. Properties change hands, managers change, and I've been both disappointed and pleasantly surprised at places where I thought I knew what I was going to get.

## Form 5. Your Bottom Line

So what does it all come down to? As the saying goes: Do the math. You can get most of the latest prices for places you intend to visit from the internet, and plan on some extra money for spontaneous stops. Theme parks are the most expensive item here, ranging from $30 or so to more than $70 per person per day. But these are items you can figure in advance. If you use a travel agent, he or she can help you plan with precision, too.

# Form 5—Your travel budget

$_____1. Travel expenses

*From forms 1 or 2. Airfare, train tickets, or driving expenses, including meals during layovers or on the train or road, and overnight accommodation if you're driving a long distance.*

$_____2. Accommodations

*From Form 3 or 4. If you're driving, include the cost of parking your car in this category.*

$_____3. Food: meals and snacks

*If you're staying in a hotel, you'll probably eat two or three meals per day in restaurants. If that's the case, allow $20 to $40 per person, per day for meals, depending on the ages of your children and what kinds of places you like to eat.*

*If you're renting an apartment and plan to fix breakfast and supper at home most of the time, eating only lunch out, figure $15 to $20 per person, per day, a figure which also takes the purchase of groceries into account. It's possible to spend much more, of course, but these figures should provide for you comfortably.*

*Per person/per day ____x number of days ____x number in family = $_____*

$_____4. Attractions and sightseeing

*The big-ticket items are the theme parks, but smaller attractions add up, too. Unlike many other destinations, Florida doesn't offer many free attractions except the beach. Check websites for the most current admission prices, total it up, and put the result here.*

$_____ 5. Shopping and souvenirs

*This is a very personal category. Give each child a fixed amount, perhaps $20 to $50, or a sum of perhaps $5 to $10 per day to pay for souvenirs, snacks, etc. They can, of course, supplement that with their own money if they wish. Mom and Dad can set their own budget in this category. However, it is best to set a fixed amount in advance. Give the money to your children when you arrive, perhaps a little at a time for younger ones.*

$_____ Total Expenses in Categories 1 through 6

Take the total and add a 10 percent contingency fund, because some things will cost more than you expect, or you'll decide at the last moment to do something not on your list. There's nothing wrong with that; I do it on almost every trip I take, and it's nice to know I've already figured it in to my budget. With luck, you won't spend it all, but it's better to return from a long trip with money left in your budget than to spend the last two hundred miles of the drive wondering if you'll get enough money from selling your car to pay off your vacation debts.

The last thing you want on your holiday is stress, and you won't worry about money if you know you've done good planning and have your expenses covered. Now there's nothing left to do but get out the sunscreen and hit the beach!

## Recommendations

❧ Ask hotel desk clerks, restaurant wait staff, and other locals where *their* favorite family places are in the area. You'll uncover some gems that way.

❧ Travel agents can do much of your planning for you for a small fee, even then it helps to do some basic research yourself to understand the process and price ranges that are possible.

❧ Almost every price can be lowered by asking the right questions or by declining options you don't need.

# Appendix: Websites

Listed below are helpful links and official websites of attractions, as well as selected unofficial websites I think are especially useful. If you find a broken link, or a web address that's changed, please let me know so it can be updated.

## Getting There
**Amtrak**
fares, schedules, and other information about the national passenger rail service
*www.amtrak.com*

**Cheaptickets**
discount airfare
*www.cheaptickets.com*

**FareReport**
compare airfares from multiple sites
*www.farereport.com*

**Kayak**
search engine for multiple travel sites
*www.kayak.com*

**Lowestfare**
discount airfare
*www.lowestfare.com*

**Microsoft Expedia**
popular general travel site
*www.expedia.com*

**Orbitz**
popular general travel site
*www.orbitz.com*

**Priceline**
name your own price for airfare & hotels, but watch restrictions
*www.priceline.com*

**SideStep**
search engine for multiple travel sites
*www.sidestep.com*

**Travelocity**
good general travel site
*www.travelocity.com*

## Arrival

**Immigration and Naturalization Service**
U.S. government site with free downloadable forms,
but hard to navigate.
*www.ins.gov*

**Immigration Services**
visa requirements. Also offers immigration forms for a fee.
*www.visa-forms.com*

**Airports of Florida**
links to official websites of major Florida airports
*www.dot.state.fl.us/aviation/commercialairports.htm*

## Accommodations

**Hotels and Motels**
*www.hotels.com*
*www.hotelscheap.org/hotel/*
*www.smoothhound.co.uk/usa/florida/index.html*

**Rental Homes, Apartments, and B&Bs**
*www.vacationhomerentals.comvacation-rentals/*
*Florida.htm*
*www.superiorsmalllodging.com*
*www.bbonline.comfl/*
*www.nomorehotels.com*
*geo.craigslist.org/iso/us/fl*
*www.resortsandlodges.comlodging/usa/florida/index.html*

**Camping in Florida**
*www.floridacamping.com*

**RV and Mobile Home Rental**
*www.koa.comrvfinder/rental/fl.htm*

## Getting Around

**Florida Transit Links**
official municipal and commercial bus, rail, and ferry websites statewide
*www.apta.comlinks/state_local/fl.cfm*

**Key West transportation**
ferry to Key West from Fort Myers or Miami
*www.seakeywestexpress.com*

**Shuttle from major cities to Key West**
*www.transfloridian.comindex.html*

**I-Ride Trolley, Orlando**
*www.iridetrolley.com*

*Major Rental Car Companies*

**Alamo**
*www.alamo.com*

**Avis**
*www.avis.com*

**Budget**
*www.avis.com*

**Dollar**
*www.dollar.com*

**Enterprise**
*www.enterprise.com*

**Hertz**
*www.hertz.com*

**National**
*www.nationalcar.com*

**Thrifty**
*www.thrifty.com*

*Media*

**Newspapers**
links to major Florida newspapers
*www.usnewslinks.comnewspapers/fl.html*

**Radio Stations**
links to major Florida radio stations
*www.usnewslinks.comradiostations/fl.html*

**Television Stations**
links to TV stations in Florida
*www.usnewslinks.comtvstations/fl.html*

## City and State Websites

**Florida Tourism Official Websites**
*www.visitflorida.com*
*www.media.visitflorida.org* [media information]

**Apalachicola**
*www.apalachicolabay.org*

**Boca Raton**
*www.bocaraton.com*
*www.ci.boca-raton.fl.us/vis/*

**Clearwater**
*www.floridasbeach.com*

**Daytona Beach**
*www.daytonabeach.com*

**Fort Lauderdale**
*www.sunny.org*

**Fort Myers**
*www.fortmyers-sanibel.com*
*www.fortmyers.com*

**Fort Walton Beach**
*www.destin-fwb.com*

**Gainesville**
*www.visitgainesville.net*

**Jacksonville**
*www.jaxcvb.com*

**Key West**
*www.keywest.com*
*www.fla-keys.com*

**Miami**
*www.gmcvb.com*

**Miami Beach**
*www.visitmiamibeach.us*

**Naples**
*www.naples-florida.com*

**Palm Beach**
*www.palmbeachfl.com*

**Panama City**
*www.panamacity.orgvacation/index.htm*

**Pensacola**
*www.visitpensacola.com*

**St. Augustine**
*www.staugustine.com*

**St. Petersburg**
*www.stpete.com*
*www.stpete.org/50things.htm*

**Sarasota**
*www.sarasotafl.org*

**Sebring**
*www.sebringflchamber.com*

**Tallahassee**
*www.visittallahassee.com*

**Tampa**
*www.visittampabay.com*
*www.tampaguide.com*

**Tarpon Springs**
*www.tarponsprings.com*

**West Palm Beach**
*www.cityofwpb.comvisitwpb/index.html*

*Attractions*

**Adventure Landing & Shipwreck Island Water Park, Jacksonville**
*www.adventurelanding.comjaxbeach/index.html*

**Ah-Tah-Thi-Ki Museum, Big Cypress Seminole Reservation**
*www.ahtahthiki.com*

**Air Florida Helicopters, Orlando**
*www.airfloridahelicopters.com*

**American Police Hall of Fame, Titusville**
*www.aphf.org*

**Ancient Spanish Monastery, N. Miami Beach**
*www.spanishmonastery.com*

**Andretti Thrill Park, Melbourne**
*www.andrettithrillpark.com*

**Angell & Phelps Chocolate Factory, Daytona Beach**
*www.angellandphelpschocolates.comindex.htm*

**Astronaut Hall of Fame, Titusville**
*www.kennedyspacecenter.comvisitKSC/attractions/fame.asp*

**Aviary and Zoo, Naples**
*www.aviaryofnaples.com*

**Bailey-Matthews Shell Museum, Sanibel**
*www.shellmuseum.org*

**Bar-B-Ranch, Davie**
*www.bar-b-ranch.com*

**Baseball Grapefruit League**
*www.floridaspringtraining.com*

**Big Cat Rescue, Tampa**
*www.bigcatrescue.org*

**Boca Raton Children's Museum, Boca Raton**
*www.cmboca.org*

**Brevard Museum of Art and Science, Melbourne**
*www.artandscience.org*

**Brevard Museum of History and Science, Cocoa**
*www.brevardmuseum.org*

**Brevard Zoo, Melbourne**
*www.brevardzoo.org*

**Bulow Plantation Ruins State Park, Ormond Beach**
*www.floridastateparks.org/bulowplantation/*

**Burt Reynolds & Friends Museum, Jupiter**
*www.burtreynoldsmuseum.org*

**Busch Gardens, Tampa**
*www.buschgardens.comBGT/default.aspx*

**Butterfly World, Fort Lauderdale**
*www.butterflyworld.com*

**Cà d'Zan, Ringling Estate, Sarasota**
*www.ringling.org/ca_mansion.asp*

**Canaveral National Seashore, Titusville**
*www.nps.gov/cana/*

**Capitol Building, Tallahassee**
*www.inusa.comtour/fl/tallahas/capitol.htm*

**Captain Memo's Pirate Cruise, Clearwater**
*www.captmemo.com*

**Casements, The (Rockefeller Home), Daytona Beach**
*www.obht.org/casements.htm*

**Castillo de San Marcos, St. Augustine**
*www.nps.gov/casa*

**Castle Otttis, Vilano Beach**
*www.castleotttis.com*

**Children's Museum of Tampa, Tampa**
*www.flachildrensmuseum.com*

**Circus Museum, Ringling Estate, Sarasota**
*www.ringling.org/circus_museum.asp*

**Civil War Soldiers Museum, Pensacola**
*www.cwmuseum.org/main.asp*

**Classic Car Museum, Sarasota**
*www.sarasotacarmuseum.org*

**Clearwater Beach & Pier**
*www.clearwaterbeach.com*

**Clearwater Marine Aquarium, Clearwater**
*www.cmaquarium.org*

**Colonial Spanish Quarter, St. Augustine**
*www.historicstaugustine.comcsq/history.html*

**Cummer Museum and Art and Gardens, Jacksonville**
*www.cummer.org*

**Cypress Gardens, Winter Haven**
*www.cypressgardens.com*

**Daytona Beach**
*www.daytonabeach.comwhattosee.cfm/mode/beach*

**Daytona International Speedway**
www.daytonainternationalspeedway.com

**Daytona Lagoon, Daytona Beach**
*www.daytonalagoon.com*

**DaytonaUSA**
*www.daytonausa.com*

**Edison and Ford winter homes, Fort Myers**
*www.efwefla.org*

**Emerald Coast Science Center, Fort Walton Beach**
*www.ecscience.org*

**Ernest Hemingway Home, Key West**
*www.hemingwayhome.com*

**Everglades Alligator Farm, Florida City**
*www.everglades.com*

**Everglades, The**
*www.nps.gov/ever*

**Fantasy of Flight, Polk City**
*www.fantasyofflight.com*

**Fishing Hall of Fame, Dania Beach**
*www.igfa.org*

**Flagler Museum, Palm Beach**
*www.flaglermuseum.us/*

**Flamingo Gardens, Davie**
*www.flamingogardens.org*

**Florida Aquarium, Tampa**
*www.flaquarium.org*

**Florida International Museum, St. Petersburg**
*www.floridamuseum.org*

**Florida Museum of Natural History, Gainesville**
*www.flmnh.ufl.edu/*

**Florida's Gulfarium, Fort Walton Beach**
*www.gulfarium.com*

**Fort De Soto Park, Tierra Verde**
*www.pinellascounty.org/park/05_Ft_DeSoto.htm*

**Fort Matanzas National Monument, St. Augustine**
*www.nps.gov/foma*

**Fountain of Youth Archaeological Park, St. Augustine**
*www.fountainofyouthflorida.com*

**Gamble Plantation, Ellenton**
*www.floridastateparks.org/gambleplantation/default.cfm*

**Gameworks, Ybor City, Tampa**
*www.gameworks.comlocations/tampa.php*

**Gasparilla Island**
*www.floridastateparks.org/gasparillaisland/*

**González-Alvarez House ("Oldest House"), St. Augustine**
*www.staugustinehistoricalsociety.org*

**Great Explorations, St. Petersburg**
*www.greatexplorations.org*

**Gulf World Marine Park, Panama City**
*www.gulfworldmarinepark.com*

**Henry B. Plant Museum, Tampa**
*www.plantmuseum.com*

**Heritage House Museum, Key West**
*www.heritagehousemuseum.org*

**Historic Cocoa Village, Cocoa**
*www.cocoavillage.com*

**Historic Pensacola Village, Pensacola**
*www.historicpensacola.org*

**Imaginarium, Ft. Myers**
*www.cityftmyers.comimaginarium/index.aspx*

**International Drive, Orlando**
*www.internationaldriveorlando.com*

**International Swimming Hall of Fame, Fort Lauderdale**
*www.ishof.org*

**Jackie Robinson Ballpark, Daytona Beach**
*www.daytonacubs.comballpark-jackie.php*

**Jacksonville Beach**
*www.jacksonvillebeach.org*

**Jacksonville Landing, Jacksonville**
*www.jacksonvillelanding.com*

**Jacksonville Museum of Modern Art, Jacksonville**
*www.mocajacksonville.org*

**Jacksonville Zoo, Jacksonville**
*www.jaxzoo.org*

**Kennedy Space Center**
*www.nasa.gov/centers/kennedy/home/index.html*

**Koreshan State Historic Site, Estero**
*www.floridastateparks.org/koreshan/*

**Lake Okeechobee**
*www.visitflorida.comdestinations/area.php/ca=60*

**Las Olas Boulevard, Fort Lauderdale**
*www.lasolasboulevard.com*

**Lightner Museum, St. Augustine**
*www.lightnermuseum.org*

**Lion Country Safari, West Palm Beach**
*www.lioncountrysafari.com*

**Little Havana, Miami**
*www.gmcvb.comvisitors/little_havana.asp*
*www.gonomad.comdestinations/0106/monk_miami_fl.html*

**Little White House, Key West**
*www.trumanlittlewhitehouse.comabout.htm*

**Lowry Park Zoo, Tampa**
*www.lowryparkzoo.com*

**Loxahatchee Everglades Tours, Boca Raton**
*www.evergladesairboattours.com*

**Magical Midway, Orlando**
*www.magicalmidway.com*

**Manatee Observation Center, Fort Pierce**
*www.manateecenter.com*

**Manatee World, Ft. Myers**
*www.manateeworld.com*

**Marineland, St. Augustine**
*www.marineland.net*

**Mary Brogan Museum of Art and Science, Tallahassee**
*www.thebrogan.org*

**Mel Fisher Maritime Heritage Museum, Key West**
*www.melfisher.org*

**Mel Fisher's Treasures, Sebastian**
*www.melfisher.com*

**Merritt Island National Wildlife Refuge, Titusville**
*www.fws.gov/merrittisland/*

**Miami Metrozoo, Miami**
*www.miamimetrozoo.com*

**Miami Museum of Science and Space Transit, Miami**
*www.miamisci.org*

**Miami Seaquarium, Key Biscayne**
*www.miamiseaquarium.com*

**Miccosukee Indian Village, Miami**
*www.miccosukee.comindian_village.htm*

**Monkey Jungle, Miami**
*www.monkeyjungle.com*

**Mote Marine Aquarium, Sarasota**
*www.mote.org*

**Museum of Art, Ringling Estate, Sarasota**
*ringling.org/museum_art.asp*

**Museum of Discovery and Science, Fort Lauderdale**
*www.mods.org*

**Museum of Fine Arts, St. Petersburg**
*www.fine-arts.org*

**Museum of Florida History, Tallahassee**
*www.flheritage.commuseum*

**Museum of Science & History, Jacksonville**
*www.themosh.org*

**Museum of Science and Industry, Tampa**
*www.mosi.org*

**Naples, 5th Avenue South Shopping**
*www.fifthavenuesouth.com*

**Naples Zoo at Caribbean Gardens**
*www.napleszoo.com*

**National Museum of Naval Aviation, Pensacola**
*www.navalaviationmuseum.org*

**National Wildlife Refuge and Bird Sanctuary, Sanibel**
*www.fws.gov/dingdarling*

**Navy Seal Museum, Fort Pierce**
*www.navysealmuseum.com*

**Old Capitol Museum, Tallahassee**
*www.flheritage.commuseum/sites/oldcapitol/*

**Old St. Augustine Historic District**
*www.oldcity.com*

**Old St. Augustine Village**
*www.old-staug-village.com*

**Oldest Wooden Schoolhouse, St. Augustine**
*www.oldestwoodenschoolhouse.com*

**Palm Beach Zoo, West Palm Beach**
*www.palmbeachzoo.org*

**Parrot Jungle Island, Miami**
*www.parrotjungle.com*

**Pensacola Lighthouse, Pensacola**
*www.lighthousefriends.comlight.asp?ID=589*

**Pirate Soul Museum, Key West**
*www.piratesoul.com*

**Ponce de Leon Inlet Lighthouse, Daytona Beach**
*www.ponceinlet.org*

**Riley Museum of African American History & Culture, Tallahassee**
*www.rileymuseum.org*

**Ringling Estate, Sarasota**
*www.ringling.org*

**Ripley's Believe It or Not! Museum, Key West**
*www.ripleyskeywest.com*

**Ripley's Believe It or Not! Museum, St. Augustine**
*www.staugustine-ripleys.com*

**Ripley's Believe it or Not! Odditorium, Orlando**
*www.ripleysorlando.com*

**Riverwalk, Fort Lauderdale**
*www.goriverwalk.com*

**St. Augustine Alligator Farm**
*www.alligatorfarm.us*

**St. Augustine Lighthouse and Museum**
*www.staugustinelighthouse.com*

**St. George Island**
*www.apalachicolabay.org/stgeorgehome.php*

**St. Nicholas Greek Orthodox Cathedral, Tarpon Springs**
*www.epiphanycity.org*

**St. Petersburg Museum of History, St. Petersburg**
*www.spmoh.org*

**St. Petersburg Pier, St. Petersburg**
*www.stpete-pier.com*

**Salvador Dali Museum, St. Petersburg**
*www.salvadordalimuseum.org*

**Sanibel Island**
*www.sanibelisland.com*

**Sarasota Jungle Gardens, Sarasota**
*www.sarasotajunglegardens.com*

**Sea Life Safari, Clearwater**
*www.cmaquarium.orgsealife%20safari%20page.htm*

**SeaWorld Orlando**
*www.4adventure.comSWF*

**Sebring International Raceway, Sebring**
*www.sebringraceway.com*

**Seminole Okalee Indian Village and Museum, Hollywood**
*www.seminoletribe.comenterprises/hollywood/okalee.shtml*

**Skydiving Wind Tunnel, Orlando**
*www.bodyflight.net/skyventure.html*

**South Beach and Ocean Drive, Miami Beach**
*www.visitsouthbeachonline.com*

**South Florida Science Museum, West Palm Beach**
*www.sfsm.org*

**Southwest Florida Museum of History, Ft. Myers**
*www.cityftmyers.commuseum/index.aspx*

**Spanish Military Hospital St. Augustine**
*www.spanishmilitaryhospital.com*

**Sponge Docks, Tarpon Springs**
*www.spongedocks.net*

**Suncoast Seabird Sanctuary, Indian Shores**
*www.seabirdsanctuary.org*

**Sunken Gardens. Petersburg**
*www.stpete.org/sunken/index.htm*

**Sunsets at Pier 60, Clearwater Beach**
*www.sunsetsatpier60.com*

**Swap Shop, Fort Lauderdale**
*www.floridaswapshop.com*

**Tallahassee Antique Car Museum, Tallahassee**
*www.tacm.com*

**Tampa Bay History Center, Tampa**
*www.tampabayhistorycenter.org*

**Tampa Museum of Art, Tampa**
*www.tampagov.net/dept_Museum*

**Tin City, Naples**
*www.tin-city.com*

**Titanic, the Experience, Orlando**
*www.titanicshipofdreams.com*

**Tomoka State Park, Ormond Beach**
*www.floridastateparks.org/tomoka/default.cfm*

**Train Land International, Orlando**
*www.airfloridahelicopters.comtrainland/welcome.html*

**Universal Orlando**
*www.universalorlando.com*

**Walt Disney World**
*disneyworld.com*

**Wannado City, Fort Lauderdale**
*www.wannadocity.com*

**Warbird Air Museum, Titusville**
*www.vacwarbirds.org*

**Weeki Wachee Springs, Weeki Wachee**
*www.weekiwachee.com*

**WonderWorks, Orlando**
*www.wonderworksonline.com*

**World Chess Hall of Fame, Miami**
*www.chessmuseum.org*

**World Golf Hall of Fame, St. Augustine**
*www.wghof.com*

**Worth Avenue, Palm Beach**
*www.worth-avenue.com*

**Ybor City State Museum, Tampa**
*www.ybormuseum.org*

**Ybor City, Tampa**
*www.ybor.org*
*www.centroybor.com*

**Young at Art Children's Museum, Davie**
*www.youngatartmuseum.org*

**ZooWorld, Panama City**
*www.zoo-world.us*